WAR TAX RESISTANCE

A Guide To Withholding Your Support From The Military

BY ED HEDEMANN

FOURTH EDITION EDITED BY RUTH BENN

WAR RESISTERS LEAGUE
New York, NY

NEW SOCIETY PUBLISHERS
Philadelphia, PA

First Edition, December 1981
Second Edition, January 1983
Third Edition, February 1986
Fourth Edition, January 1992, Edited by Ruth Benn
First through Third editions published under the title
Guide to War Tax Resistance

Published by
The War Resisters League
339 Lafayette Street
New York, NY 10012
and
New Society Publishers
4527 Springfield Avenue
Philadelphia, PA 19143

Copyright © 1992 War Resisters League

Library of Congress Catalog Card Number: 92-80407
International Standard Book Numbers
US Paper 086571-245-X
Cloth 086571-244-1
Canada Paper 155092-187-8
Cloth 155092-186-X

Typesetting by
Kemper Roach, Pixels
Charlottesville, Virginia

Cover and text designed by
Rick Bickhart

Cover graphic by
Stephen Kroninger © 1991.

Printed by
Capital City Press, Inc.
Montpelier, Vermont

Contents

Introduction **5**
1. Why Resist War Taxes? **8**
2. Philosophical and Political Questions **11**
3. The Budget and War **15**
4. How to Resist **25**
    How Much Not to Pay **25**
    The Telephone Tax **25**
    Income Tax Resistance **27**
    Withholding **30**
    Organizational Resistance **36**
5. The IRS Audit and Appeal Process **38**
    Examination Procedure **38**
    Tax Court **39**
    The Constitutional Arguments **41**
    Tax Resistance as Eliminating Complicity **43**
6. The Collection Process **45**
7. Resisting Collection **53**
8. Alternative Funds **57**
9. History of War Tax Resistance in the United States **62**
10. Global War Tax Resistance **69**
11. Personal Histories **78**
12. Resistance Actions **100**
13. Other Tax Resisters **106**
14. National Campaigns and Legal Tax Objection **109**
    Alternative Revenue Service **109**
    The Peace Tax Fund **110**
    War Tax Resisters Penalty Fund **112**
    Paying Under Protest **112**
15. Conducting a Session on War Tax Resistance **114**
16. The National Resistance Network **116**
War Tax Resistance Resources **118**
The War Tax Resistance Network **120**
War Resisters League and New Society Publishers **125**
Index **126**

Charts, Tables, and Graphs

Guns or Butter? **10**
Military Spending Throughout United States History **16**
Military Spending 1940-1996 (without inflation) **18**
How Federal Taxes Are Raised **19**
Military Spending as a Percentage of Total Federal Funds **20–21**
The Cloaking of Military Spending **22–23**
Federal Funds Outlays By Function **24**
The No Withholding Wage Limits **31**
W-F Form **32–33**
Income Tax Appeals Procedure Chart **40**
Possible Penalties **47**
Statutes of Limitations **55**

Acknowledgements

Through the four editions of this book there have been many people to thank and resources to note. Since this Fourth Edition maintains much of what has come before, Ed Hedemann's original acknowledgements are reprinted first:

First Edition

The following four books were indispensable for certain sections of this book: *Handbook on the Nonpayment of War Taxes* (provided the basis for "Political and Philosophical Questions" and several biographies in "Personal Histories"), *Ain't Gonna Pay for War No More* (the Nuremberg arguments, background for the three consequences chapters), *People Pay for Peace* (provided the tax court segment, as well as helped with the legal consequences sections), and Barbara Andrews' thesis *Tax Resistance in American History* (very helpful for parts of "History of WTR in the U.S.," "Other Tax Resisters," and "Budget and War" chapters). The section on "Feminist Tax Resistance" is copyrighted by BettyJohanna.

Ernest Bromley's extensive knowledge of war tax resistance and its history improved this book significantly. Karl Meyer offered detailed comments in the "How To" and "Consequences" chapters, particularly the discussion relating to not filing and W-4 resistance.

Steve Gulick, Juanita and Wally Nelson, Marion Bromley, Rob Nippert, Sallie Marx, Michael Gasster, Susan Furry, Susan Wilkins, Maris Cakars, Ralph DiGia, and Wendy Schwartz made numerous valuable suggestions. In addition, Steve Gulick, Lori Nessel, Alan Eccelston, Larry Bassett, Kathy Levine, Bob Smith, Paul Monsky, Vincent Tranquilli, Lyle Snider, Robin Harper, Bruce Chrisman, Betty Johanna, and Richard Catlett all cooperated by turning in their pieces, sometimes with a short deadline.

Susan Pines aided with proofing and preparation for typesetting, as well as overseeing the final stages of production. —*1981*

Third Edition

Kate Renner collected and put together the vastly improved "Global War Tax Resistance" chapter, a job that took many months of correspondence.

Kathy Levine and Larry Bassett, whose knowledge of the national war tax movement is unsurpassed, provided essential information without which this book would be incomplete.

—*1986*

Fourth Edition

Rick Bickhart designed and pasted-up the third and fourth editions. His suggestions and help were invaluable.

Vicki Metcalf updated and corrected the legal sections for this edition as well as for the Third Edition.

Thanks to Carolyn Stevens for her work on the "Resisting Collection" chapter and to Karen Marysdaughter for helping with the contact list. And to many people who offered review and comment on various chapters including Charles Scheiner, Joe Maizlish, Sallie Marx, Steve Gulick, Lisa Harper, Barbara Hirshkowitz and others at New Society Publishers, and the folks at Northern California War Tax Resistance. Judy Kowalok updated the charts in Chapter 2 and put together the history chronology in Chapter 9. Thanks to Donna Johnson, Tom Wilson, Randy Kehler and Betsy Corner, and Clare Hanrahan for the work on their personal stories and to all the others for their updates.

Mary Jane Sullivan proofread the final copy from our great typesetter Kemper at Pixels. Thanks to all the groups and individuals who sent in photos and graphics.

Elliot Linzer donated his time to produce the index for the first three editions. Thanks to Vicki Revere for the fourth edition index.

And special thanks to Ed Hedemann for reading the whole thing yet again and offering his thoughtful comments.

—*Ruth Benn*
January 1992

Introduction

BY ED HEDEMANN

One sunny December morning an unassuming young minister walked into the Bath, North Carolina post office, purchased a money order for $2.09, and without fanfare mailed it to the Methodist Commission for Overseas Relief. Thus began the modern war tax resistance movement.

Fifty years ago that $2.09 check was supposed to be for a "defense tax stamp" which all motorists were required to display on the windshields of their cars. The minister, Ernest Bromley, spent sixty days in jail for his refusal. But his courage in the face of almost universal condemnation during the early years of the second world war and the example of the other war tax resisters throughout the 1940s laid the groundwork for the resourceful and informed movement we have today.

Ten years ago when this *Guide* was first published many people became war tax resisters rather than stand aside and watch in horror and frustration as the two superpowers played nuclear chicken.

Today, with the fourth edition of the *Guide* just off the press, the balance of power has shifted dramatically. The United States stands alone as the world's nuclear bully. However, in seeking to justify a bloated and festering budget built on the "threat" of international Communism, a desperate Pentagon is more inclined to engage in adventuristic campaigns such as those waged in recent years against Grenada, Panama, and Iraq. Spurred on by flag-waving militarists and their stooges in Congress, who among us will stand in the way of a U.S. invasion of, say, Cuba, or Libya, or Columbia? . . . People like Betsy Corner and Randy Kehler.

Randy is currently serving a six-month jail term for refusing to turn over to the IRS the house he shared with Betsy and their daughter Lillian for unpaid war taxes. Betsy and Randy have resisted war taxes since they first owed income taxes thirteen years ago.

This *Guide* is for the Randys and Betsys in this country who disagree with the military priorities of the United States, who are not content to wait for the government to make things better, and who are willing to take an initiative against military spending.

(Continued)

Founders of the modern war tax resistance movement (l to r) Wally Nelson, Juanita Nelson, Ernest Bromely, Marion Bromley, and Maurice McCrackin attending an October 1991 conference in Voluntown, Connecticut. Photo by Ed Hedemann.

Introduction

Unlike many people who begin tax resistance to reduce their complicity with the war-making machinery of the U.S., my complicity was so small* back in 1970 that I had a telephone installed in order to have the opportunity to resist war taxes.

War tax resistance is an opportunity—an opportunity to be reckoned with.

I felt then as I do now that the government would be perfectly content if protesters and critics confined their dissent to voting, letter writing, and rallies. For most people, nothing is more demoralizing that to feel that no matter what you do, you will have no impact.

However, war tax resistance has an almost magical ability to force a confrontation and make the government pay attention. Not much danger of being ignored. And in the unlikely even that the state looks the other way, tax money rerouted from the military to community programs guarantees an impact.

But what about the *hassle* of those threatening notices from the IRS and the *inconvenience* of the IRS trying to seize your bank account or salary, or the *fear* that maybe one day you'll be taken to court just because you tried to follow your conscience?

I think about the *hassle* suffered by a soldier forced to leave his home and job to fight in a war not of his making.

I think about the *inconvenience* suffered by a woman in Baghdad who lost her house and all its possessions to a "smart" bomb.

I think my greatest *fear* is that someone—with whom I had no quarrel—has died because I contributed to the military spending of the United States.

—*January 1992*

---

*Being a student, I owed no income taxes.

If a thousand men (and women) were not to pay their tax-bills this year, that would not be a violent and bloody measure, as it would to pay them, and enable the State to commit violence and shed innocent blood.

—Henry David Thoreau
"On the Duty of Civil Disobedience"

1 Why Resist War Taxes?

People are drafted through Selective Service. Money is drafted through the Internal Revenue Service.

Billboard displayed in Greenfield, Massachusetts by the War Tax Refusers Support Committee. Designed by artist Richard DiMatteo, the advertising company donated the space to the Committee for one month in 1990.

"If you don't believe in it, why pay for it?" This is the title of a flyer that was sent to peace movement people encouraging their participation in war tax resistance activities at the Internal Revenue Service (IRS). This title also represents the primary reason why people refuse to pay taxes which contribute to war.

As long time war tax resister Wally Nelson once explained to a visiting IRS agent, "We don't intend to cooperate with the IRS in its attempts to make us pay for killing. What would you do if I came into your office tomorrow with a cup in my hand, asking for contributions to enable me to buy guns and kill a group of people I don't like?"*

For many, the only difference between paying for war and physically participating in war is that the former is less messy and more convenient. Paraphrasing A.J. Muste, in order to conduct a war or build a military, the government requires two chief resources: soldiers and money. People are drafted through the Selective Service System, and money is drafted through the Internal Revenue Service. During the Civil War draftees could join the army or buy their way out with $300. It isn't much different today, except it is an almost universal draft of one's labor, and $300 would be a bargain, even if you account for inflation.

The technology of warfare has undergone

*New Roots, p. 33, April 1981.

dramatic, even revolutionary, changes. These changes have created a military with a far greater need—almost an addiction—for money rather than soldiers. This addiction has resulted in unprecedented "peacetime" military spending.

Proponents of high tech weaponry argue that wars can be fought with fewer casualties. Computer-guided missiles are fired far from their intended targets, protecting the soldiers who fire the missiles. But when the missiles explode, they can still kill thousands of combatants and civilians alike.

Military spending takes its toll in other ways: through the moral and cultural deterioration of our society; the deaths from starvation here and around the world; the racism, sexism, and violence promoted by a society which glorifies militarism and domination; the lack of jobs, poor education, inadequate health care, insufficient housing, and so forth.

World politics began changing dramatically in the late 1980s with the collapse of the Berlin Wall and then the break-up of the Soviet Union. The threat of nuclear war was reduced, but the weapons to wage it still exist. We may see cutbacks in military personnel and major weapons systems over the next years, but the Pentagon's development of forces that are quickly deployed to "hot-spots" around the world is a dangerous

April 20, 1971

To the Editor of the Boston Globe:

For thirty years, as religious pacifists and advocates of the way of love and nonviolence in all human relationships, my husband and I have been active in the search for peace. It is, therefore, with special dismay that we watch the increase in lawlessness and violence in the country in recent months.

A particular case in point has been brought to our attention recently by a group that claims to be "in the business of peace." We have received a number of appeals, or more realistically demands, for funds in support of the group's program despite our repeated response in the negative. The demands come from a small town in Massachusetts, but we have reason to believe that the organization has much larger ramifications in Washington. It has been suggested, furthermore, that this group is involved in various illegal and violent activities, including the use of both bombs and willful arson as well as outright murder of innocent people. It is said that this group advocates forceful overthrow of governments and coercion or overt repression of those who disapprove of its activities.

It is evidence of this repressive behavior that we are anxious to bring to public attention. In the last few weeks we have received notes that read like ultimata from these people asserting that if we are not willing to contribute to their program voluntarily, they will take steps to help themselves to our funds or our personal possessions.

We would like to know whether other readers of The Globe have had this experience, and what they have done to stop this outrage. The group refers to itself as "IRS."

Elizabeth Boardman

(Reprinted from Ain't Gonna Pay for War No More, *edited by Robert Calvert, p. vii, 1972; originally printed in the* Boston Globe, *April 20, 1971.)*

Why Resist War Taxes?

Military spending not only increases the risk of war, but people are dying now from our military economy.

---

trend. The greatest threat of war still lies in the use of conventional weapons in regional conflicts.

The significant changes needed to stop this slide to war will not occur without a continued outpouring of protest, including dramatic actions by many people. War tax resistance is one of the strongest and most dramatic nonviolent statements an individual can make.

People become war tax resisters for a variety of reasons. Although not pacifists, some have been motivated to act because of the nuclear war threat and the immoral misuse of government spending. However, many war tax resisters also do not believe that killing or threatening to kill is an acceptable way to solve social or political problems. New resisters frequently report feeling a gain in personal power over their own lives upon becoming war tax resisters.

Historically, war tax resisters have been moved by strong religious convictions in their nonpayment. Segments of the Society of Friends, the Church of the Brethren, and the Mennonite Church—the historic peace churches—have felt that to pay war taxes is to participate in war, violating the teachings of Jesus. Only since World War II, and especially since the Vietnam War, have there been significant numbers of war tax resisters motivated by political or secular beliefs. No matter what motivates those of us who resist war taxes, every one of us is responsible for reducing our complicity in war and preparation for war.

However, for a lot of war tax resisters reducing

We are all responsible to reduce our complicity in war preparation.

Some people use war tax resistance as a means to *confront* the government with their opposition.

GUNS OR BUTTER?

Building 4 duplex houses, renovating 10 units of abandoned housing, and weatherizing 22 homes	**$940,000**	1 Harpoon missile
Feeding 1 million children through the National School Lunch Program for 1 year	**$141 million**	Feeding troops in the Middle East during the Gulf War for one month
Support 1600 rape crisis and battered women's shelters	**$200 million**	6 hours of military spending
Immunization and basic health supplies for 50 million children in Asia, Africa, and Latin America	**$500 million**	1 B-1 bomber
Clean up 15 of the worst hazardous waste dumps	**$500 million**	370 Tomahawk cruise missiles
Provide nutrition assistance to 75 million children in Asia, Africa, and Latin America	**$750 million**	1 Stealth bomber
Provide nutritional supplements and prenatal care for 2,127,000 low income families	**$1 billion**	1 day of the Persian Gulf War
30,800 civilian jobs (such as building light rail for mass transit)	**$1 billion**	24,000 military related jobs (such as building M-1 tanks)
Provide comprehensive pre-school for 769,000 disadvantaged children	**$2 billion**	2 Army Reserve Divisions
Rehabilitate 150,000 units of low income housing	**$3 billion**	2 Trident submarines
Mass transit subsidized in nine cities	**$4.5 billion**	1992 request for research on Star Wars missile defense plan
Providing Aid to Families with Dependent Children (AFDC) benefits for 1,500,000 families	**$5 billion**	35 MX missiles on rails

Sources: The Women's Budget, 4th edition, Women's International League for Peace and Freedom; Mother Jones, *March/April 1991*; Jobs with Peace; SANE/Freeze, January 1991; Budget of the U.S. Government, FY 1992.

The ability to motivate other people makes war tax resistance more than just a personal action.

complicity is only one of many reasons why they refuse to pay war taxes. Another major reason is to register a protest—a protest which cannot be ignored. They do not simply strive for moral purity, but seek to *confront* the government with their opposition. Living below the taxable income denies the government funds for war; resisting war taxes by filing and refusing to pay incorporates the element of confrontation.

The ability to motivate other people makes war tax resistance more than just a personal action. The classic case of this phenomenon is that of Henry David Thoreau. His personal act of tax refusal and subsequent essay had, and continue to have, enormous impact. War tax resisters are not reticent about what they are doing and why. Such dramatic acts of protest will not move all who are in sympathy to act in kind, but many will take steps they would not otherwise have taken.

Finally, most resisters want to put their tax money to constructive use. Their nonpayment and redirection of tax money is a way to correct the deficiencies of government spending. Alternative or People's Life Funds have been set up across the country by communities of resisters as a means to maximize their fiscal and public impact.

Philosophical and Political Questions

The questions below are typical of those often posed to war tax resisters. The responses to them are not intended to be the final word, or something with which all war tax resisters will agree. They are there merely to stimulate thinking for those who are just beginning to deal with resistance. Many of the questions and responses were derived from the *Handbook on Nonpayment of War Taxes* (Peacemakers, pp. 10-13, 1981) and *Ain't Gonna Pay for War No More* (War Tax Resistance, pp. 33-38, 1972).

We're Not at War, Why Resist?

It is entirely possible that as you read this, the U.S. is involved in a war again, and the question may be moot. U.S. military strategy changed after the Vietnam War to quick strikes, covert or proxy wars, and massive, rapid air attacks. Hidden or short actions allow less time for antiwar sentiments to grow. While a protracted war or one with many U.S. casualties is less likely, the government continues to prepare for limited engagements around the world. Our tax dollars also contribute to many of the ongoing wars fought by smaller nations.

Opposing wars *before* they begin (e.g., by resisting their causes) is far better than trying to stop them once underway. High military spending is certainly one such cause. In fact, since World War II we have had a "permanent war economy," to borrow a phrase from Seymour Melman.

Today's tax dollars are contributing to the preparation for future wars; in addition, citizens are asked to pay interest on the debts created by many past wars.

Why Use Illegal Methods?

Many feel that it is more important to violate a law than to violate their conscience (or religious beliefs) when the two conflict. Most war tax resisters are compelled by conscience to stop contributing to preparations for mass murder. Some people feel that protests they make through legal channels are frequently ignored, but resisting taxes registers a protest the government cannot ignore. Furthermore, open conscientious breaking of a law often generates public curiosity, affording resisters more opportunities to present their views.

If Everyone Were to Obey Only Those Laws They Like, Wouldn't It Lead to Chaos?

That's a common argument against civil disobedience. There are times in every society when obeying laws perpetuates injustice and disorder. Disobeying Hitler's laws might not have disrupted the order in Nazi Germany, but it certainly would have contributed a lot toward creating a better world. Disobeying segregationist laws in this country provided a step towards a less racist society. At times, disobeying "neutral" laws aids in calling attention to injustice.

Historically, civil disobedience has not led to people running amok in the streets, disobeying all laws. In fact, war tax resisters consider those who prepare for war to be in violation of international laws and contributing to a breakdown of a just social order. War tax resisters seek to build community through responsible use of their resisted money, not a society where people just do their own thing.

There is nothing in the federal budget which even comes close to military spending in size. So those who object to federal spending on other items (e.g., abortion or welfare) are throwing in red herrings. Nevertheless, even if there are those who wish to take the same risks as war tax resisters, this does not negate the validity of refusing to pay money for wars and militarism.

Besides, who should determine how the people's money is to be spent—the people or a small clique in Washington, D.C.? A society is strengthened by questioning, criticism, and focused resistance, not by blind obedience.

What About the Good Things a Taxation System Provides?

The taxes you pay to the government cannot be earmarked for the constructive functions of the government. Anything you hand over to the IRS will, in large part, go to the military. Also, a lot of expenditures in the nonmilitary part are of questionable value from the perspective of most war tax resisters: nuclear power, prisons, FBI, CIA, unnecessary bureaucracy, and so forth. Many war tax resisters redistribute their unpaid taxes to constructive programs on a local, national, and international level, and many do pay state and local taxes.

While you may feel that you should participate in the established taxation system, the use of tax money for war completely overshadows the fairness of any tax system. If one favors paying taxes no matter how the money is to be spent merely because one feels that the income tax is democratic in its impressment of money, then one may just as well favor conscription which can be equally democratic in its impressment of men and women.

Philosophical and Political Questions

The power and validity of war tax resistance is not diminished even if the government succeeds in collecting.

War tax resistance doesn't expect perfect consistency; it seeks to become an effective force against war.

Graphic from The First Freedom: Freedom of Conscience and Religion in Canada, *published by Conscience Canada, 1989.*

One good feature of an evil institution ought not to blind us to the monstrous evil of the institution itself. The fact that war has stimulated the advancement of medical science does not lead us to approve the social institution of war.

Doesn't the Government Eventually Collect?

A war tax resister should anticipate that the government will attempt to collect and may eventually succeed. However, it is *not* true that the government will necessarily succeed in collecting for every year you resist. In fact, despite how up front your resistance is, your case may simply get lost in the bureaucracy. Also, some tax resisters make it so difficult for the IRS to collect, the case is written off as "uncollectible." Finally, there is a statute of limitations for collection (ten years from the point of assessment) beyond which the IRS can no longer proceed.

Even if the IRS eventually succeeds in collecting, it often costs them more to deal with a resister than they get from the collection. Every act of resistance, every letter to the IRS, every refusal to pay, every interaction with an IRS employee strengthens the political and moral point that U.S. citizens will no longer support the illegal and immoral actions of the U.S. government. The more public our resistance, the more other people will be challenged to think about their complicity with state-sponsored violence. The power and validity of war tax resistance is not diminished even if the government eventually succeeds in collecting.

With Interest and Penalties Added, Doesn't the Resister Pay More to War?

Interest and penalties are irrelevant if the government cannot collect. Even if the IRS does collect this larger amount, it does not necessarily mean that more will be contributed to militarism and war. Except in rare instances (e.g., when extremely large amounts of money are owed) the extra money taken by the IRS will not cover the collection costs. In dealing with tax refusers the IRS often has spent more than it has collected.

The IRS cannot afford to go after all people it thinks owe taxes. Thus, if tens of thousands of people refused taxes in opposition to war, the cost of collections and attempted collections would be so great that the resistance would be significant because of this factor alone.

Since Other Federal Taxes Are Unavoidable, Isn't Income Tax Resistance Inconsistent?

Refusing to pay all war taxes is not possible. A completely consistent war resister would probably have to leave the country or live without money in the wilderness. If we have anything to do with the national economy, we contribute in some way to federal revenue, hence to war. However, individual income taxes provide about two-thirds of the revenue needed for federal funds. And it is through these taxes that the average citizen is most directly connected with war. Is not a person who refuses such taxes more consistent than a person who opposes war yet pays whatever is asked for the military? War tax resistance doesn't expect perfect consistency. It seeks to become an effective force against war.

Didn't Jesus Pay Taxes? Doesn't "Render Unto Caesar" Mean That Christians Should Pay Taxes?

We are told in the Gospels that Jesus paid the Temple Tax, a half shekel exacted annually from every Jew over twenty years old, as a "contribution to the Lord." Once, the disciple Peter went to Jesus and said that the tax man had come. Jesus said: "Pay the tax for us both."

It seems understandable that Jesus would pay this tax. The unusual thing about the incident, however, is not that he paid it, but that the tax gatherer first of all had said to Peter: "Does your master pay the Temple Tax?" Commentaries point out that there was evidently a belief abroad that Jesus did not pay this tax. After the tax man had left, Jesus told Peter that because his mission seemed so much greater than that of the Temple, he did not feel a moral responsibility for paying the tax. "Pay the tax for us both, rather than give offense," he said. The decision to pay seems to have been based on the words, "rather than give offense." (Matthew 17:27)

At a later time and in a different circumstance he was asked: "Is it right for us to pay the poll tax to the emperor?" (Luke 20:22) This head tax was levied by Rome on every person who was a resident of Judea. Payment was regarded as a badge of servitude to Rome. Jesus was a resident of Galilee, so was not even subject to the tax. Therefore, he was merely being asked whether someone else should pay this poll tax. He quickly asked for a Roman denarius and held it up before those "who sought to entrap him," and asked: "Why do you put me to such a test?"

By holding the coin aloft he drew attention to the fact that it bore the image of Caesar, a fact long repugnant to the rabbis, who considered such imagery idolatrous, hence a transgression of the Second Commandment. Before giving the coin back to the one who trafficked in such coins, he said: "Pay the emperor what belongs to the emperor, and pay God what belongs to God." The account says: "They could not fasten on what he had said before the people, and they were amazed at his answer, and said nothing more." A distinct impression is given in all the Gospel accounts of this incident that the people who heard his answer did not know whether he had advised payment or nonpayment.

If he had merely answered, "Yes," to the question of paying taxes to the emperor, or "No" to the question, they would have known; there would have been little amazement. The askers of the question were banking on the assumption that he would say "No," in which case they could seal his fate at the hands of Rome. But they apparently thought there was some possibility of his saying "Yes," in an effort to save himself from the possible sentence of death. When his answer came out, they didn't know which of the two replies he had given, because his answer had only seemed to say, "Decide for yourselves."

In the absence of an answer saying expressly that you should pay taxes to Rome, the entrappers went out and said he was guilty of "forbidding the payment of taxes to the emperor." In a few hours he was dead upon the cross, with this as one of the three charges lodged against him. (Luke 23:2)

There Are Not Enough People to Make War Tax Resistance Effective

Effectiveness is always difficult to measure. It is true that war tax resistance *alone* is unlikely to make significant change in society. But tax resistance combined with the other tactics available to nonviolent movements can contribute considerable effectiveness to achieving change. It was an effective tactic in India's campaign for independence, a useful means to protest the Indochina War, and an important component of the Palestinian *intifada* (see Chapter 10). Thoreau's tax resistance and subsequent civil disobedience essay has had a remarkable impact on the world.

Most movements begin with a small number of dedicated people hammering away at what often appears to be a hopeless situation. If Rosa Parks had been concerned about the effectiveness of her refusal to leave the white section of the bus, she may not have remained seated and the Montgomery bus boycott may never have happened. The four men who sat-in at a Greensboro, North Carolina, Woolworth lunch counter in 1960 had no idea the effect their sit-in would have.

None of this is to argue against trying to determine the most effective strategy, but simply to caution against thinking that there is a *sure way* to know what will be effective and what won't. Besides, every dollar redirected away from the military into alternative funds is doubly effective.

Furthermore, people resist taxes for more than reasons of effectiveness. Even if an action was shown to be ineffective, it might be valid simply because it is the right thing to do politically, ethically, or morally. Those considerations are what motivated Henry David Thoreau and Rosa Parks.

War tax resisters have often encouraged others either to resist or do things they would not have done without an example to inspire them.

Even if Tax Resistance Were Effective, Wouldn't Domestic Programs Suffer and Not the Military?

It is true that the military is among the last to be cut when the government is short of funds. But money denied the government by war tax resisters is redirected to community (and other) programs which suffer because of government spending priorities. So the more effective war tax resistance becomes, the more human service programs are aided.

Will I Go To Jail?

War tax resistance involves little risk of jail. Since World War II, only about twenty people have been

Though effectiveness is tough to determine in advance, tax resistance will contribute to the overall strength of the movement.

Jesus' answer had only seemed to say, "Decide for yourselves."

The military is among the last expenditures to be cut when the government is short of funds.

jailed for reasons *related* to war tax resistance—generally not for the resistance itself. The primary interest of the IRS itself is to get the money, not jail the resister, so war tax resisters must be prepared to accept some financial risk.

The IRS has a lot of power. One way it wields its power is through the fear that has been instilled in every adult in this country. Overcoming that fear and acting on one's conscience can be very liberating.

In Conclusion

People considering war tax resistance often worry about what friends and relatives will say. They wonder if they will lose their jobs or if their credit rating will suffer. Anytime you take a stand of conscience questions such as these arise. It is helpful to remember that the "worst-case" scenario is rarely realized.

Choosing whether to resist and how, and knowing some of the risks, is what this book is about. War tax resistance is an individual choice, but there *are* groups around the country to look to for support and for organizing actions.

War tax resistance is not always easy, but there are humorous elements and a supportive network. Many have found that being a war tax resister has challenged them in ways they didn't expect and led them to a deeper understanding of nonviolence and personal power.

Overcoming fear of the IRS and acting on one's conscience can be very liberating.

The Budget and War

Military and war spending have dominated the federal budget historically. While a particular war or military action may inspire individuals to war tax resistance, it is useful to put government priorities and budgeting in a wider perspective. This chapter offers an overview of the history of military spending and helps to unravel the tricks of calculating the military percentages in the current budget.

The History of Taxation and Military Spending

In examining the history of taxation in this country a pattern emerges. As revenue is needed to wage a war or even pay for the debts of a previous war new systems of taxation appear. Often those taxes, initiated as necessities during wartime, are retained after the war is over.[1] Military spending after every war has dropped sharply (except following the Korean and Indochina wars), but *never* to the prewar level. Nonmilitary spending increases after every war filling some of the "void" left by the reduced war spending (see charts on pages 16 and 20).

Since the Revolutionary war was funded largely through loans (e.g., from France), federal spending in the postwar years was literally dominated by the war debt. Interest on the debt amounted to 60% of all federal spending. So current and past military spending hovered around 80% to 90%. Customs duties provided the majority of revenue until the Civil War.

Tobacco, alcohol, and other excise taxes were added to help pay for the building of the Continental Navy (1798-1801). These excise taxes were repealed after the navy was built.

With the War of 1812 (1812-15) military expenditures quadrupled (to 80% of all spending) and Congress again resorted to excise taxes (e.g., tobacco and alcohol) to supplement the customs duties. Because of their unpopularity the excise taxes were repealed following the War, necessitating an increase in customs duties. However, none of these measures were sufficient to pay for the war, resulting in a dramatic rise in the national debt (to two-and-a-half times its former level). For the next twenty years there were no wars, military spending leveled off (to 50% to 60% of the budget) and the national debt almost disappeared.

During the war for Texas independence (1836) military spending doubled. But with the Mexican War (1846-48) military expenditures quadrupled (to 80% of all federal spending). However, taxes were not increased so again the national debt rose dramatically.

Military spending during the Civil War (1861-65) increased almost *forty times* its previous level — amounting to 93% of the budget! As a result, customs taxes were doubled, excise taxes were reinstituted, and the first income tax (affecting less than 3% of the people) was established with a permanent tax collection agency (the forerunner of the IRS). Because all this was insufficient to meet the expenses of the war, the debt increased to thirty-five times its prewar level. Though military spending dropped to about 20% of the budget, the cost of the Civil War (veterans' benefits and interest on the debt) amounted to about 50% of each year's budget. Thus 70% of the postwar budget went to current military and Civil War expenses. Because of its unpopularity the income tax (as well as many of the other taxes) was removed. Once again customs duties provided most of the revenue. The Civil War debt was reduced but never eliminated in the years following.

During the Spanish-American War (1898) military spending tripled, and a series of excise (e.g., tobacco and alcohol) and other taxes was instituted to pay for it. Due to the taxes and the shortness of the war the debt rose very little. But after the war the military budget rose from its prewar 20% (of the budget) to about 45%.

Military expenditures increased to about thirty times their former level with U.S. entry into World War I (1917-19). The enactment of the Sixteenth Amendment four years earlier established a permanent income tax for the first time. But all these taxes only accounted for one-third of the revenue needed to finance the war. War bonds, liberty loans, and other forms of borrowing provided the balance of the money. Though ostensibly voluntary, "bond drives" became a form of taxation because self-appointed patriots took it upon themselves to collect such monies from unwilling citizens.[2]

As a result of all this borrowing, the war debt increased the national debt to twenty times the prewar level, and yearly interest on that debt went up to forty-five times its former level. The debt (and interest on it) never dropped significantly, and in fact rose due to the Depression and increased social expenditures. Because of the antiwar mood of the country, the Depression, and a dramatic increase in social spending, military spending as a percentage of the federal budget dropped to an all-time low of 11% in 1934.

Military outlays during World War II increased to almost *eighty times* the prewar level! Direct spending on the war accounted for over 80% of all gov-

New systems of taxation appear as revenue is needed to wage a war or even pay for the debts of a previous war.

Military spending drops sharply after most wars, but never to the pre-war level.

Customs duties provided the majority of revenue until the Civil War.

Military outlays during World War II increased to almost 80 times its pre-War level!

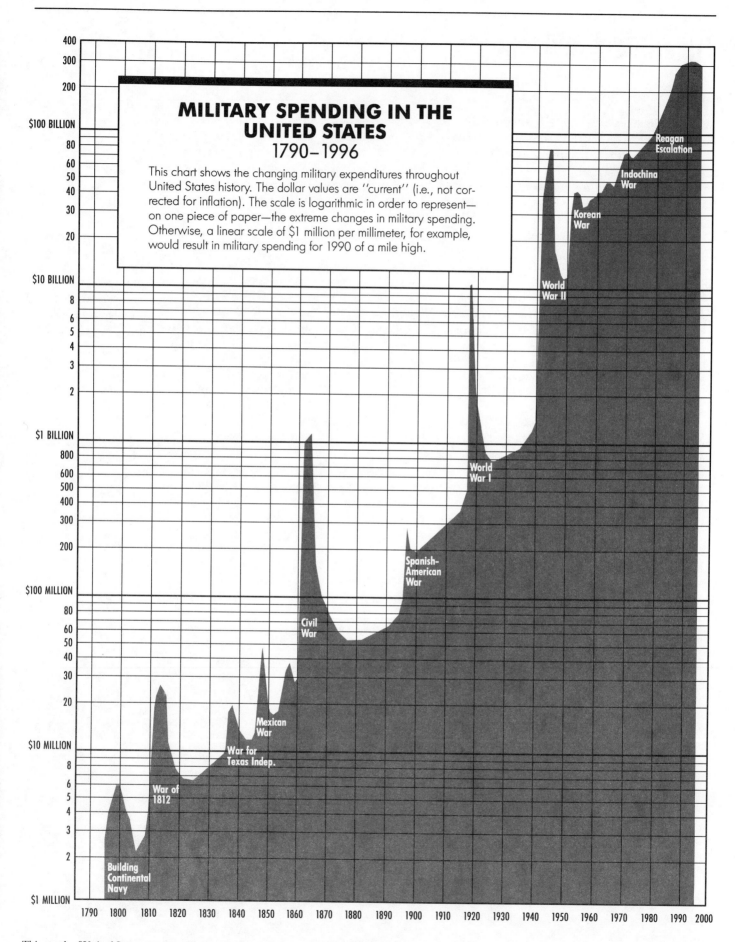

This graph of United States current military spending is in current dollars (therefore, effects of inflation are not removed). Figures are from *Historical Statistics of the United States, Colonial Times to 1970* and recent issues of the *Budget of the United States*.

ernment expenditures (or 95% if war-related costs are added for the 1940-46 period[3]) or 42% of the gross national product. The institution of the employee withholding system in 1943 increased the number of persons filing an income tax return from 11% in 1940 to 36% in 1945[4]— resulting in a twelve-fold increase in revenue from individual income taxes. However, all these taxes could only take care of two-fifths of this unprecedented government spending. As a result, the debt jumped to six and a half times its 1940 level, and interest on the debt went up five-fold.

Although military outlays declined following the war, they did not drop as sharply compared to all previous wars. Something new had been created—a peacetime centralized military institution, symbolized by the Pentagon. The war had constructed a powerful military bureaucracy which had no interest in dismantling itself and sought perpetuation of its power. The enactment of peacetime conscription in 1948, the build-up of anti-communist hysteria, followed by the Korean War, and the growth of the military industries during the Cold War resulted in an entrenchment of the postwar military establishment.

Military spending doubled during the Korean War (1950-53), dropping very little in the Cold War period which followed. Because President Truman had raised taxes sufficiently to pay for the war, the debt did not increase significantly. But military spending continued to rise steadily.

So as not to alienate Americans from U.S. involvement in Vietnam, President Johnson avoided raising taxes. As a result not only military spending, but the debt also rose during the Indochina War.

Following the war inflation increased dramatically. Again, military spending did not drop significantly even with the effects of inflation taken out (see the chart on page 18). But beginning with the Carter administration and continuing through the Reagan years, military spending increased significantly as the graphs in this chapter illustrate. The increase in annual military spending from 1980 to 1991 amounted to $164 billion. During this period—considered "peacetime"—the U.S. spent over $3 trillion on the military.[5]

In 1991 George Bush announced the dismantling of some nuclear weapons. Military bases at home and abroad have been closed. The number of troops is scheduled to be reduced from 2.1 million to 1.6 million. Despite these hopeful signs, continued spending on costly weapons systems is likely to offset other types of cutbacks. Besides, the White House and Pentagon are not about to dismantle the military. The 1991 Persian Gulf War provided a convenient rationale for maintaining a high level of military spending. Other proposals such as a Pentagon-led drug war, are designed to convince military critics that a weakened military would leave Americans vulnerable to drugs and international terrorism, if not communists.

War Taxes

There are many different kinds of taxes and not all are war taxes. Taxes can be federal, state, or local in origin. They can be in the form of income taxes, customs duties, sales taxes, excise taxes, social security taxes, property taxes, etc. As bad as state or local governments can be, they do not conduct wars. The closest state or local taxes get to being war taxes are through their contribution to the national guard, which amounts to very little of state budgets. State and local taxes usually manifest themselves in the form of sales taxes, property taxes, and some excise taxes. Several states and a few cities also have income taxes.

Federal taxes are the war taxes. But no single federal tax goes directly to war; they are mixed. Some federal taxes *do not* contribute to military spending, even in part. Those are the *trust funds*. Trust funds are, in theory, collected by the federal government and then held in trust, eventually to be spent only on that for which they were collected. The largest such fund is the social security trust fund, contributions to which are removed from each paycheck as FICA (Federal Insurance Contributions Act). The airport trust fund which is collected as an excise tax on air travel, and the highway trust fund which is collected as an excise tax on each gallon of gasoline, are examples of other federal trust funds. In 1981 a military trust fund to finance Pentagon programs was proposed. However, it is unlikely such a trust fund will be created in the near future.

All federal collected taxes which do not go into trust funds contribute to military spending. These taxes are spent as federal funds. The largest such tax is the individual income tax which makes up three quarters of all federal funds. Other taxes which contribute to military spending are corporation income taxes, some excise taxes (e.g., tobacco, alcohol, telephone), estate and gift taxes, customs duties, etc. Savings bonds, which used to be called war bonds, though not a tax, are a means through which the government can borrow money from the people for federal

The White House and the Pentagon are not about to dismantle the military.

World War II created a powerful military bureaucracy which had no interest in dismantling itself and sought perpetuation of its power.

Taxes collected and spent as federal funds are the war taxes.

Trust funds such as social security do not contribute directly to military spending.

The Budget and War

The largest and most important of all the war taxes is the individual income tax.

Not all spending on the military shows up in the Department of Defense budget.

programs such as the military.

The problem is how to resist these taxes. In order to avoid customs duties, do not bring taxable items back into this country. If you refuse payment, the item(s) will likely be confiscated at the port of entry. Avoiding estate and gift taxes is a bit trickier. Having property, etc., distributed before death (at least three years) may be the only way. In order to refuse corporation income taxes, you must first have some control over the corporation. Unfortunately, there are few corporations that are inclined to resist. (See page 36 for one corporation which did.)

The most famous excise tax to be resisted is the telephone tax (see Chapter 4). Alcohol and tobacco federal excise taxes (there are also state taxes on these items) have dominated the excise taxes from 1792 on. In 1990 the alcohol federal excise tax brought in about $6 billion, the tobacco federal excise tax amounted to about $4 billion, and the telephone federal tax resulted in $3 billion in revenues. There are federal excise taxes (usually in the form of manufacturers' taxes) on guns, bullets, fishing rods, coin-operated gaming devices, bows and arrows, windfall profit tax, etc.

Obviously the largest and most important war tax of them all is the individual income tax. Most of this book is devoted to resisting that tax.

Analyzing the Budget

Analyzing the federal budget to determine how much is spent for the military and past wars, and what percentage of the budget that represents, is not particularly straight forward for a number of reasons. First, not all military spending is listed under the Department of Defense. Second, the effect of past wars on current spending is difficult to calculate. Third, since 1964 federal funds have been mixed with trust funds, making it hard to separate the two. Also, details such as "interfund transactions" and "undistributed offsetting receipts" tend to make precise calculations difficult or questionable.

Military Expenses

Obviously everything which comes under the Department of Defense is a military or war expenditure. But federal spending contained within some other department (or agency) heading can be part of the "defense function." Currently the most significant one is spending within the Department of Energy for nuclear warheads and nuclear reactors in submarines. When he first took office President Reagan tried, unsuccess-

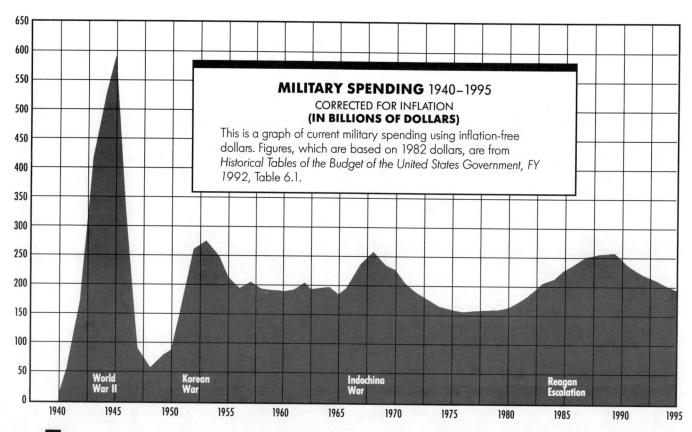

MILITARY SPENDING 1940–1995
CORRECTED FOR INFLATION
(IN BILLIONS OF DOLLARS)
This is a graph of current military spending using inflation-free dollars. Figures, which are based on 1982 dollars, are from *Historical Tables of the Budget of the United States Government, FY 1992*, Table 6.1.

fully, to abolish the Department of Energy and shift nuclear items to the Department of Commerce. The original reason nuclear weapons spending was kept separate (in the Atomic Energy Commission) was to place nuclear weapons under "civilian control."

Though not particularly significant compared to the Department of Defense, the following departments, agencies, or separate "accounts listings" contribute in a small way to military spending: Department of Transportation (for the Coast Guard, though some analysts feel this is more civilian than military), CIA, Selective Service System, Federal Emergency Management Agency (civil defense), General Services Administration (stockpiling of critical materials for war time), Intelligence Community Staff, Funds Appropriated to the President (military assistance to foreign countries), NASA (military satellites and many space shuttle flights).

Expenses of Past Wars

Current expenditures for past wars are reflected in veterans' benefits and interest on the national debt. Veterans' benefits are clearly itemized in all budgets since 1789. However, knowing what percentage of the debt results from wars or military spending is not always easy.

During and immediately following every war (and sometimes just before) the national debt rose dramatically, except in the case of the Korean War as noted earlier. Until recently a significant rise in the debt was rare during nonwar years (one striking exception was during the Depression when social spending increased rapidly). Historically the national debt has been a by-product of wars. Therefore, interest on that debt as a rule has been an expense of past wars.

For twenty-five years following the end of World War II (1945-70), the national debt hovered between $250 and $350 billion. Interest on the debt was probably at least 80% war-created. During the Indochina War the debt went into another climb, because the government did not raise sufficient taxes to offset the war expenses. However, following the war the debt continued to rise dramatically (surpassing $1 trillion in fiscal year 1982 and $3.2 trillion in 1990). Part of that was due to inflation, but even after subtracting inflation (see chart on page 18), military spending began climbing in 1977, a climb that rapidly accelerated.

Since the Indochina War ended in 1975, the U.S. has been involved directly in fairly brief interventions—Panama and the Persian Gulf War.

HOW FEDERAL TAXES ARE RAISED
FEDERAL FUNDS RECEIPTS BY SOURCE (FY 1992)
(IN BILLIONS OF DOLLARS)

Individual Income Tax	$530	72%
Corporation Income Tax	$102	14%
Excise Taxes	$48	6.5%
Estate & Gift Taxes	$13	2%
Customs Duties	$19	2.5%
Miscellaneous (Primarily earnings from Federal Reserve System)	$24	3%
Total	$736	100%

- INDIVIDUAL 72%
- ESTATE & GIFT 2%
- CUSTOMS 2.5%
- MISC. 3%
- EXCISE 6.5%
- CORP. 14%

Therefore, the rise in the debt is not primarily *war*-created and current interest on the national debt might be as little as 40% to 50% *war*-created. *However,* recognizing that following World War II, the Korean War, and the Indochina War military spending did not drop off as sharply and deeply as following all previous wars; and realizing that the Cold War, the arms race, and a military establishment (in the form of the Pentagon and industries which rely on military contract) seeking to perpetuate itself have kept military spending high and soaring; it is worth estimating how much this bloated military spending has affected the national debt.

But first some decisions need to be made on how to calculate the military portion of the debt. Let me use the following example to illustrate two possible methodologies. Suppose that for a particular year military spending was $300 billion and total spending was $600 billion, and the deficit for that year was $100 billion. Methodology A: Since military spending was 50% of total spending, you could argue that the military portion of that debt was 50% or $50 billion. Methodology B: Or you could argue that if there were no military spending, there would be no debt—in fact, we would have a surplus; therefore, the debt for that year is

Veterans' benefits and most of the interest on the national debt represent spending for past wars.

If there were no wars or military spending, there would be little or no debt.

The Budget and War

entirely military-created.

Using the first methodology, the Center on Budget and Policy Priorities (Washington, DC) calculated that the interest payments in the 1980s on the accumulated national debt should be considered 50% to 60% military and war-created[6]. They began their calculations using FY 1940 as the base year because at that point the accumulated debt was very small compared to current standards. Then each subsequent year the military-created contribution to the deficit of that year (if there was one) was added to the total accumulated military debt. In this way, the military-created portion of the total national debt was calculated.

If methodology B is used, the military-created portion of the national debt would be 100%. This is because in every year since 1940 the military spending exceeded the deficit if there was one.

As a compromise WRL has used 80% of the interest on the national debt as being military and war-created.

Recalculating the Budget

Once the dollar amounts for past and present military spending are determined you can calculate the percentages. But first you have to decide "percentage of *what*." In other words, is the military percentage to be of the gross national product (GNP, or all spending—public and private—in the country), federal funds (the administrative budget of the federal government), or the unified budget (trust funds and federal funds). Shown on this page is an example of how those percentages differ.

The percentages the president uses each year in the unveiling of the budget are those from the unified budget. This sort of calculation has the distinct advantage from the president's perspective of making military spending appear smaller and social spending larger. However, from the viewpoint of the taxpayer it is deceptive. *If you want to know where the money that you pay on April 15 (or from each paycheck) goes, it is the federal funds percentage which more accurately reflects the spending.* Money for the trust funds is raised separately and is spent specifically on what it was raised for.

In order to get a proper perspective on military spending you cannot rely on the president's yearly budget[7] or on the media which simply parrots the president's figures. You must rely on alternative groups (e.g., Women's International League for Peace and Freedom, Friends Committee on National Legislation, Council for a Livable World, National Priorities Project, Center for Defense Information, and WRL) and periodicals to supply the more accurate percentages, or work them out yourself.

To make your own calculations you must refer directly to the annual *Budget of the U.S. Government* available from Government Printing Offices or in libraries. The *Budget* contains a table of about 200 pages called "Federal Programs by Agency and Account." This listing includes line item expenditures by department. It shows which are federal

> The budget percentages the government uses each year cover up the extent of its military priorities.

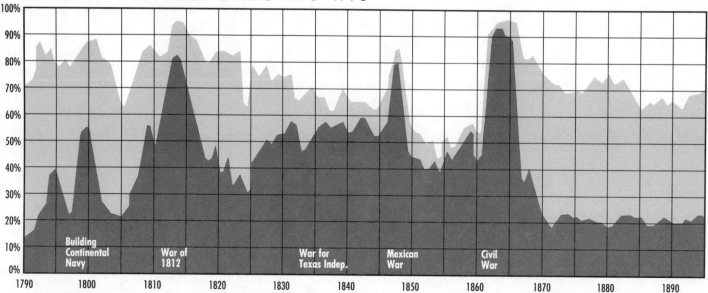

Dark section of the graph represents current military spending. Lighter section represents estimated cost of past military spending.

fund items and which are trust fund items and indicates what function each listing belongs to. For example, the Department of Agriculture can be split into a health function, income security function (e.g., food stamps), natural resources and environment functions, international function, and of course an agriculture function. Most of what is allocated for the Department of Treasury is really for interest on the national debt.

Each function is given a code, and you can trace the military codes and corresponding budget outlays through each department. Direct military expenses are found in the Department of Defense, Department of Energy, Funds Appropriated to the President, and some percentage of NASA, Treasury, Coast Guard, and other small items.

If you want to calculate just the military percentages: Add the Department of Defense to the military part of the Department of Energy, for current military spending[8]. Add veterans' benefits to 80% of the interest on the national debt, for past military spending. Divide by the total federal funds.

It should be noted that budget figures are usually either "outlays" or "budget authority." Outlays represent just what is to be spent for that particular year; whereas budget authority is spending *authorized* that year and some future years. So to reflect accurately what is spent each year, outlays are the appropriate figures to use.

To calculate percentages, interfund transactions need to be taken care of. Interfund transactions represent federal fund monies which are spent as trust funds or trust fund monies which are spent as federal funds. The fiscal year 1991 budget outlays are:

Federal funds...$1.1 trillion
Trust funds...$453 billion
Interfund transactions...$148 billion
Unified budget total...$1.4 trillion

Most of the interfund transactions are monies raised by federal funds and spent by trust funds according to the table in the back of the *Budget*.

MILITARY PERCENTAGE OF DIFFERENT BUDGETS
FISCAL YEAR 1991
(IN BILLIONS OF DOLLARS)

	% of GNP ($5,958)	% of Unified Budget ($1,409)	% of Federal Funds Outlays ($1,104)
Present Military ($330)	6%	23%	30%
Past & Present Military ($589)	10%	42%	53%

To get a proper perspective on military spending, you must rely on alternative groups or work the figures out yourself.

1 *Tax Resistance in American History*, Barbara Andrews, B.A. thesis, Goddard College, p. 278, 1976.
2 Ibid, p. 288.
3 *Encyclopedia Americana*, volume 22, p. 685, 1981.
4 Andrews, op cit., p. 289.
5 *World Military and Social Expenditures 1991*, Ruth Leger Sivard, World Priorities, Inc.
6 *The Military Tax Bite*, Paul Murphy, Center on Budget and Policy Priorities, 1985.
7 This budget is what the president wants to spend. Congress always approves a slightly different budget. And what is ultimately spent for that fiscal year is something else.
8 There are some other small items which are part of the "defense function," but can be ignored if you are willing to settle for a good approximation.

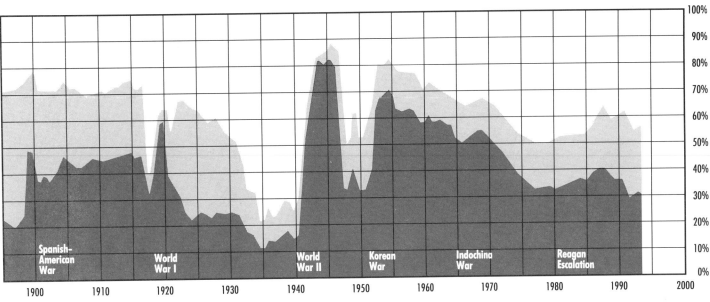

Figures are from *Historical Statistics of the United States, Colonial Times to 1970* and recent issues of the *Budget of the United States*.

THE CLOAKING OF MILITARY SPENDING

Although the yearly proposed budget (from the President) runs hundreds of pages, all the public usually notices is the simple little pie chart printed in most newspapers. Consequently, it is worth observing what message that pie chart communicates to people about how their tax money is spent. Note that the two most significant changes occurred with the release of the Fiscal Year (FY) 1964 Budget (during the Kennedy Administration) and the FY 1971 Budget (Nixon Administration).

The below pie charts have been taken unaltered directly from *The Budget of the United States Government* for FY 1963, 1964, 1970, 1971, 1975.

1963

FY 1963
How it used to be. Notice that military spending is separated along with "interest" and "veterans" from the rest of the federal budget pie.

- 63% National Defense, International, and Space
- 10% Fixed Interest Charges
- 6% Veterans
- 6% Agriculture
- 6% Health and Welfare
- 9% All Other

1964

FY 1964
One year later, the government shoves "Social Security and other trust funds" into the pie. Notice how the military portion has magically shrunk from 63% to 51% of the budget. However, the tables inside the budget still list trust funds separately until FY 1969 when the "unified" budget is created, combining trust funds and federal funds.

- 51% National Defense, International, and Space
- 6% Fixed Interest Charges
- 5% Veterans
- 23% Social Security and Other Trust Funds
- 5% Agriculture
- 10% Other

1970

FY 1970
The pie chart has changed little since the FY 1964 budget except that "Vietnam" has been listed explicitly (beginning with the FY 1967 budget).

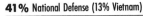

- **41%** National Defense (13% Vietnam)
- **4%** Veterans
- **22%** Social Insurance Trust Funds
- **12%** Education and Other Major Social Programs
- **2%** Debt Reduction
- **2%** International
- **6%*** Interest
- **11%** Other

1971

FY 1971
"Veterans" and the trust funds slices of the pie suddenly disappear into a new super-category called "Human Resources." So *for the first time*, thanks to this graphic sleight-of-hand, military spending is no longer portrayed as the largest slice of the pie.

- **36%** National Defense
- **41%** Human Resources
- **10%** Physical Resources
- **1%** Debt Reduction
- **7%*** Interest
- **5%** Other

1975

FY 1975
Finally completing the transformation, "Human Resources" is subsumed into a still larger and innocuous-sounding category called "Benefit Payments to Individuals." The pie chart categories will remain basically unchanged for all subsequent years.

- **29%** National Defense
- **37%** Benefit Payments to Individuals
- **17%** Grants to States and Localities
- **10%** Other Federal Operations
- **7%** Net Interest

*Excludes interest paid to trust funds

The Budget and War

FEDERAL FUNDS OUTLAYS BY FUNCTION
FISCAL YEAR 1991

100% TOTAL FEDERAL FUNDS
1.1 Trillion

29% Current Military	23% Past Military	23% Human Resources	10% General Government	9% Savings and Loan Bailout	6% Physical Resources
$330 Billion	**$259 Billion**	**$259 Billion**	**$112 Billion**	**$101 Billion**	**$70 Billion**
Military personnel $79 Retired pay $11 Operation & maintenance $86 Family housing $3 Construction $5 Procurement $79 Research & development $36 Nuclear weapons (DoE) $10 International military assistance $9 Coast Guard $3 NASA (military portion 50%) $7 Other (CIA, SSS, FEMA, etc.) $2	Veterans benefits $30 Interest on national debt (80% estimated to be created by military spending) $229	(Education, Health and Human Services, HUD housing subsidies, Labor Department)	(Government, Justice Department, International Affairs, Peace Corps, 20% interest on national debt, civilian portion of NASA)	FDIC and Resolution Trust Corporation	(Agriculture, Commerce, Energy, HUD administration/community development, Interior Department, Transportation, Environmental Protection)

Source: Budget of the U.S. Government, FY 1992

How to Resist

All the techniques listed below have been successful one time or another in resisting war taxes. New government rules, regulations, procedures, or laws may make some of these methods less appropriate in the future. On the other hand, regulation changes may create new means to stop the flow of money to the military. It is wise to ask a war tax resistance counselor to help you sort through the pros and cons of the various methods. See the resource lists at the back of this book, and contact an organization near you.

There are basically three steps to income war tax resistance: first, stop or limit the withholding system (if money is withheld from each paycheck, there is little you can do to resist taxes); second, don't pay; and third, redistribute the resisted money into some socially useful function (e.g., community alternative fund; see Chapter 8).

How Much Not to Pay

How much you don't send to the IRS is, of course, your decision assuming you have control over your taxes. Some resisters begin by refusing a symbolic amount and then in future years resist more.

Symbolic. Some refuse to pay $10 as a small gesture of defiance and protest to the war-making machinery. Some refuse an amount of money equivalent to what the average family spends in taxes for the military each week ($35 in 1991). Some tax resisters refuse to pay the estimated 10% of their taxes which goes to the nuclear military (nuclear warheads and their delivery systems). Others might choose a symbolic figure based on the amount of U.S. military aid to Latin America, Asia, or the Middle East. The Alternative Revenue Service's EZ Peace form was designed to encourage at least a symbolic resistance (see Chapter 14).

Current Military. Some tax resisters refuse to send about 30% of their taxes to the IRS, which represents current spending on the military.

Past and Current Military. Many war tax resisters refuse the percentage of both current and past military spending which has varied between 50% and 65% during the past decade. Past military and wars are reflected in two major budgetary items: veterans' benefits and interest on the national debt. Though veterans' benefits represent a basically humanitarian expenditure, many war tax resisters refuse to pay for it because that expense is just as much a part of military spending as a soldier's salary, and the benefits are used as a recruiting incentive. All people should be entitled to medical and other benefits regardless of whether they were in the military or not. Since the national debt is mostly war- or military-created, the majority of the interest on that debt is a war expenditure. Money borrowed during wartime is a war expense. So past military and war spending amounts to about 20% of what a taxpayer would send to the IRS on April 15.

All Federal Income Taxes. Many war tax resisters refuse to send any money to the IRS, even for the so-called "good" parts of the budget. The basic logic here is that any money paid will go in part to wars and the military. You cannot earmark money you send to the IRS and say "please spend this only on nonmilitary things" and expect they will do that. Further, the nonmilitary part includes prisons, nuclear power, CIA, FBI, etc. In addition, if the money not sent to the IRS is routed by the resister into community programs, it will have a much greater positive effect, having not been whittled down by a huge bureaucracy.

The Telephone Tax

The federal excise tax on telephone service has been associated with war spending throughout most of its history. The first telephone tax— on toll calls only—was imposed in 1898 (the Spanish-American War era). It was repealed in 1902, but a tax on long distance calls was reinstated by the War Tax Revenue Act of 1914. This was repealed in 1916, but reimposed in 1917 along with other war taxes. Then it was repealed in 1924 and reimposed in 1932. The first tax on local telephone service came during World War II. The war brought a 25% tax on long distance calls and a 15% tax on local service. This tax was retained during the Korean War. The tax was reduced to 10% on all telephone service in 1954. In 1965 Congress approved a reduction of the phone tax to 3% and planned to phase it out entirely in 1969.

However, in 1966 the Johnson Administration needed money for the escalating war in Vietnam. Congress passed a special tax bill which included a reimposition of the 10% phone tax. Wilbur Mills, Chairman of the House Ways and Means Committee explained during the floor debate that "it is Vietnam, and only the Vietnam operation, which makes this bill necessary."[1] The tax was extended in 1968 for two more years. In late 1970 another two-year extension was approved, but with the proviso that it be reduced by 1% each year thereafter and repealed entirely on January 1, 1982.

In January 1981 the tax was extended another year at 2%. The tax was due to expire on January

How much you don't send to the IRS is your decision assuming you have control over your taxes.

Any money paid through your income tax will go in large part to the military.

The federal excise tax on telephone service has been associated with war throughout most of its history.

How to Resist

There were as many as a half million phone tax resisters during the Indochina war.

1, 1983 but instead jumped to 3%—the first increase since 1966! The 3% telephone tax was then scheduled to expire at the end of 1987, but was again extended, this time through 1990. Through the 1980s the phone tax income served the general treasury, but clearly it was needed to help offset the Reagan administration's huge military build-up.

In 1990 instead of letting the tax expire, the 101st Congress extended it *permanently* at 3%, and this time with a new twist. Sponsors of the Act for Better Child Care seized the phone tax extension as a source of *new* funding for their programs (new sources being a requirement under Gramm-Rudman rules to reduce the federal deficit). The permanent phone tax was then attached to this bill and passed by Congress. Nevertheless, the phone tax revenues go into the general fund as they always have and in no way are earmarked for child care programs. Telephone taxes are available to the military in the same way as income taxes. War tax resisters continue to encourage telephone tax resistance; some groups redirect resisted phone taxes directly to child care themselves.

From April 1966 through 1990 the total revenues from the federal excise tax on telephone service have amounted to $42 billion.[2] According to the IRS the telephone tax raised over $3 billion in 1990, and the Congressional Budget Office has estimated that the tax will amount to a total of $13 billion for the years 1991 through 1995.[3]

Refusing the Phone Tax. To refuse the federal excise tax on telephone service simply deduct that amount from your monthly phone bill(s). If you receive one bill covering both local and long distance calling, the federal tax is usually itemized in two separate places: the local portion and the long distance portion. If you have a long distance telephone service separate from local service, that bill will itemize a federal excise tax. When you pay the bill(s) less the tax, enclose a note explaining that you are not paying the tax because of opposition to military spending, etc. Some phone companies require that you notify them each time you pay or else the unpaid tax will accumulate as "balance due." Others have actually refunded the tax when accidentally paid! Do not allow the tax to accumulate as a balance due. If it does contact the phone company and complain. The phone company should credit your account and report the unpaid tax to the IRS.

The idea for not paying the telephone tax was suggested by Doris Sargent in a letter to the *Peacemaker,* April 2, 1966. Karl Meyer started promoting it around the Chicago area and suggested to Maris Cakars that it might make a good national campaign of the Committee for Nonviolent Action. Shortly afterwards the War Resisters League picked it up and began a national campaign to refuse payment of the telephone tax. WRL printed up cards that telephone tax resisters could enclose with their bill payment each month and produced the brochure "Hang Up On War," first drafted by Karl Meyer. Telephone tax resistance grew to an estimated half million people by 1972.

From the beginning of the telephone war tax resistance movement in 1966 telephone company response was simply to notify the IRS of the nonpayment, *not* shut off telephone service. The telephone company position is that the nonpayment is a matter between the tax resister and the IRS. In fact, telephone companies would rather not have the tax on telephone service or have to collect it.

However, there have been some small telephone companies (and recently the new long distance companies) unaware of policy and law, which have discontinued telephone service to resisters. To set them straight, the tax resister should refer to IRS Procedural Rules (section 601.403 (c) (2) in the *Code of Federal Regulations,* title 26):

> If the person from whom the tax is required to be collected refuses to pay it . . . the collecting agency (e.g., the telephone company) is required to report to the district director of internal revenue for the district in which the returns are to be filed the name and address of such person, the nature of the service . . . rendered, the amount paid thereof, and the date on which paid. Upon receipt of this information the district director will proceed against the person to whom . . . the services (were) rendered to assert the amount of tax due, affording such person the same protest and appellate rights as are available to other excise taxpayers.

Two cases are of special interest:

In the case of Martha Tranquilli of Mound Bayou, Mississippi, who had her telephone service cut off in 1968 for nonpayment of her telephone tax, the Federal Communications Commission stated that:

> [T]he IRS does not hold the telephone company responsible for the amount . . . In this situation it cannot be considered that the tax is a "sum due the telephone company," within the meaning of Section 2.4.3 of American Telephone Company's Tariff FCC No. 263 which provides for disconnection of service upon non-payment. Therefore, a serious question

To refuse the federal telephone tax, simply deduct it from your monthly bill.

is raised as to whether the disconnection was not a denial of interstate telephone service in violation of the tariff, and therefore Section 203 (e) (3).[4]

Under section 203 (e), the telephone company could be penalized $500 and $25 for each day telephone service is shut off. Martha Tranquilli's phone was shut off for almost 700 days. The FCC hinted that Tranquilli might wish to sue the phone company for damages. Her phone service was restored immediately.

In a 1972 decision the FCC did order the company to pay a penalty in Martha Tranquilli's case. The commission noted that the IRS did not "by practice or regulation, require [AT&T] to enforce payment of the tax and...the company was without authority to enforce such payment." Citing the protest and appeal rights contained in the IRS procedural rules, the FCC stated, "[AT&T] could not eliminate such taxpayer rights by paying the tax and enforcing reimbursement by means of a service disconnection."[5]

Since 1971 telephone tax resisters have relied upon the *Tranquilli* case to prevent disconnection of their telephone service. However, a 1990 informal decision of the FCC raises questions about the legality of service disconnections by phone companies other than AT&T. Wayne Lottinville of Eugene, Oregon filed an informal complaint with the FCC when his long distance company, Call U.S., disconnected his phone service. Call U.S. argued that its billing system does not distinguish between taxes and telephone service, and that it disconnected Lottinville's service because he failed to pay his bills in full, not because he refused to pay the tax. In its response to the information complaint, the FCC allowed the disconnection, stating that it was "not unreasonable" and noting that Call U.S. is a "nondominant carrier" (i.e., a company that lacks the power to control prices).[6] The *Tranquilli* case was distinguished on the ground that it was based on AT&T's tariff, which does not apply to Call U.S. Because Lottinville's complaint, unlike Tranquilli's, was informal, the decision does not have the same precedential value.

All phone companies besides AT&T are considered nondominant carriers. All companies have tariffs, but only AT&T's is on file with the FCC. The others are filed with state public utility commissions, and it is state law and regulation which determine the circumstances under which these companies may disconnect service.

One aspect of the Lottinville decision was incorrect. The decision asserts that IRS regulations have changed since 1972 to require telephone companies to collect the tax. This is not true—the companies have *always* been required to collect the tax. What they are not required (or authorized) to do under the tax law is to *enforce* collection of the tax. The IRS statute and procedural rules regarding this are the same ones that were in effect when *Tranquilli* was decided. And, as the FCC pointed out in the *Tranquilli* decision, enforced collection through service disconnection denies people their protest and appeal rights under the IRS regulations.

If your telephone company threatens to disconnect your service (or even accumulates the tax on subsequent bills) call to talk with a supervisor (if the first person you reach is uncooperative). Refer to the IRS procedural rules and the *Tranquilli* decision that do not give a phone company any right or authority to enforce collection of the tax by shutting off service. Point out that the IRS rules only required them to report you to the IRS and that the FCC has said a phone company cannot deny people their IRS appeal rights by disconnecting service. Check with your state public utility commission to see what your company's tariff and your state's regulations say about disconnection of service.

If your company does shut off your service you may be able to appeal to your state public utility commission, as well as to the FCC. Because of the uncertainty of the law at this point, it would be wise to seek assistance from a national war tax resistance organization or a counselor or lawyer before filing an appeal.

Though telephone tax resisters have never been jailed, during the Indochina War they were frequently harassed with salary or bank account levies, auto seizures, etc.—all for $5 or so in telephone tax. The cost of each collection was estimated to be $300-$400.[7] Since the end of the Indochina War the number of telephone tax resisters has declined, but so has harassment. Telephone tax resisters may receive a notice of nonpayment from the IRS although collections for the small amounts of this tax are still rare.

Income Tax Resistance

Listed below are methods used in refusing payment of income war taxes. While the choice of method is primarily a matter of style and personal preference, there are distinct advantages and disadvantages as noted in each section. Resistance methods generally include an act of civil disobedience, but some people within the war tax

> The phone company may notify the IRS of your non-payment but should not disconnect your service.

> Resistance methods generally include an act of civil disobedience.

resistance network have chosen to stop paying war taxes legally by living below the taxable income level. A discussion of the pros and cons of that choice is included in this section also.

There is no intention here to pass judgment on which is the best or the "right" way to deal with war taxes (filing vs. nonfiling, resisting vs. living below the taxable level, etc.), but to point out the arguments and debates so that people can make the best choice for their situations.

File Normally, But Refuse Payment. Most war tax resisters use this method. It involves simply filling out your return according to IRS rules and refusing to pay whatever amount you have chosen to resist. Always include a letter of explanation as to why you are refusing to pay. This method has no value unless there is a tax due, so controlling your withholding may be necessary (see details below). This form of tax resistance bypasses the Examination Division and goes straight to the Collection Division of the IRS.

Arguments for this method include:
- Conscientious war tax refusal relies upon open disobedience and acceptance of consequences. The moral and political impact of such refusal comes in part from openly informing the government of our protest and the reasons for it. If we refuse taxes without informing the government, we will not be distinguishable from millions of others who evade taxes for reasons of personal benefit.

> **Openly informing the government of the protest enhances the moral and political impact of war tax refusal.**

> **If you alter your tax return, you may be assessed with the $500 "frivolous" fine.**

Drawing by Signe Wilkinson, a Philadelphia cartoonist.

- The act of open resistance is more significant than how much is refused.
- Our dispute is not with the system of taxation but with how tax money is spent.
- The IRS has only three years to dispute the figures on your return. The statute of limitations for collection is ten years from the date of assessment.

Arguments against filing:
- Those who file income tax returns provide the IRS with a lot of information thus making collection more likely. Unless self-employed, their W-2 forms disclose the amount and source of their income, and the filer may list the location of assets such as bank accounts or stocks.
- IRS employees are unlikely to pay attention to the protest. There is more political and social impact by talking openly about our tax refusal to friends and co-workers, who are more likely to be influenced by us.
- Filling out forms for the IRS is not a good use of time when you don't believe in how the money is distributed in the first place. Spend the time volunteering for something you believe in instead.

A warning note: Beginning in 1983 some war tax resisters were slapped with a $500 "frivolous filing" fine, because they had written war tax deductions, credits, or other messages on their IRS 1040 or EZ forms. For a few years this fine was applied liberally by the IRS, and resisters who appealed usually lost in court. Include your reasons for refusing to pay or other comments on a separate sheet of paper. See "Other Methods" below.

Not Filing. Some refusers decide not to file tax returns at all. They may choose to send a letter to the IRS at tax time explaining their resistance or ignore the IRS completely. This method may be most effective for those who are self-employed or have income which is not reported to the IRS on W-2 or 1099 reports.

Arguments for this method include:
- It is effective noncooperation with the entire income tax collection system. It does not require submitting information to the IRS. Because of the dominance of militarism the U.S. tax system has become so perverse and distorted that it does not serve a positive social purpose.
- The IRS may not notice a person who hasn't filed, and the money may be free and clear from the military. The nonfiler may "get lost in the shuffle."
- The collection process is slowed when you do not file your own income tax return and refuse

to cooperate with the IRS in assessment.

Arguments against nonfiling:

• There is no statute of limitations for assessment. Once an assessment is made, the IRS has the standard ten years to collect.

• Nonfilers run the risk of having the IRS invent a ridiculously high income and claim an absurd tax (see Robin Harper's story, Chapter 11).

• The penalty for failure to file is in addition to, and accumulates ten times faster than, the penalty for late payment.

• For those self-employed resisters who want to pay social security taxes, there is no easy way to do so without filing.

• A nonfiler may feel reluctant to be vocal about his/her resistance for fear of being noticed by the IRS. Nonfilers may fear joining in collective acts of resistance such as alternative funds.

Before 1987 many of those who did not file never heard from the IRS at all. Sometimes they received notices asking them to file but there was little follow-up to those notices. However, since 1987 it appears that the IRS has developed a better capability to file skeleton returns automatically, using information provided by employers and other income payers on annual W-2 and 1099 reports.

There is a slightly higher chance of criminal prosecution for nonfilers, but among the thousands of principled war tax refusers in the last fifty years only two have been indicted for failure to file a tax return (Catlett in 1979 and Chrisman in 1980; see Chapter 11).

Other Methods. A number of other methods for war tax resistance were popular in the past, but all carry risks of the $500 frivolous filing fine. Using the *War Tax Deduction*, individuals filed the 1040 and included a "war tax deduction" itemized on Schedule A under "Miscellaneous Deduction." The deduction could be made large enough to reduce the tax to zero. The *War Tax Credit* was written into the credit section of the 1040 form, taking a "credit" of the amount of taxes one chose to resist. The filer did not have to itemize, but the IRS sometimes considered this a mathematical error and sent it directly to the Collection Division. A similar method was the *War Tax Adjustment* written into the "Adjustments to Income" section of the 1040. Some resisters claimed *Extra Dependents* in the upper part of their return. For example, Martha Tranquilli claimed six peace organizations as dependents (see Chapter 11). The effect of the number of dependents comes into the "Tax Computation" section of your return. This method is little used now because of the significant danger of being charged and convicted of fraud, besides the likelihood of a frivolous fine. The *Fifth Amendment or Blank Return* was especially popular among right-wing tax refusers (see Chapter 13). It involves simply writing on every line which required monetary information "Fifth Amendment." A variation on this method is to file a signed and dated blank return, including a note of explanation. In either case the resisters claim that they have legally filed. The IRS position is that such resisters are liable both for the frivolous filing penalty *and* for the nonfiling penalties. (See "Not Filing" section above.)

Living Below Taxable Level. Some war tax opponents have chosen to lower their income to below the legally taxable level. For tax year 1991 this means:

• $5,000 for a married person (under 65) filing separately,

• $5,550 for a single person under 65,

• $10,000 for a married couple under 65,

• $10,650 for a married couple, one of whom is over 65,

• $11,300 for a married couple, both over 65.

Generally, those who make less than these amounts do not have to file.[8] If you are legally entitled to deductions, tax credits, etc., or have dependents, then the ceiling below which you are not taxed rises.

Basically, what is involved is to minimize the taxable part of your income and maximize the nontaxable part. If you file you can also claim every possible deduction and credit. You may need to consume less, grow some of your own food, conserve, purchase economically, do your own repairs, barter for services, and/or make your own gifts. For most people legal avoidance of taxes for war would require substantial changes in their lifestyles.

Arguments for lowering one's income include:

• This is the surest way to avoid paying taxes to the military since no money is owed and there is no risk of collection.

• It's a positive step towards creating a less materialistic society free from an oppressive economic system and can lead to a more ecological lifestyle.

• It is effective noncooperation with the entire income tax collection system.

> The General Accounting Office (GAO) reported that almost half the people with annual incomes over $100,000 who fail to file tax returns are escaping investigation by the IRS. Nonfilers with incomes below $100,000 are more likely to be assessed for taxes by the agency. The GAO acknowledged the IRS's shortage of investigators, but pointed to the irony of pursuing those from whom the financial gain would be lower.
> *Wall Street Journal*, March 14, 1991.

Not filing is noncooperation with the entire income tax collection system because of the dominance of militarism in the economy.

If you don't file, the IRS may invent a ridiculously high income for those years.

For most people legal avoidance of war taxes would require substantial changes in their lifestyles.

Keeping income low is a positive step towards creating a less materialistic society.

Arguments against this method as resistance:
- It lacks the confrontational element of directly refusing to pay what the government wants. Since it is legal, the government will be unaware of the protest.
- A.J. Muste, among others, felt that living below the taxable level solely to avoid taxes is allowing the government to choose your standard of living.
- For most people in this country, this is not a realistic option, and it leaves them little room to incorporate war tax resistance into their lives. Promotion of this method may discourage people who might otherwise be sympathetic to war tax resistance.

Some people try to avoid paying taxes by forming "family corporations," in which only the profits and capital gains would be taxable and the material needs of the family would be part of the corporation's expenses. The IRS considers such arrangements to be a "scam," denies the sought-after tax benefits, and sometimes adds 20% negligence penalties.

Some resisters have chosen dramatic changes in their lifestyles while continuing to be vocal in their opposition to military spending. One person living below the taxable level sent a letter to the IRS stating, "I am including no information on my income for 1980." She did this because she wanted to resist war taxes, not just avoid them.[9] Though she was not required to give the IRS any information, in any civil or criminal proceedings the burden of proof is on the taxpayer. Some resisters have lowered their incomes to circumvent collection after a number of years of nonpayment; many continue vocal and public resistance as the IRS continues its collection efforts.

Withholding

With the desperate need for more revenue during World War II the government hit upon a clever scheme: instead of relying on the citizen to pay taxes, take the money at the source by withholding from each paycheck. The employer becomes tax collector, and the burden is shifted to the taxpayer to recover any excess taxes withheld. Not only does this method guarantee collecting from most wage earners, but should the taxpayer fill out the return incorrectly or even fail to fill it out, the government comes out ahead. Further, even if the government has to return some of the withheld money, it has had it for many months as an *interest-free loan.*

Withholding puts a real crimp into the ability of the tax resister to decide whether or not to pay. The freedom to choose is essentially eliminated. The huge military budget that created a need for the withholding system also set in motion the seeds of the modern war tax resistance movement. Before World War II very few people legally paid income taxes for the relatively small (except during wars) military budget.

Before the Vietnam War the primary ways war tax resisters avoided withholding were by being self-employed or doing labor not subject to withholding. When it was discovered that withholding could be stopped by inflating the W-4 form, this became the primary means to avoid withholding for war tax resisters.

How the W-4 Works

Every time a person gets a job for a wage or salary, she or he must fill out a W-4 form ("Employee's Withholding Allowance Certificate") and give it to the employer. This form allows the employer to determine how much is to be withheld from each paycheck. The employee must figure the number of "allowances" to be claimed. Allowances include:
- 1 for employee,
- 1 for each dependent, unless claimed by someone else (e.g., the spouse),
- 1 "special withholding allowance" for a single person with one job, or married person whose spouse does not work,
- 1 or more for "estimated deductions or tax credits." The latter, determined on a worksheet on the back or top of the W-4 form (see page 33), is designed to reduce withholding for people who pay fewer taxes than normal because of significantly large deductions or credits. The employee only puts the *total number* of allowances being claimed on the portion of the W-4 turned into the employer, *not* where those allowances come from. Before 1972 the W-4 forms made explicit the source of allowance, forcing war tax resisters to claim dependents they obviously did not have.

Employees who submit a W-4 to their employer must sign the following statement: "Under penalties of perjury, I certify that I am entitled to the number of withholding allowances claimed on this certificate, or if claiming exemption from withholding, that I am entitled to the exempt status." Conviction for perjury can result in a maximum sentence of three years and/or $250,000 (IRC § 7206). There are other lesser and more common penalties for altering the W-4 form, such as the $500 civil penalty for "filing false information with

NO WITHHOLDING WAGE LIMITS

ALLOWANCES CLAIMED	WEEKLY SINGLE	WEEKLY MARRIED	BIWEEKLY SINGLE	BIWEEKLY MARRIED	SEMIMONTHLY SINGLE	SEMIMONTHLY MARRIED	MONTHLY SINGLE	MONTHLY MARRIED
0	25	70	50	140	55	150	105	300
1	70	115	135	225	145	240	290	480
2	110	155	215	310	235	330	460	640
3	150	195	300	390	320	420	640	840
4	195	240	380	470	410	500	840	1000
5	230	280	460	560	500	600	1000	1200
6	280	320	540	640	600	680	1200	1360
7	320	360	620	720	680	780	1360	1560
8	360	400	720	800	780	860	1560	1720
9	400	440	800	880	860	960	1720	1920
10	440	490	880	960	960	1040	1880	2080

Source: Circular E (IRS Publication 15), January 1991

respect to withholding" (IRC § 6682). So far, no war tax resister has been convicted of perjury for altering a W-4 form, but several people have gotten the $500 civil penalty.

There is also a criminal misdemeanor penalty for filing a "false or fraudulent" W-4 form (IRC § 7205). The maximum penalty under this provision is one year's imprisonment and a $100,000 fine, although actual sentences are almost always much lower than the maximum. A number of war tax resisters were convicted under Section 7205 during the 1970s, but none has been charged under this section since the early 1980s, when the $500 civil penalty was enacted.

When W-4 resistance is used in conjunction with the nonfiling method (see p. 28), there is a possibility of a 75% civil fraud penalty (and a remote chance of a criminal tax evasion charge).

Controlling Withholding

In order to have control over how much, if anything, you will pay the government, you must first control withholding. Listed below are half a dozen ways that have worked to give the resister control over her or his taxes.

Inflating the W-4. Known as "W-4 resistance" this is the most common method used by war tax resisters. Enough allowances on the W-4 form are claimed to reduce withholding to zero or whatever level wanted. In order to determine this number you need access to Circular E (IRS Publication 15), the "Employer's Tax Guide." You can get a free copy from the IRS, look at your employer's copy, or contact a war tax resistance counselor. The tables are divided by pay period (weekly, biweekly, etc.) and marital status. By finding the appropriate table and knowing the gross (i.e., total, before anything is taken out) salary, you can determine how many allowances you need in order to reduce your withholding to zero. If you want to reduce your withholding to half, first determine what should normally be withheld, then look for how many allowances are necessary to reach half that withholding figure. Note that the IRS requires employers to submit to it W-4 forms claiming more than ten allowances (but not those claiming under eleven).

The table above, taken from a recent Circular E (January 1991), gives the salary limit below which *nothing will be withheld* for various allowances. The Circular E also includes tables for daily payroll periods.

Without the tables you can calculate the reduction or prevention of withholding with the following formula:
- Gross weekly salary x 52 weeks = Annualized salary
- *Minus* $2,150 (single exemption for 1991) or $4,300 (married exemption for 1991) = amount subject to withholding
- *Divided* by $2,150 (value of each withholding allowance) = Number of allowances needed to prevent all withholding. Round off the result to the next highest whole number.

Once the number of allowances you want to claim is determined, file your W-4 (or a new one if you have one on file). Do not tell your employer why you are doing this or how you calculated the

Use the Circular E to determine how many allowances to claim in order to reduce your withholding.

1992 Form W-4

Department of the Treasury
Internal Revenue Service

Purpose. Complete Form W-4 so that your employer can withhold the correct amount of Federal income tax from your pay.

Exemption From Withholding. Read line 7 of the certificate below to see if you can claim exempt status. *If exempt, complete line 7; but do not complete lines 5 and 6.* No Federal income tax will be withheld from your pay. Your exemption is good for one year only. It expires February 15, 1993.

Basic Instructions. Employees who are not exempt should complete the Personal Allowances Worksheet. Additional worksheets are provided on page 2 for employees to adjust their withholding allowances based on itemized deductions, adjustments to income, or two-earner/two-job situations. Complete all worksheets that apply to your situation. The worksheets will help you figure the number of withholding allowances you are entitled to claim. However, you may claim fewer allowances than this.

Head of Household. Generally, you may claim head of household filing status on your tax return only if you are unmarried and pay more than 50% of the costs of keeping up a home for yourself and your dependent(s) or other qualifying individuals.

Nonwage Income. If you have a large amount of nonwage income, such as interest or dividends, you should consider making estimated tax payments using Form 1040-ES. Otherwise, you may find that you owe additional tax at the end of the year.

Two-Earner/Two-Jobs. If you have a working spouse or more than one job, figure the total number of allowances you are entitled to claim on all jobs using worksheets from only one Form W-4. This total should be divided among all jobs. Your withholding will usually be most accurate when all allowances are claimed on the W-4 filed for the highest paying job and zero allowances are claimed for the others.

Advance Earned Income Credit. If you are eligible for this credit, you can receive it added to your paycheck throughout the year. For details, get Form W-5 from your employer.

Check Your Withholding. After your W-4 takes effect, you can use **Pub. 919**, Is My Withholding Correct for 1992?, to see how the dollar amount you are having withheld compares to your estimated total annual tax. Call 1-800-829-3676 to order this publication. Check your local telephone directory for the IRS assistance number if you need further help.

Personal Allowances Worksheet

People often neglect to take this allowance.

For 1992, the value of your personal exemption(s) is reduced if your income is over $105,250 ($157,900 if married filing jointly, $131,550 if head of household, or $78,950 if married filing separately). Get Pub. 919 for details.

- **A** Enter "1" for **yourself** if no one else can claim you as a dependent . . . . **A** _____
- **B** Enter "1" if:
  - You are single and have only one job; or
  - You are married, have only one job, and your spouse does not work; or
  - Your wages from a second job or your spouse's wages (or the total of both) are $1,000 or less.

  B _____
- **C** Enter "1" for your **spouse.** But, you may choose to enter -0- if you are married and have either a working spouse or more than one job (this may help you avoid having too little tax withheld) . . . . **C** _____
- **D** Enter number of **dependents** (other than your spouse or yourself) whom you will claim on your tax return . . . . . **D** _____
- **E** Enter "1" if you will file as **head of household** on your tax return (see conditions under "Head of Household," above) . **E** _____
- **F** Enter "1" if you have at least $1,500 of **child or dependent care expenses** for which you plan to claim a credit . . **F** _____
- **G** Add lines A through F and enter total here. Note: *This amount may be different from the number of exemptions you claim on your return* ▶ **G** _____

For accuracy, do all worksheets that apply.
- If you plan to **itemize or claim adjustments to income** and want to reduce your withholding, see the Deductions and Adjustments Worksheet on page 2.
- If you are **single** and have **more than one job** and your combined earnings from all jobs exceed $29,000 OR if you are **married** and have a **working spouse or more than one job,** and the combined earnings from all jobs exceed $50,000, see the Two-Earner/Two-Job Worksheet on page 2 if you want to avoid having too little tax withheld.
- If **neither** of the above situations applies, **stop here** and enter the number from line G on line 5 of Form W-4 below.

---------- Cut here and give the certificate to your employer. Keep the top portion for your records. ----------

Your employer gets only the lower half of this form.

Form W-4
Department of the Treasury
Internal Revenue Service

Employee's Withholding Allowance Certificate

▶ For Privacy Act and Paperwork Reduction Act Notice, see reverse.

1992

Notice that you do not specify where the allowances come from.

1 Your first name and middle initial	Last name	**2** Your social security number

Home address (number and street or rural route)	**3** ☐ Single ☐ Married ☐ Married, but withhold at higher Single rate
City or town, state, and ZIP code	Note: *If married, but legally separated, or spouse is a nonresident alien, check the Single box.*
	4 If your last name differs from that on your social security card, check here and call 1-800-772-1213 for more information . ▶ ☐

- **5** Total number of allowances you are claiming (from line G above or from the Worksheets on back if they apply) **5** _____
- **6** Additional amount, if any, you want deducted from each paycheck . . . . **6** $ _____
- **7** I claim exemption from withholding and I certify that I meet **ALL** of the following conditions for exemption:
  - Last year I had a right to a refund of **ALL** Federal income tax withheld because I had **NO** tax liability; **AND**
  - This year I expect a refund of **ALL** Federal income tax withheld because I expect to have **NO** tax liability; **AND**
  - This year if my income exceeds $600 and includes nonwage income, another person cannot claim me as a dependent.

  If you meet all of the above conditions, enter the year effective and "EXEMPT" here . . . ▶ **7** 19___
- **8** Are you a full-time student? (Note: *Full-time students are not automatically exempt.*) . . . . **8** ☐ Yes ☐ No

Under penalties of perjury, I certify that I am entitled to the number of withholding allowances claimed on this certificate or entitled to claim exempt status.

Read pages 30-34 for information on penalties.

Employee's signature ▶ _____ Date ▶ _____, 19___

9 Employer's name and address (Employer: Complete 9 and 10 only if sending to the IRS) | **10** Office code (optional) | **11** Employer identification number

Cat. No. 10220Q

Form W-4 (1992) Page 2

Deductions and Adjustments Worksheet

Note: *Use this worksheet only if you plan to itemize deductions or claim adjustments to income on your 1992 tax return.*

1. Enter an estimate of your 1992 itemized deductions. These include: qualifying home mortgage interest, charitable contributions, state and local taxes (but not sales taxes), medical expenses in excess of 7.5% of your income, and miscellaneous deductions. (For 1992, you may have to reduce your itemized deductions if your income is over $105,250 ($52,625 if married filing separately). Get Pub. 919 for details.) ... **1** $ _____

2. Enter:
   - $6,000 if married filing jointly or qualifying widow(er)
   - $5,250 if head of household
   - $3,600 if single
   - $3,000 if married filing separately

   ... **2** $ _____

3. **Subtract** line 2 from line 1. If line 2 is greater than line 1, enter -0- ... **3** $ _____
4. Enter an estimate of your 1992 adjustments to income. These include alimony paid and deductible IRA contributions ... **4** $ _____
5. **Add** lines 3 and 4 and enter the total ... **5** $ _____
6. Enter an estimate of your 1992 nonwage income (such as dividends or interest income) ... **6** $ _____
7. **Subtract** line 6 from line 5. Enter the result, but not less than -0- ... **7** $ _____
8. **Divide** the amount on line 7 by $2,500 and enter the result here. Drop any fraction ... **8** _____
9. Enter the number from Personal Allowances Worksheet, line G, on page 1 ... **9** _____
10. **Add** lines 8 and 9 and enter the total here. If you plan to use the Two-Earner/Two-Job Worksheet, also enter the total on line 1, below. Otherwise, **stop here** and enter this total on Form W-4, line 5, on page 1. ... **10** _____

Two-Earner/Two-Job Worksheet

Note: *Use this worksheet only if the instructions for line G on page 1 direct you here.*

1. Enter the number from line G on page 1 (or from line 10 above if you used the Deductions and Adjustments Worksheet) ... **1** _____
2. Find the number in **Table 1** below that applies to the **LOWEST** paying job and enter it here ... **2** _____
3. If line 1 is **GREATER THAN OR EQUAL TO** line 2, subtract line 2 from line 1. Enter the result here (if zero, enter -0-) and on Form W-4, line 5, on page 1. **DO NOT** use the rest of this worksheet ... **3** _____

Note: *If line 1 is **LESS THAN** line 2, enter -0- on Form W-4, line 5, on page 1. Complete lines 4–9 to calculate the additional dollar withholding necessary to avoid a year-end tax bill.*

4. Enter the number from line 2 of this worksheet ... **4** _____
5. Enter the number from line 1 of this worksheet ... **5** _____
6. **Subtract** line 5 from line 4 ... **6** _____
7. Find the amount in **Table 2** below that applies to the **HIGHEST** paying job and enter it here ... **7** $ _____
8. **Multiply** line 7 by line 6 and enter the result here. This is the additional annual withholding amount needed ... **8** $ _____
9. Divide line 8 by the number of pay periods remaining in 1992. (For example, divide by 26 if you are paid every other week and you complete this form in December of 1991.) Enter the result here and on Form W-4, line 6, page 1. This is the additional amount to be withheld from each paycheck ... **9** $ _____

Table 1: Two-Earner/Two-Job Worksheet

Married Filing Jointly		All Others	
If wages from **LOWEST** paying job are—	Enter on line 2 above	If wages from **LOWEST** paying job are—	Enter on line 2 above
0 - $4,000	0	0 - $6,000	0
4,001 - 8,000	1	6,001 - 10,000	1
8,001 - 13,000	2	10,001 - 14,000	2
13,001 - 18,000	3	14,001 - 18,000	3
18,001 - 22,000	4	18,001 - 22,000	4
22,001 - 26,000	5	22,001 - 45,000	5
26,001 - 30,000	6	45,001 and over	6
30,001 - 35,000	7		
35,001 - 40,000	8		
40,001 - 60,000	9		
60,001 - 80,000	10		
80,001 and over	11		

Table 2: Two-Earner/Two-Job Worksheet

Married Filing Jointly		All Others	
If wages from **HIGHEST** paying job are—	Enter on line 7 above	If wages from **HIGHEST** paying job are—	Enter on line 7 above
0 - $50,000	$340	0 - $27,000	$340
50,001 - 100,000	640	27,001 - 58,000	640
100,001 and over	710	58,001 and over	710

Privacy Act and Paperwork Reduction Act Notice.—We ask for the information on this form to carry out the Internal Revenue laws of the United States. The Internal Revenue Code requires this information under sections 3402(f)(2)(A) and 6109 and their regulations. Failure to provide a completed form will result in your being treated as a single person who claims no withholding allowances. Routine uses of this information include giving it to the Department of Justice for civil and criminal litigation and to cities, states, and the District of Columbia for use in administering their tax laws.

The time needed to complete this form will vary depending on individual circumstances. The estimated average time is: **Recordkeeping** 46 min., **Learning about the law or the form** 10 min., **Preparing the form** 70 min. If you have comments concerning the accuracy of these time estimates or suggestions for making this form more simple, we would be happy to hear from you. You can write to both the **Internal Revenue Service,** Washington, DC 20224, Attention: IRS Reports Clearance Officer, T:FP; and the **Office of Management and Budget,** Paperwork Reduction Project (1545-0010), Washington, DC 20503. **DO NOT** send the tax form to either of these offices. Instead, give it to your employer.

*U.S. Government Printing Office: 1991 — 285-081

allowances unless your employer does not mind being complicit in your tax resistance.

If you make an unauthorized alteration or addition to your W-4 form or make any statements to your employer that the information is false, then your W-4 form is invalid (IRC 31.3402 (f)(2)–1 (e)). In these cases the employer is supposed to disregard your W-4 and withhold as if you were single and claiming no withholding allowances. Or if an earlier W-4 is on file, the employer should withhold according to that one.

"To curb the filing of false federal income tax withholding forms by persons claiming unreasonable number of allowances or total exemption," the IRS issued the following regulations: the employer is required to send to the IRS any W-4 form which claims "exempt" for an employee making over $200 per week, or claims for more than ten allowances (see IRS Publication 15). The IRS may also require an employer to submit copies of W-4 forms from a particular employee or group of employees thought to be trying to avoid withholding.

If your W-4 form is sent to the IRS, it will remain in effect until the employer hears in writing from the IRS. The IRS may instruct the employer to alter the withholding. The employer must abide by the IRS instructions until they are revoked by the IRS. It is up to the employee to convince the IRS in writing why she or he is entitled to additional allowances.

We do not know whether most employers are aware of these regulations or whether they abide by them. If they do, this means that single employees earning more than about $22,500 a year (in 1991) will no longer be able to prevent the withholding of *all* taxes by this particular method. Individuals who are anxious to be total income tax resisters may need to lower their salary, work part-time jobs and file more than one W-4, experiment with other forms of stopping withholding (see below), or even discover a new method.

The W-4 resistance method was suggested in 1965 by Ken Knudson[10] and later popularized by Karl Meyer, but before 1972 war tax resisters could only claim extra dependents. Lyle Snider holds "the record" of having claimed the most dependents on a W-4 form: three billion, for the population of the earth. He was convicted of fraud in 1973. But a year later the conviction was overturned. The U.S. Court of Appeals observed that Snider was engaging in hyperbole, and obviously not attempting to deceive anyone (see page 66).

Since claiming extra dependents could easily be proven false, the government indicted several war tax resisters in the early 1970s (sixteen that we have record of) for W-4 resistance, and eventually six were jailed (from one month to nine months). However, in 1972 the W-4 forms were changed to allow employees to claim additional allowances for "estimated itemized deductions" or tax credits. As a result it became very difficult to prove falsification or fraud. Very few war tax resisters have been prosecuted for inflating the new W-4 forms. In fact, Paul Monsky (see Chapter 11) is the only one we are aware of, *so far*. In the early 1980s thousands of auto workers in Michigan inflated their W-4 forms to stop payment of what they considered unconstitutional taxes. However, the government cracked down on a few of them, handing out sentences of up to thirty months (see page 108).

W-4 Exempt. If you legally owed no taxes last year and *expect* to owe none this year, you can claim exempt on your W-4 form, and no taxes will be withheld (see the W-4 form on pages 32-33). Many war tax resisters believe they can truthfully affirm that no tax was owed last year and none will be owed this year, because they believe they have the right not to pay for militarism and war preparation. But since the IRS may be able to prove easily that money was owed *last year*, these resisters are opening themselves up to charges of perjury for filing a "false or fraudulent" W-4 form. Whether you will owe taxes for the current year is more a matter of opinion, however. Some of the autoworkers mentioned above were claiming exempt, thus precipitating the crackdown on them and the new rules from the IRS.

Self-Employed. If you are self-employed, you have complete control over withholding. Occupations which lend themselves to self-employment include doctors, dentists, lawyers, music teachers, tutors, therapists, counselors, writers, illustrators, performers, musicians, entertainers, lecturers, and farmers. Other occupations lend themselves to setting up small businesses, such as printers, messenger services, decorators, hairdressers, barbers, bakers, woodworkers, upholsterers, electricians, typesetters, mechanics, engineers, architects, computer programmers, and truck drivers. Being a consultant is another way to avoid withholding.[11]

The line between an employee and being self-employed is not always clear. The IRS uses a series of twenty "common-law control factors" which act as *guides* to distinguish between an employee and an independent contractor.[12] The IRS describes an employer as a person for whom a worker performs

---

Employers are supposed to notify the IRS of any employee who claims more than 10 allowances, or who claims "exempt" when making over $200 per week.

Lyle Snider claimed three billion dependents, for the population of the earth.

In the early 1970s several war tax resisters were indicted for claiming too many dependents.

service as an employee. The employer usually provides the tools, place of work, has the right to fire an employee, sets the hours, makes regular payments, pays business expenses, provides training and direction, etc. The employee makes regular reports to an employer, does not suffer a profit or loss in the business, does not make her/his services available to the public, can quit, has a continuing relationship with the employer, cannot hire assistance (except as a foreperson), etc. The more of the these factors that apply to you, the more likely that the IRS will rule that you are an employee rather than an independent contractor, and require your "employer" to withhold taxes from your pay.

To help avoid confusion, independent contractors should have their own letterhead, phone, and office; submit invoices; set their own hours; have their own tools; and institute other practices opposite of those mentioned for defining employees.

Those who receive a significant income through self-employment are required to file and pay estimated tax (including social security taxes) on a quarterly basis. The penalty for not making quarterly payments of estimated tax consists of interest added to the unpaid amount from the date due. This penalty does not apply if 1) the total tax liability for the year is less than $500, 2) the person had no tax liability in the previous year, or 3) the total of estimated taxes paid plus taxes withheld during the year equals 90% of the tax due for the year or 100% of the previous year's tax.

Non-Withheld Labor. There is no withholding from ministers, domestic workers, newspaper vendors, most agricultural laborers, and some day-labor.

Employment Agency. If your work does not meet the criteria for self-employment described above, you might try forming an employment agency—a small scale model of Kelly Services or Manpower—in order to gain control over withholding. As your employer the agency would be responsible for withholding, not the company which pays for the labor. The employment agency could be formed as a partnership by two or more people. According to the Internal Revenue Code section 701, "persons carrying on business as partners shall be liable for income tax only in their separate or individual capacities."

The IRS could rule that your employment agency is not a legitimate employer or subcontractor. Therefore, your employment agency should try to satisfy as many of these employer criteria as possible. Obviously, some do not apply to the employment agency arrangement. Having an office or a post office box, letterhead (to send bills for services rendered for each pay period), and a phone would be a good start. Your agency should pay employees at regular intervals, pay business expenses where appropriate, and employees could even submit reports—anything which will give the agency more of an official employer appearance.

One of the keys to having it work would be to convince your current employer to agree to pay for your services to this agency rather than directly to you.

One drawback of this approach is that your employment agency could end up being subject to other laws applicable to employers—such as Occupational Safety and Health (OSHA) regulations, workers' compensation, and unemployment insurance.

Employer Refuses to Withhold. The advent of withholding in effect drafted every employer in the country as a "deputy tax collector" for the IRS. Many socially and politically progressive employers are not enamored with the idea of forcing their

---

THE CASE OF ONE RESISTING EMPLOYER
WAR RESISTERS LEAGUE

In 1956 after beginning work with the War Resisters League, Ralph DiGia asked WRL's board not to withhold federal taxes from his paychecks. The organization agreed and thus began WRL's direct involvement in resistance.

The IRS ignored Ralph for some time, but in 1974 they froze WRL's bank account for the resisted tax dollars of other employees. They took the whole account, $2,537.43, still $1,000 less than they claimed was owed.

After some years of his resistance Ralph began to receive personal visits from collection agents, then a levy was placed on his salary at WRL for tax years 1971, 1972, 1974, and 1975 (1973 got lost in the shuffle). Because the WRL has a policy of not honoring IRS levies, WRL was summoned to U.S. District Court in 1978 to show cause why the organization should not be required to honor the levy. The Court ruled in December of 1979 that it did not "challenge the sincerity of the defendant's professed opposition to war. ...The only issue for decision is a legal one: does the defendant have a constitutional right to refuse taxes because of religious or conscientious objection to one of a myriad uses to which revenue is put? On this issue, the government is entitled to judgement as a matter of law."

On April 15, 1981 the IRS asked WRL to list its assets as a means of finding the bank account. WRL refused to cooperate. Then on April 18, 1983 the U.S. Department of Justice seized $1,228.23 from WRL's bank account for the four tax years mentioned above.

The War Resisters League resists the federal telephone tax. Although the IRS continues to send salary levies to WRL for other individuals, the relationship has not been a close one in recent years.

If you are self-employed, you have complete control over withholding.

There is no withholding from domestic workers and agricultural laborers.

Withholding drafted every employer in the country as a deputy tax collector for the IRS.

Some churches and organizations will stop withholding at the request of an employee or refuse to honor salary levies.

Savings bonds are war bonds in disguise.

employees to pay for war. A few have openly fought that role. For example, the American Friends Service Committee (AFSC) and two of its employees sued the government to stop it from forcing the AFSC to withhold taxes from employees who conscientiously were opposed to paying for war. A federal district court judge in 1974 ruled in favor of the AFSC only to be overturned quickly by the Supreme Court in an 8 to 1 decision. Some churches and a few organizations, such as the War Resisters League, Clergy and Laity Concerned, CCCO, and Sojourners, will stop withholding at the request of an employee and refuse to honor levies on an employee's salary.

Employers have been taken to court or have had their bank accounts levied for taxes of employees (see box this chapter). The IRS has been known to punish such employers with a 50% penalty (§6332 (2)) for refusing to honor a levy, and even 100% penalty (§6672) for not withholding. However, the 100% penalty for failure to withhold is really a collection device rather than a penalty. It simply authorizes the IRS to collect from the employer 100% of taxes not withheld. It does not subject the employer to an additional penalty. In addition to the 100% "penalty," there is also a 10% civil penalty for failure to pay over withheld taxes.

There is also the possibility of criminal penalties for the willful refusal to honor a levy or to withhold taxes from employees. Although the IRS has occasionally threatened to revoke the tax exempt status of organizations cooperating with their members' or employees' war tax resistance, it is unlikely that the IRS could legally follow through with this threat against organizations otherwise meeting the criteria for tax exempt status.

Organizations cooperating with resisters may also be subject to penalties if they fail to submit required "information returns." Organizations are required, for example, to file a Form 1099 if they make payments totalling more than $600 during the year to an individual providing services as an independent contractor. Under the 1986 tax law, the penalty for failure to file required information returns is $50 for each return; if the failure is due to "intentional disregard" of the filing requirement, the penalty is the greater of $100 per return or a specified percentage (generally 10%) of the amount not reported (IRC §6721).

War tax resisters facing salary levies may choose to use this opportunity to explain their resistance to an employer or organizational board. Even when employers have ultimately decided to honor levies, a discussion around the possibility of refusal can have educational benefits. In some cases the IRS has collected the taxes from other sources or simply dropped levies after a protest by the employer or while the employer was considering its response.

Resisting Other War Taxes

Alcohol and Tobacco. Smokers who consume a pack of cigarettes each day will cough up about $90 a year in federal excise taxes. People who drink two beers or a couple of glasses of wine a day will be contributing $70 to $150 a year in federal excise taxes. Since these are by far the biggest revenue sources for federal excise taxes, many war tax resisters have tried (without much success) to resist payment. Aside from abstaining the best that can be done to avoid these taxes is to make your own wine or beer (up to 200 gallons per person per year) and roll your own cigarettes (papers and loose tobacco are free of federal excise taxes).

Savings Bonds. Though transformed through a miraculous face-lift from being "war bonds," the function of savings bonds remains the same: to allow the government to borrow money for federal spending. These are as much war—or military—bonds as ever.

Air Travel, Gasoline, Social Security. Technically, these are not war taxes since they are collected for trust funds, and do not go into federal funds out of which all military spending comes. However, during the Indochina War, some people successfully refused to pay the federal tax on air travel, thinking it was a war tax. Some religious sects are exempt from social security taxes. Gasoline taxes — good luck! The federal government has borrowed from trust funds, particularly the Social Security, to help offset deficits. In those instances the trust funds indirectly helped war and military spending.

Organizational Resistance and Complicity

A number of organizations have been resisters themselves—primarily through nonpayment of the telephone tax. By refusing to withhold or not honoring levies they are also complicit with the war tax resistance of their employees.

One corporation, Collective Impressions Printshop organized by the Community for Creative Nonviolence in Washington, D.C., refused to pay its corporate income taxes from 1977 to 1980 in opposition to nuclear weapons and power development. The money was sent to the U.S. Arms Control and Disarmament Agency, but returned. Their accounts were seized four times.[13]

Some organizations have written policies about war tax resistance. This policy may be to state the group's own resistance (i.e., regarding phone tax or withholding), and to clarify the organizational relationship to individual staff members who are war tax resisters. A good resource for *any* organization is *Fear God and Honor the Emperor: A Manual on Military Tax Withholding for Religious Employers* available from Friends Committee on War Tax Concerns, 1506 Race Street, Philadelphia, PA 19102.

Some organizations resist the telephone tax.

1 *Congressional Record*, February 23, 1966.
2 *Internal Revenue Report of Excise Taxes*, reported at CCH Federal Excise Tax Reporter para. 6805.
3 Congressional Budget Office Report, "An Analysis of the President's Budget Proposals for Fiscal Year 1991," March 5, 1990.
4 FCC 71-668, Docket 19271, FCC Reports, 30 FCC 2nd, pp. 835-839, 1971.
5 38 FCC 2d, pp. 192-198, 1972.
6 FCC, 63203, IC-89-05837, Feb. 26, 1990.
7 *WIN* Magazine, November 15, 1970.
8 People who receive more than $400 in self-employment income in a year are required to file. A number of other factors also affect filing requirements. People should check the specific requirements for each year.
9 *Peacemaker*, September 1981.
10 *Peacemaker*, page 6, September 11, 1965.
11 This list is from the *Handbook on Nonpayment of War Taxes*, Peacemakers, page 16, 1981.
12 For example, see the Social Security Claims Manual, chapter 1200, '120 1212.5; or the Social Security Handbook, §804-824, pp. 140-144.
13 *People Pay for Peace*, pp. 19-20, 1984.

5 The IRS Audit and Appeals Process

The possibility of an IRS audit[1] creates fear and trembling in most Americans. However, many war tax resisters see an audit as an opportunity to communicate their views to the government.

Some tax returns are chosen randomly or by formula for examination. In the past many war tax resisters used the "war tax deduction" or "war tax credit" methods (see p. 29) in order to have their returns selected for examination and to take advantage of the appeals process. Since 1983, however, many resisters have been deterred from claiming war tax deductions or credits because the IRS now assesses $500 "frivolous" return penalties when these methods are used. Examiners are also supposed to check for W-4 compliance during an audit, therefore, an audit can lead to penalties for W-4 resistance and to disallowance of one's W-4 certificate. In addition, people who bring war tax cases in tax court could be charged penalties of up to $5,000 for troubling the Court with "frivolous or groundless" suits.

After what may be a long and tedious process of appeals, you should expect your return will arrive at the Collection Division, with possible additional penalties for taking this route. So why bother with the Examination Division at all, you may ask. Some war tax resisters still find it advantageous to use this process for its educational and consciousness-raising potential. Also collection is delayed throughout the whole process, which may last up to three or four years, and the system is gummed up for awhile.

There are also legal reasons for using the appeals process—if one disputes the amount of tax the IRS wants to assess. For instance, if you don't file a return, the IRS can "file" one for you. If they do this, you can expect them to overestimate your income and underestimate your exemptions and deductions—resulting in a higher tax bill than if you had filed. Challenging an erroneous amount in tax court will not subject you to "frivolous" case penalties. (But if you also argue that you should not be required to pay war taxes, you can expect a "frivolous" case penalty for making that argument.)

Examination Procedure

If your return is selected for audit, the examination may take place by mail, at the IRS office, or at your home or place of business (called a field examination). Returns that are challenged by the IRS because they contain "unallowable items" (such as a war tax deduction or credit) are generally examined by mail.

You can bring a representative (such as a lawyer, accountant, or your tax preparer) and witnesses to an office or field examination. You can also use a tape recorder if you give the IRS ten days written notice of your intention to do so. Some war tax resisters have brought friends and supporters with them and have used the examination as an opportunity to express their moral and political views about war. There is no penalty for doing this, but examiners will likely try to limit your presentation to matters they consider germane to your tax liability.

The purpose of the examination is to seek "additional information to verify your correct tax." Following the examination, a "Report of Individual Income Tax Examination Changes" containing adjustments to your return will be sent to you.

If you do not accept the "finding" of the report, you have thirty days (from the date of the report) to request an appeals conference with the Appeals Office of your IRS region. The IRS may disallow the hearing if they feel your "reasons for disagreement do not come within the scope of the internal revenue law; for example, disagreement based solely on moral, religious, political, constitutional, conscientious, or similar grounds." If you do not respond within thirty days, your case will be processed "on the basis of adjustments shown in the examination report."

Whether or not you take advantage of this appeal, a "Notice of Deficiency" (or ninety-day letter) will eventually be issued by the IRS. You have ninety days from the date of this notice to file a petition with the U.S. Tax Court (see below). After losing there you can go to the U.S. Court of Appeals and then to the U.S. Supreme Court.

After you have exhausted the appeals procedures or if you do not petition the tax court within ninety days, the IRS will send you a "final assessment of tax due" (form 4188). If you do not pay within ten days, your file will be sent to the Collection Division. The Collection Division has ten years from the date of this "assessment" to collect the tax, or bring a collection action in court. If they do not succeed in that period of time, the tax is no longer due and cannot be collected.

If you filed your return showing a tax due and you refused to pay it, and the IRS accepts your return as filed, the tax can be assessed by the IRS immediately; the ten-year clock begins ticking at this point.

Normally the IRS has three years from the date of filing in which to begin the process of examination. If they do not challenge it within this period, the return stands as filed. But if your return contained false or fraudulent information, or if you did not file a return, there is no time restriction on when the IRS can begin the examination. However, once a "final assessment" has been made, the Collection Division still has ten years to collect.

Refund Procedures

Another route of appeal is to request a refund after the tax has been paid or collected by the IRS. A request for refund must be filed with the IRS within two years after the tax was paid or three years after the return was filed, whichever deadline is later. A refund request is made by filing an "amended return" (form 1040X), which risks the $500 "frivolous" return penalty if a war tax deduction or credit is claimed.

A refund claim can be filed in federal district court or the U.S. Court of Claims within two years after the IRS denies a request for refund. If the IRS doesn't respond to the refund request within six months, a court action may be filed anytime. Under Rule 11 of the Federal Rules of Civil Procedure, the government can be awarded damages if a person brings a case that is not "well grounded in fact" and "warranted by . . . law" (i.e., a "frivolous" case penalty). Damages under this rule have been awarded against lawyers who represented war tax resisters competently and in good faith.

You can expect the same outcome in the district courts and Claims Court as in tax court (see following sections).

Tax Court[2]

You can go to tax court with or without a lawyer. If you are going *pro se* (without a lawyer), the first step is to write or call the U.S. Tax Court, 400 Second St., NW, Washington, D.C. 20217, addressing the Clerk of the Court. Ask for a copy of the current rules of practice and procedure because you have a case coming up. After you get the rule book, you must decide whether your case will be a small tax case or not. If the amount in dispute is over $10,000, the case cannot be conducted as a small tax case, but if it is less you have this option. If you do choose the small tax case route, then *you have waived your right of appeal to higher courts,* and any decision made will not serve as a precedent.

Next you need to file a petition explaining why you want to be in tax court. You must adhere rigidly to time limits set for submission of various documents. You have exactly ninety days from the mailing date of the IRS "Notice of Deficiency" until the filing date with the tax court. If you are late you cannot have your case heard by tax court. It is also essential to send all items by certified mail with a return receipt requested. After your petition has been filed by the tax court with a copy to the IRS, the IRS has sixty days to file an answer or forty-five days to make a motion. When you get the answer, you may submit a reply, for which you have another forty-five days. There are other possibilities for other kinds of motions. It is quite likely that the tax court will not allow any oral statements or presentation of witnesses. Eventually you will have a time set for your hearing.

In cases claiming a right to refuse to pay for war the tax court has determined that what exists is only a "matter of law" not a "matter of fact"; that is, there are no disputed facts (for example, mathematical differences), but only a question as to whether one may take a deduction for this purpose. The tax court considers it irrelevant whether you sent your refused taxes to a worthy cause or not. The IRS usually moves for a Judgment on the Pleadings, Summary Judgment, or Dismissal of the case. This means that all things being admitted, you have no case because there is no such war tax deduction or credit. It is the policy of the tax court not to hear any evidence (because there are no matters of fact) and only to hear your argument. You may file a brief explaining your argument in writing. Invariably the government's motion, as described, is granted, and you find yourself out of the tax court with a right of appeal to the appellate court.

The appellate court invariably upholds the tax court regardless of any constitutional arguments. The appellate court holds that the constitutional requirements do not take precedence over the IRS regulations because the constitutional rights of the First and other amendments are not absolute. This position, however, seems to assume that the IRS code is absolute! Further, if your arguments are not based on religious reasons, but political reasons, you will run into issues called "standing" and "justiciability," which means that as an "individual" taxpayer relying on political arguments (e.g., Nuremberg Principles or International law) you cannot bring such a case at all.

If you lose in tax court and want to appeal, you must file a notice of appeal within ninety days with the appellate court. If you lose at the appellate court level, you have ninety days to file a petition for Writ of Certiorari with the U.S. Supreme Court. This writ need not be granted and up to this point

If the IRS does not challenge your return within three years of the filing date, the return stands as filed.

In tax court you must adhere rigidly to time limits set for submission of various documents.

The position of the courts seems to assume that the IRS Code is absolute.

The IRS Audit and Appeals Process

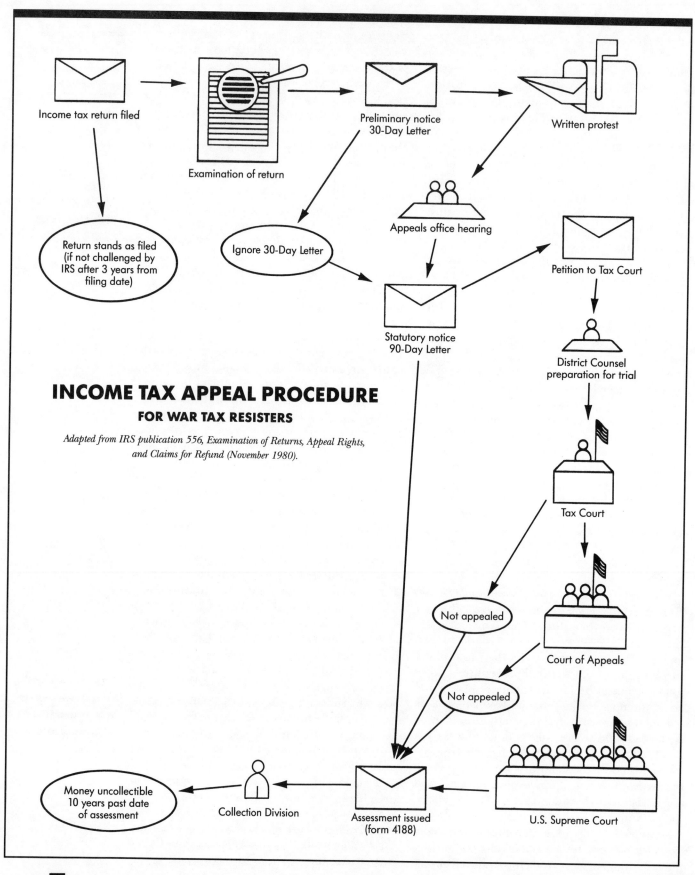

has not been.

The tax court can assess penalties of up to $25,000 for bringing a "frivolous or groundless" case. The tax court considers war tax resistance cases "frivolous" and "groundless." The $25,000 "frivolous case" penalty may also be imposed on people who "unreasonably failed to pursue available administrative remedies" before bringing a case to tax court. This means that people are expected to seek relief in every available way from the IRS itself before going to tax court. The appellate court can also assess "double damages" for filing a "frivolous" appeal.

Taking a case to court is up to the resister. Many have chosen not to use the courts at all because they see these institutions as protecting the military and perpetuating militarism.

The Constitutional Arguments

What follows is a brief review of the basic constitutional arguments used in tax resistance court cases. Some resisters, however, ignore constitutional arguments and rely solely on political or moral arguments.

First Amendment

Congress shall make no law respecting an establishment of religion, or prohibiting the free exercise thereof;...
Many religious pacifists, beginning with A.J. Muste in 1961, have argued that this amendment protects their right not to pay taxes for war. However, the right to free exercise of religion has never been held to be absolute, and a long line of tax court and federal district court decisions has denied war tax resisters a First Amendment right to refuse war taxes.[3]

Most of these cases were actions brought by war tax resisters to establish a right to exemption from war taxes. First Amendment arguments have also been raised in cases initiated by the government. In 1990 Philadelphia Yearly Meeting unsuccessfully defended against an IRS levy enforcement action by arguing that it could not constitutionally be required to violate the religious beliefs of its employees by collecting refused taxes from them.[4]

In 1989 Don Mosley and Max Rice of Jubilee Partners in Comer, Georgia, refused to comply with an IRS summons on the ground that compliance would violate their First Amendment right to free exercise of religion by compelling them to support indirectly the expenditure of funds for military purposes. Although reluctant to punish them for being faithful to their religious convictions, the judge sentenced them to sixty days in jail for contempt. They were released before their sentences were completed.

Most of the First Amendment cases were decided during the time when the courts were applying the "compelling state interest" test to free exercise claims. Under this test when religious practices were made illegal by any law, courts had to decide first whether there was a "compelling" state interest justifying the burden on religion. If they found that there was a compelling interest, they then had to decide whether any "less restrictive means" were available to the government to achieve its interest without burdening religious practice.[5]

Applying this standard the courts readily determined that the government's interest in tax collection is compelling, but (to the great frustration of resistance lawyers) none bothered to address the question whether less restrictive means (such as a Peace Tax Fund) could be used by the government to achieve its interest without burdening religious freedom.

In the 1990 *Smith* case[6] the Supreme Court abandoned the compelling state interest test and adopted a standard that is even less favorable to war tax resistance. Under the new test any "neutral law of general applicability" may be enforced even against people whose religious convictions will be violated by compliance. Since the tax law is a neutral law of general applicability it can be applied to conscientious objectors to taxation for military purposes regardless of the impact on religious practice.

Although the Supreme Court has never accepted a war tax resistance case, the Court in *Smith* repeated a previous statement indicating that it would not recognize a First Amendment right to conscientious war tax refusal: "The tax system could not function if denominations were allowed to challenge the tax system because tax payments were spent in a manner that violates their religious belief."[7]

The *Smith* standard has been applied by a lower federal court in a tax collection case involving war tax resisters. In the *Philadelphia Yearly Meeting* case mentioned above, the judge, although clearly sympathetic to the Yearly Meeting's position, was constrained by the *Smith* ruling to hold that the Yearly Meeting was required to honor IRS levies against the salaries of war tax resisters on its staff.[8] She noted in her opinion:

> It is ironic that here in Pennsylvania, the woods to which Penn led the Religious Society of Friends to enjoy the blessings of religious liberty,

The First Amendment can be *interpreted* as protecting nonpayment of taxes because of conscience.

Judges have been sympathetic to some war tax resistance cases but are constrained by the letter of the law.

neither the Constitution nor its Bill of Rights protects the policy of that Society not to coerce or violate the consciences of its employees and members... or to act as an agent for our government in doing so.

There is an effort underway to reinstate the "compelling state interest" test through Congressional passage of the "Religious Freedom Restoration Act." Whether or not that standard is restored, war tax resisters should not expect the courts to uphold a First Amendment right to refuse military taxation.

Fifth Amendment

No person... shall be compelled in any criminal case to be a witness, against him/herself.... War tax resisters who produce records or answer questions of the IRS in court might aid their prosecution since they did not pay taxes, a criminal act as defined by the Internal Revenue Code. Even though the Fifth Amendment refers to "any criminal case," it can apply "in any proceeding, civil or criminal, administrative or judicial, investigatory or adjudicatory."[9] Financial records summoned by the IRS can show that a resister had the ability to pay taxes, thereby helping the IRS to prove that the resister's nonpayment was "willful." Using these and other arguments, Margaret Haworth succeeded in preventing the IRS from compelling her to produce records and answer questions in court.[10]

Also in *United States v. Harper*,[11] war tax resister Robin Harper succeeded in stopping the government's attempt to compel him to produce records. In 1985 a federal judge in New York City ruled that Larry Bassett could not be compelled to provide financial records to the IRS Collection Division since the records might incriminate him. In 1990 Allen Moss of Baltimore also won a Fifth Amendment case after refusing to provide information in response to an IRS summons. This was the first case involving war tax resisters since Fifth Amendment protections were cut by recent Supreme Court rulings.

However, in some cases the government has granted immunity from prosecution, then jailed resisters for contempt for continued failure to produce their records. In 1989 Max Rice and Don Mosley were jailed for refusing to obey an IRS summons. However, they had chosen to base their defense on the First Amendment right of freedom of religion rather than the Fifth Amendment privilege against self-incrimination. Although several war tax resisters have successfully relied upon the Fifth Amendment to resist IRS summonses and subpoenas, the Court has declared that the Fifth Amendment is not a basis to refuse to file a tax return. (*U.S. v. Sullivan*, 274 U.S. 259 (1927).)

Ninth Amendment

The enumeration in the constitution, of certain rights, shall not be construed to deny or disparage others retained by the people. War tax resisters claim that the listing of specific rights in the Constitution for the people does not mean that the people are not entitled to various other rights just because they are not specifically listed—in particular the right to refuse participation in war, e.g., by refusing to pay war taxes.

In contracting to enter into a state of society, the people collectively, and the person individually, only divest themselves of those natural rights which they expressly relinquish by enumeration. That this fundamental proposition of natural rights was of primary importance to the framers of the Constitution is evident from the attention given the concept at the time. In a letter to Jefferson, Madison wrote, "The rights of conscience, in particular, if submitted to public definition would be narrowed more than they are likely to be by an assumed power." Thus Madison clearly stated that those unenumerated rights under the Ninth Amendment are or include the right of conscience.

Bill Durland, Center on Law and Pacifism, in *Lull and Herby v. C.I.R.* (605 F.2d 1166 (4th Cir. 1979)) argued:

> From the history of adoption of the Ninth Amendment it is clear that it can be viewed as the constitutional affirmation of unenumerated rights as well as a rule of construction stating that the enumeration of some rights does not deny others. For example, the right of conscience not to kill or pay for killing is retained by a person when he or she enters into a state of society. Such rights are absolute and thus cannot be abridged by any qualifying, court-made tests such as has been the case with the First Amendment. They are not subject to any judicial qualification and extend to the payment for killing just as to the killing itself.
>
> It is absurd to think the government would pass a law prohibiting murder but not convict someone of murder who paid for a murder to be done by another person. The power to tax, obviously, is not absolute. It is a power delegated to the government and as such it is qualified. The Ninth Amendment, however, is absolute

and is not to be exercised by the government but by the individual. Therefore the Ninth Amendment takes precedence over Article 1, Section 8 —the taxing power of the United States.[12] Unfortunately, the appellate court rejected the argument and the Supreme Court refused to hear the case.

Fourteenth Amendment

No State shall make or enforce any law which shall...deny to any person within its jurisdiction the equal protection of the laws. Conscientious objection to war in any form is protected by the Universal Military Training and Service Act, but not by the Internal Revenue Code. This argument was also made and rejected in *Lull and Herby*.

Article VI of the Constitution

All treaties made, or which shall be made, under the authority of the United States, shall be the supreme law of the land.... Since international treaties are the supreme law of the land, resisters argue that they are refusing war taxes on the basis of the following treaties:

- United Nations Charter, Article I, section 2. All member nations agree "to develop friendly relations among nations based upon respect for the principles of equal rights and self-determination of people."
- United Nations Charter, Article II, section 3. All member nations agree to "settle their international disputes by peaceful means in such a manner that international peace and security, and justice are not endangered."
- United Nations Charter, Article II, section 4. "All members shall refrain...from the threat or use of force against the territorial integrity or political independence of any state."

The Nuremberg Principles[13]

These principles delineate the scope of individual responsibility in the face of illegal activities by a government. The three principles relevant to individual responsibility are:

II. The fact that internal law does not impose a penalty for an act which constitutes a crime under international law does not relieve the person who committed the act from responsibility under international law.

IV. The fact that a person acted pursuant to order of his government or of a superior does not relieve him from responsibility under international law, provided a moral choice was in fact possible to him.

VIII. Complicity in the commission of a crime against peace, a war crime, or a crime against humanity as set forth in Principle VI is a crime under international law.

Principle VI, which defines crimes against peace and war crimes, states:

The crimes hereinafter set out are punishable as crimes under international law:
a. Crimes against peace:
(i) Planning, preparation, initiation or waging of a war of aggression or a war in violation of international treaties, agreements or assurances;
(ii) Participation in a common plan or conspiracy for the accomplishment of any of the acts mentioned under (i).
b. War Crimes:
violations of the laws or customs of war which include, but are not limited to, murder, ill-treatment or deportation to slave-labor, or for any other purpose of civilian population of or in occupied territory, murder or ill-treatment of prisoners of war or person on the seas, killing of hostages, plunder of public or private property, wanton destruction of cities, towns, or villages, or devastation not justified by military necessity.

Nashville lawyer, Fyke Farmer, was the first to use the Nuremberg Principles in his refusal to pay taxes on his 1949 income. In 1958 the Supreme Court refused to hear his case, which had gone against him in lower courts.[14] Section 7852(d) of the Internal Revenue Code, also affirms the fact that international treaties are the supreme law of the land. A case under section 7852(d) was brought by Gene and Mary Doyle in 1982, with representation by the Center on Law and Pacifism. The tax court and appellate court ruled against them.

Tax Resistance as Eliminating Complicity[15]

Complicity, both in general usage and in law, refers to one who aids, helps, or is an accomplice to a wrongdoer. If the wrongdoer commits a crime, the accomplice is just as responsible as the one who actually commits the crime. An example involves the draft board raid by the Baltimore Four during the Vietnam War. One of the four, Reverend James Mangel, did not actually pour blood on the draft files. However, his conviction was upheld by the Court of appeals, which stated:

Just as one may not supply a weapon to another with knowledge that it will be used to commit a crime, here the appellant could not with impunity give his blood knowing the unlawful

> The Internal Revenue Code denies equal protection to COs.

> International treaties are the supreme law of the land. Therefore the UN Charter and Nuremberg Principles forbid participation in war preparation and war crimes.

purpose to which it would be put.

This principle is not altered when the criminal is a nation, rather than an individual.

Certainly, no valid distinction can be drawn between giving someone a gun and giving the money to buy a gun. In either case if it is known that the one will commit a crime with the gun once it is obtained, the other would be an accomplice.

At the present time U.S. taxpayers are giving the United States money to buy nuclear weapons and other weapons of mass destruction. There is no possible use of these weapons (and others) which would not constitute a violation of international law. War tax resisters have argued that the choice to end this complicity by resisting war taxes is mandated by the Nuremberg Principles, and hence, it cannot be illegal.

Telford Taylor, Professor of Law at Columbia University and Chief Counsel for the prosecution at the Nuremberg war crimes trials, has written:

[T]he notion of individual accountability before the bar of international law lies at the heart of the Nuremberg judgements, and the reluctance of the Germans to resist oppressive acts of state is widely held to have greatly aided the Nazi seizure of power.[16]

Richard A. Falk, Milbank Professor of International Law and Practice at Princeton University, has suggested in the passage quoted below that an American taxpayer may properly refuse to pay taxes to a government believed to be acting in an illegal, criminal fashion:

The war crimes tribunals, most notably the Nuremberg Tribunal, were exclusively concerned with defendants who occupied positions of leadership and responsibility in the state apparatus. However, the wider logic of Nuremberg extends to embrace all those who knowingly, at any rate, participate in a war effort they have reason to believe violates international law. *The degree of complicity with such an aggressive war effort needed to establish criminal responsibility* has never been established authoritatively... *Those who seek access to the courts in order to test the legality of the war—for instance, by refusing to pay all or a part of their income taxes—are also, it would seem, entitled to a substantive determination of the issue.*[17]

It is unrealistic to suggest that U.S. citizens aware of these implications should wait until the Supreme Court rules on the legality of current military preparations for war. It is very clear that individuals must make the moral and legal judgments which the Allies required (after the fact) of the Germans. However, unlike the Germans, U.S. citizens now have the benefit of the Nuremberg Principles. And unlike the Germans who may not have known, then, what the Third Reich was doing, the U.S. public is well aware of the activities of the United States.

This chapter was updated and revised by Vicki Metcalf. For more information see NWTRCC's War Tax Manual for Counselors and Lawyers.

---

1 The IRS has phased out the term "audit" in favor of the apparently less threatening "examination." Nevertheless, the results are the same. We use the terms more or less interchangeably. See Publication 556, "Examination of Returns, Appeal Rights, and Claims for Refund" for what to expect from the Examination Division.

2 This section was adapted and updated from *People Pay for Peace,* (pp. 19-21, 1980) by Vicki Metcalf.

3 E.g., *Muste v. C.I.R.*, 35 T.C. 913 (1961); *Graves v. C.I.R.*, T.C. Memo 1976-353, aff'd, 579 F.2d 392 (6th Cir. 1978).

4 *U.S. v. Philadelphia Yearly Meeting*, 753 F.Supp. 392 (E.D.Pa. 1990.)

5 *Sherbert v. Verner*, 374 U.S. 398 (1963); *Wisconsin v. Yoder*, 406 U.S. 205 (1972).

6 *Oregon State Employment Division v. Smith*, 108 L.Ed.2d 876.

7 Id. at 886-887, quoting *U.S. v. Lee*, 455 U.S. 242, 260 (1982).

8 753 F.Supp. 1300.

9 *Kastigar v. United States*, 406 U.S. 441 (1972).

10 *United States v. Margaret Haworth*, M-18-304 (S.D.N.Y. 1975). Since this is a memorandum, not an official decision, it is not on record.

11 397 F.Supp. 983 (E.D.Pa. 1975).

12 *Friends Journal*, op. cit., p. 16-17.

13 This section was taken, with some modifications, from a piece written by John David Egnal (a lawyer from Springfield, MA) and printed in *Ain't Gonna Pay for War No More* edited by Robert Calvert, p.29, 1972.

14 *Handbook on the Nonpayment of War Taxes,* Peacemakers, p. 39, 1981.

15 This section is an edited version of John Egnal's piece which appeared in *Ain't Gonna Pay for War No More*, pp. 30-31. Originally written about U.S. war crimes in Vietnam, it was edited for broader application.

16 *Nuremberg and Vietnam: An American Tragedy,* p. 16, 1970.

17 *The Vietnam War and International Law,* Vol. 2, pp. 250-54, emphasis added, 1969.

The Collection Process
What the IRS Can Do to You

Once you have exhausted (or ignored) the IRS appeals process and have been assessed a tax due, the IRS will allow ten days to pay. After that, the Collection Division of the IRS takes over. However, there are times when "accelerated billings" are made if the IRS thinks the normal ten-day notice will allow the resister to shift assets. This is called a "jeopardy collection" and will come with little or no notice.

From the date of assessment a statutory lien is in effect against your property. This chapter outlines collection procedures the IRS can use against you to satisfy that lien, roughly in order of most likely to least likely. IRS publication, 586A, "The Collection Process," summarizes what the Collection Division can do to you.

Interest and Penalties

Resisters who file showing a tax due but simply do not pay are likely to get a nonpayment penalty of ½%-1%[1] of the tax due for every month past the due date (up to a maximum of 25%). In addition interest is tagged on to the unpaid taxes and penalties.[2]

War tax resisters who use the war tax deduction or credit methods usually get assessed a $500 "frivolous" return penalty and may also get a 20% "negligence" penalty added to their tax, in addition to the ½%-1% per month (up to 25%) nonpayment penalty and interest.

The IRS could also attempt to charge the resister with fraud and add a 75% penalty to the tax. Fraud is interpreted as bad faith and an intent to evade taxes through deception. However, war tax resisters are generally out in the open about what they are doing and why, so a fraud charge is unlikely. Contact the IRS immediately to protest a fraud or any other penalty you think was added erroneously.

Resisters who did not file are likely to have a penalty of 5% per month added to their tax due (up to 25%), as well as the nonpayment penalty and interest.[3] In addition, the IRS may add the 20% "negligence" penalty or try to add the 75% fraud penalty. (Failure to file may increase somewhat the otherwise slight chance of a fraud penalty.) But an even greater danger is the IRS will have to estimate your tax, since you will have given them no information to go by. See pages 28-29 for a discussion of the nonfiling tactic.

For quick reference a summary of possible civil and criminal penalties are on the following page.

Letters, Calls, and Visits

Every tax resister can expect a series of forms and (if you are lucky, *handwritten*) letters from the IRS. In fact, these letters are the most effective collection instruments for the IRS. To most people they sound particularly threatening, especially the ones with "FINAL NOTICE BEFORE SEIZURE" printed in bold. Generally, agents will call or visit your place of residence during weekday working hours. So if you are not home, you won't hear from them. Once in a while they will call evenings or weekends.

Keep in mind that collection agents have been known to walk off with property (bicycles, television sets, stereos, etc.) after being let into the residence of some war tax resisters during a visit. In at least one instance the IRS agent gained entry into a war tax resister's home by posing as a friend. There is no requirement to admit an IRS agent into one's home without a search warrant (usually called a "Writ of Entry").

With passage of the Taxpayers Bill of Rights in 1988 the IRS may not seize bank accounts, wages, or any other property until it gives a "Final 30-day Notice" (Section 6236).

> "In a recent conversation with an official of the IRS I was amazed when he told me that 'if the taxpayers of this country ever discover that the IRS operates on 90% bluff, the entire system would collapse.'"
> —Senator Henry Bellmon, OK

> A 1988 study of IRS letters to taxpayers by the federal watchdog General Accounting Office turned up so much evidence of errors that at a congressional hearing on the matter, Republican Representative Christopher Shays of Connecticut declared: "I am a little breathless. I am not used to these kinds of hearings where I learn that 47% of all the written responses to taxpayers are incorrect.... How can we even contemplate prosecuting anybody?"
> Money, April 1990, p. 86

Bank Account Levy

If persuasion has failed, the next most likely move for the IRS is to grab your bank account. If you have an interest-bearing account, your bank sends annual statements to the IRS which may allow them to locate your money quickly. If the account is not easily located, they may ask you for its location. If you refuse to tell them, they may check credit agencies, public utilities (e.g., the telephone company), or banks near where you live or work.

Aside from the general 30-day warning to pay up before seizure (made through a form letter and sometimes verbally), you probably will not be given notice that your bank account is about to be levied. Although there are cases where notice has

> There is no requirement to admit an IRS agent into one's home without a search warrant.

The Collection Process

A bank account levy is only valid for what is in the bank at the time of levy.

Max Sandin sat-in at the U.S. Treasury Department to protest the seizure of his social security check.

Cynthia Foster being interviewed by a reporter at the Union Warren Bank in Boston protesting her account being seized. Photo courtesy of New England WTR.

been given in advance, the bank will not allow you to close out the account after it has received a levy notice from the IRS. If the account does not contain sufficient funds to cover the levy, other sources will be sought to satisfy the remainder.

The levy (form 668A) is valid only for amounts owed to you on the date and at the time it was served on the bank. For example, if the levy is for $1,000 and at the time it was served your account contained $10, then $10 is all that can be taken. Even if an hour later, unaware there is a levy on your account, you deposit $500, the levy can only take the $10. But if the bank unknowingly turns over to the IRS assets deposited after filing the levy, it may be very difficult to get the money back. Also, the IRS can serve successive levies as frequently as it wants.

According to a 1985 Supreme Court decision, the IRS can now seize all the money in a joint bank account, even if some of the money belongs to a depositor who doesn't owe any taxes. It would then be up to the nonresister to prove to the IRS how much money in the account belongs to her or him and not to the resister.

In some states (notably Pennsylvania) joint accounts of spouses cannot be seized for the separate taxes of either spouse. But, of course, if the couple filed a joint return, the joint account can be seized.

Bank accounts made up of social security benefits, pensions, welfare payments, etc., can be levied. However, such action would be "only in flagrant and aggravated cases of refusal to pay." Max Sandin, a painter from Cleveland who was imprisoned during World War I as a conscientious objector, first began refusing taxes in 1943. After years of successfully keeping his money from the IRS, his social security check was seized in 1961. He went to the U.S. Treasury Department and began a sit-in. He was arrested and jailed briefly. Since that time not only were social security checks taken, but also his pension checks from the painter's union.[4]

Certain types of income, including unemployment benefits, workers' compensation, and child support payments under a court order are exempt from levy under the IRS Code. It is an open question whether these payments remain exempt after they have been deposited in the bank. They should still be considered exempt, but it is often difficult to prove the source of funds in a bank account, especially when money from different sources is deposited in the same account.

Whether bank accounts held in trust by or for you are safe from levy depends upon the trust. The IRS may levy on any "property or rights to property" belonging to the person whose taxes it is collecting. A person's property rights in a trust depend upon the terms of the trust and applicable law. Parents have sometimes been harassed if the tax resister is a minor living independent of her or his parents. But legally the parents are no longer responsible.

Levy of Wages or Salary

The tax resister's wages are the next most likely target of IRS collection agents. A "Notice of Levy on Wages, Salary, and Other Income" (form 668W) is usually served on the employer. Court authorization is not required before a levy action is taken unless collection agents must enter private premises in order to serve a levy. A minimum amount is free from levy; this is equal to:
• the personal exemption ($2,150 in 1991)
• plus the applicable standard deduction ($5,700 for a joint return; $5,000 for head of household; $3,400 for a single person; and $2,850 for married filing separately in 1991)
• divided by 52.

Thus, the minimum levy-free income for a single person would be $2,150 plus $3,400 divided by 52, which equals $106.73 per week. For each dependent add the exemption amount divided by 52. A head of household with one dependent would be entitled to $178.85 exempt income per week. If

POSSIBLE PENALTIES FOR REFUSING FEDERAL INCOME TAXES

CIVIL PENALTIES		IR CODE
Refusal of employer to honor levy	50%	6332 (c) (2)
Failure to file	5% a month (up to 25%)	6651 (a) (1)
–if fraudulent	15% a month (up to 75%)[1]	6651 (f)
Failure to pay	½%–1% a month (up to 25%)	6651 (a) (2 & 3)
Negligence or disregard of rules and regulations, etc.	20% of underpayment due to negligence, etc.[2]	6662
Fraudulent* underpayment of taxes	75% of underpayment due to fraud[3]	6663
Willful failure of employer to withhold	100%	6672
False information on W-4	$500	6682
Filing a "frivolous" tax return	$500	6702
Bringing or maintaining a "frivolous or groundless" case in Tax Court	$25,000[4]	6673
Aiding and abetting understatement of tax	$1,000 per return	6701

CRIMINAL PENALTIES		
Evasion of tax**	5 yrs. &/or $250,000	7201
Willful*** failure of employer to collect	5 yrs. &/or $250,000	7202
Willful failure to file	1 yr. &/or $100,000	7203
Willful failure to pay	1 yr. &/or $100,000	7203
Willful failure to pay estimated tax	1 yr. &/or $100,000	7203
Employer willful failure to furnish correct W-2 form to employee	1 yr. &/or $100,000	7204
False and fraudulent information on W-4	1 yr. &/or $100,000	7205
Fraud or false statements (perjury)	3 yrs. &/or $250,000	7206
Fraudulent returns, etc. (not under perjury)	1 yr. &/or $100,000	7207
Failure to obey summons[4]	1 yr. &/or $100,000	7210
Corrupt or forcible interference with administration of IR laws	3 yrs. &/or $250,000	7212 (a)
Forcible rescue of seized property	2 yrs. &/or $250,000	7212 (b)

*Fraud requires bad faith, and an interest to evade tax through deception.
**Requires fraud.
***Willful is defined as the "voluntary intentional violation of a known legal duty."

1 Applies to returns due after Dec. 31, 1989. Revenue Reconciliation Act of 1989.
2 Applies to returns due after Dec. 31, 1989. Prior penalty was 5% of underpayment plus 50% of interest on underpayment. Former IRC §6653(a).
3 Applies to returns due after Dec. 31, 1989. Prior penalty was 75% of underpayment plus 50% of interest on underpayment. Former IRC §6653(b).
4 Applies to proceedings pending or commenced after Dec. 31, 1989. Former penalty was $5,000.

you do not assist your employer in determining the number of legal dependents (on form 668P) within a three-day period, the IRS will only allow the exemption for a single person.

Unlike the bank account levy, this levy remains in effect continuously through multiple pay periods until the IRS issues a release to the employer. The employer can only fulfill the levy if they are "obligated to the taxpayer for any property or funds."

An employer not honoring a levy will usually get a "Final Demand" (form 668C) ordering compliance within five days. To continue to ignore the levy, the employer risks a 50% penalty (§6332(c)(2)). The IRS may take the employer to court, or more likely, levy the employer's bank account. (See p. 36.)

Ignore You or Issue Refund

More frequently than one would expect, there are those years when a tax resister's return is not challenged by the IRS, implicitly accepting the "war tax deduction," or other protest device—even though a letter of explanation was enclosed. Similarly many war tax resisters have succeeded in getting a full refund of withheld taxes through fil-

A wage levy can remain in effect through multiple pay periods.

Some years the IRS will not challenge the resister's return.

ing their 1040 forms. If three years pass from the date of filing, the money is free and clear (unless the return involved fraud or falsified information). So it is not *inevitable*, as many people think, that the IRS will eventually get the money.

There are a number of theories as to why this happens. Obviously, error on the part of the IRS is one (particularly when the deduction method is used). Because of the large number of returns each spring, IRS employment is seasonal. Some of these people (many of whom are students working the night shift) may be sympathetic enough to allow the return to pass unchallenged.

Though the above does happen war tax resisters should assume the IRS will notice their nonpayment and come calling.

Federal Tax Lien

If unsuccessful in making a collection after trying the methods above, the IRS may file a "Notice of Federal Tax Lien" (form 668). IRS policy is to file written notice of lien whenever $2,000 or more is unpaid.[5] This notice is to make *public* to the resister's "creditors that a lien exists against your property, including property acquired after the Notice of Federal Tax Lien is filed." The notice is filed in an office designated by the state (e.g., the Registrar's Office in the resister's county).

Technically, a lien[6] is in effect from the date of assessment until the IRS has collected the money or feels it is uncollectible. Ostensibly, the filing of the "Notice of Federal Lien" is to lay claim on property the resister may have or may acquire. But in reality, the purpose of the notice is to embarrass the resister—by making the lien public—and "adversely affect your business transactions or other financial interests." For example, they hope it will hurt your credit rating. So it becomes a device to harass you into paying.

Seizure and Auction of Property

A levy on tangible property "is referred to as a seizure." *Stealing* would be a more accurate term. This method of collection is not particularly common for war tax resisters. But it happens often enough (maybe two or three dozen instances in the past decade) that the resister should be prepared for its possibility.

Any type of property may be seized. The most common property seized is the automobile. War tax resisters have had houses, bicycles, television sets, and stereos seized. Safety deposit boxes can be drilled in order to seize the contents.

Property exempt from seizure includes:

- clothes (except for luxury items, such as furs)
- school books
- for a head of a family: fuel, provisions, furniture, and personal effects (e.g., your toothbrush) not to exceed $1,500 in value
- books and tools used in your trade, business, or profession, not to exceed $1,000 in value
- undelivered mail
- certain annuity and pension payments
- workers' compensation
- certain public assistance payments, including AFDC and SSI
- unemployment benefits
- child support payments under a court order
- certain service-connected disability benefits of veterans (IRC Sect. 6334).

The complete list is carried in IRS publication 586A.

In addition, one's principal place of residence is exempt from levy unless a district director or assistant district director of the IRS approves the seizure in writing, or the IRS determines that collection is in jeopardy (§6334(a)(13),(e)).

In addition to property that is exempt from seizure under the IRS Code, the IRS has announced that it will not levy the following: welfare payments, government training and skill development allowances, and retirement benefits less than $6,000 per year. Other types of property generally not seized unless failure to pay is deemed by the IRS to be "flagrant and aggravated" include social security and medicare benefits, certain pension plans, and the cash loan value of insurance policies. Property subject to a mortgage or other lien will generally not be seized by the IRS unless the resister has enough "equity" in the property to make the seizure worthwhile to the IRS. Again, a complete list is found in publication 586A.

Once seized, the property is usually put in storage until sale at a public auction. The auction must occur between ten and forty days after public notice (e.g., in the local paper). The auction can be through sealed or open bidding, but sealed bid is more common. Those who want to enter a sealed bid must use IRS form 2222.

Proceeds from the sale are applied to the expenses of levy and sale (e.g., storage costs), to liens other creditors may have, and then to the tax bill (including interest and penalties). The balance, if any, is returned to the resister "upon request."

Before any sale the IRS determines a "minimum price" and determines whether sale to the government at the minimum price would be in the "best interest" of the government. If no one bids the

---

The purpose of a public *lien is to embarrass the resister and hurt her/his credit rating.*

Property seizures against war tax resisters are unusual. When they happen, they automobile is the most likely target.

minimum price and the sale has been determined to be in the best interest of the government, the property is considered sold to the government (and the person's tax debt reduced by the minimum price amount). Otherwise, the property is returned to the owner, still subject to the tax lien, and the expenses of the seizure and sale are added to the tax bill. The property can be redeemed at any time prior to the sale by paying the tax, etc. Real estate can be redeemed within 180 days after the sale by paying the purchaser what she or he paid plus interest of 20% a year.

Some of the real hair-raising stories about the IRS come as a result of seizures. A small business owner from Fairbanks, Alaska had a levy for $4,700 filed against his wages. He and his wife fought the assessment through some complex legal tactics. The IRS was so angered they seized the couple's ten-year-old Volkswagen. The couple, however, locked themselves in the car and refused to turn over the keys. IRS agents responded by smashing the windows and dragging the wife out of the car, over a sidewalk littered with glass, in full view of astonished bystanders and a local newspaper photographer. The car was sold for $500.[7]

A cabinetmaker and member of the Brethren church refused payment of $73,000 (according to the IRS) over a number of years by using the Fifth Amendment resistance strategy. He had been involved in a protracted dispute with the IRS about how much was owed. While he was beginning work one day in the workshop next to his house in a rural part of Maryland, a procession of unmarked cars, police vehicles, three wreckers, and an interstate moving van halted outside his house. Then forty U.S. marshals, state patrolmen, IRS collection agents—some armed with M-16 rifles, shotguns, and handguns—surrounded his property and took up positions near the house, workshop, and along the highway. A bunch of them burst into the workshop pointing their guns and shouted: "Halt! We're here to seize!" Simultaneously another armed group moved into the house, confronting his wife and daughter. The whole house was searched for cash. Neighbors, who had gathered to watch, were forced to leave at gun point. All his vehicles, machinery, tools, and stock were seized—down to soap dishes and toothbrush holders. When asked why a small army was sent, the IRS explained it was "to ensure the protection of the taxpayer, his family, the private vendors we hired to move the equipment, and innocent bystanders."[8]

Obviously, such cases represent an aberration of IRS procedures rather than policy. But excesses by individual agents do happen from time to time. Of the 112 million tax returns filed in 1988, about twelve million filers received "problem" notices from the IRS—late payment, math errors, etc. (see box on p. 45 regarding IRS inaccuracy).

Over the ten years from 1979–1989 the IRS stepped-up collection efforts due to the government's revenue needs. In 1989 the IRS had 2.8 million delinquent accounts covering various years. They filed 904,000 liens, 2.3 million salary and bank account levies, and 12,870 seizures.[9] In 1990, an IRS representative testified before the Oversight Subcommittee of the House Ways and Means Committee that the IRS had $62 billion in accounts receivable inventory (including $11 billion in interest and penalties). This amount did not include $25 billion considered uncollectible.[10]

IRS seizures of property belonging to war tax resisters had been very unusual since the end of the Indochina War—until 1984. Since then perhaps a dozen houses and a similar number of cars were seized. David Pascale holds the record for such seizures—his house in Georgia was seized by the IRS three times (the first in 1987), and when he later moved to New Mexico his car was seized.

In a few cases the IRS has cancelled sales of seized property because of opposition by resisters and their supporters. In one case the IRS released a seized house after the resister informed the collection agent that she had a retirement account containing sufficient funds to cover her taxes, even though she didn't disclose the location. (In general, the IRS would rather seize "liquid" assets.) Some resisters who have been unwilling to bid on their own houses (because that would mean paying the government) have recovered their homes by "redeeming" them from the purchasers at the tax sale. In one case neighbors of a resister purchased his farm at a tax sale, then placed the property in the name of a land trust so that he could continue to live there without risk of another seizure by the IRS. (Stories about particular seizures appear in Chapters 11 and 12.)

Criminal Court and Jail

It is very rare that the IRS will use the courts and the threat of jail to force payment or punish a war tax resister. A classified IRS directive[11] handed down on July 15, 1980, told its agents not to pursue felony prosecution of tax refusers for fraud or failure to file unless underpayments average *at least $2,500* a year for three years straight. Previously, the limit was $1,000 in unpaid taxes. Misdemeanor

An auction must occur between 10 and 40 days after public notice.

A bunch of them burst into the workshop pointing their guns and shouting: "Halt! We're here to seize!"

"Under a government which imprisons any unjustly, the true place for a just man (or woman) is also in prison."
—Henry David Thoreau

> "Though the IRS is concerned about the money, it is more concerned that the idea of people saying NO not get out of hand. That's why we have to continue to build a movement of resisting authority."
> —Ralph DiGia

prosecutions for false returns are not being pursued unless the unpaid tax involved is more than $500. Exceptions in this directive were made for "flagrant or repetitious conduct" (particularly of celebrities whose prosecution might serve as a deterrent). The IRS expects to handle the vast majority of its cases through civil procedures, since it is (at the moment) more interested in getting payment than punishing war tax resisters.

Since World War II no war tax resisters that we are aware of have been jailed for refusing to pay their taxes. However, about twenty war tax resisters have been jailed for related reasons: contempt of court for refusing to produce records or reveal sources of assets, claiming excessive dependents on the W-4 or 1040 forms, and failure to file. The length of time served is usually around two or three months. Jim Shea, Karl Meyer, and Martha Tranquilli have the distinction of having served the longest sentences—from eight to ten months. In the most recent case, Randy Kehler received a six-month contempt of court sentence for refusing to agree not to return to his home after a court ordered eviction. (See Chapter 11 for Meyer, Tranquilli, and Kehler stories).

There was a spate of criminal prosecutions for W-4 resistance in the early 1970s. These ended by 1975, however, when the IRS started imposing a $500 *civil* penalty for W-4 resistance. It is also more difficult to detect W-4 violations now, since the basis for calculating allowances has changed.

In the last few years there have been no criminal cases brought against war tax resisters to our knowledge. Considering the thousands of people who refuse to pay war taxes each year, this means the chances of prosecution are rather unlikely. If tax resistance continues to grow, government crack-downs will almost certainly grow as well.

In two prosecutions the court preferred alternative sentences to jail. In 1979 Bruce Chrisman, a Mennonite war tax resister from Illinois, was prosecuted for failure to file (he signed a blank return). He was sentenced to a year alternative service with the Mennonites and ordered to pay court costs, fines, and all back taxes (see Chapter 11). Brandeis mathematics professor, Paul Monsky, was prosecuted in 1980 for making a false and fraudulent statement on his W-4 form (he claimed 42 allowances). This was the first W-4 prosecution since the early 1970s. Monsky was sentenced to 416 hours of public service, a year's probation, and directed to stop inflating his W-4 form (see Chapter 11).

According to the Center on Law and Pacifism,[12] Supreme Court decisions have allowed some information to be admitted legally by the IRS in a trial against you, although that information may be *obtained in violation of law,* court decisions, or IRS regulation. These violations have included:
- concealed tape recordings
- phone taps
- bugging with listening devices
- opening mail through agreement with the Post Office
- investigation of your private affairs without probable cause
- threats to auditors who refuse to give information concerning you.

Harassment

The government seems to be running an ex-

A VISIT BY THE IRS

A call or visit by an IRS agent from the Collection Division is not an unusual event. However, if the IRS is having difficulty in making a collection or if they are considering criminal prosecution, the resister may well experience a different type of visit from the IRS.

Marion Bromley, a war tax resister since 1947 and a founding member of the Peacemakers, recounts one such visit to her residence outside Cincinnati, Ohio in 1958:

Seeing a big car drive in, I left the corn patch I was hoeing and approached the house. The two men in the car wore sport shirts so I thought they were not FBI, but didn't suppose they were radicals.

"Does Juanita Nelson live here?" inquired the driver.

"No."

Getting out of the car, he continued, "Did she ever live here?"

"Yes," I replied, "some years ago."

"I'd like to get her present address," said the driver.

"I don't believe I'd give it to you unless I knew why you wanted it."

"We're from the Internal Revenue Service at Hamilton."

"Oh, well, I'm sure she wouldn't want me to give it to you."

The shorter man, who had been silent up to this time, came around the front fender of the car and threatened, "Maybe you'd like a summons! Would a summons help you to give the information?"

"No, I don't think so," I replied. I probably smiled.

"Get her name, Tim."

It has been our experience that usually a man from the "intelligence" division accompanies a collector. Several

panded and more sophisticated version of the old "protection racket" scheme. Citizens are expected to come across with money for their own protection from some unknown assailant, or else who knows what horrible things will happen to them or their property. Those citizens who don't pay (the IRS) for their protection (by the Department of Defense, etc.) may suffer the consequences—not from the "Russians," but from their self-appointed "protectors," who threaten to take money, property, and even liberty.

In 1981 the IRS wanted to ask Congress for permission to publicize the returns of some tax protesters, including "pacifists who refuse to pay taxes to support military spending."[13] Because of the tremendous increase in the number of tax protesters (tripling within three years) and because the IRS felt it was being falsely accused of harassing protesters, the IRS wanted authorization for this unprecedented exposure of tax returns. To date this has not occurred.

In August 1969 the IRS set up a Special Services Staff to target "ideological organizations." The War Resisters League, National War Tax Resistance, Catholic Worker, and the Peacemakers were among the 3,000 organizations and 8,000 individuals on whom files were accumulated before it was disbanded in 1973.

Other Considerations
Professional Licensing

War tax resistance may effect professional licensing. In 1983 Vicki Metcalf was questioned about her resistance by the Colorado Board of Law Examiners. She was ultimately admitted to the Colorado Bar when she convinced the Board that her resistance did not constitute "moral turpitude." However, in 1987 Tom Wilson of Massachusetts lost his license to practice dentistry because of his resistance. (The actual basis for revocation of his license was nonpayment of state taxes, but the state tax bill was based upon an IRS determination of his federal tax liability after he refused to cooperate with federal tax collection.) As of October 1991 Tom is continuing to practice dentistry, without a license (see Chapter 11). In 1987 the Presbyterian Church reinstated Rev. Maurice McCracken to the ministry, having suspended him twenty-five years before because of his war tax resistance (see Chapter 11).

Passport and Green Card Applications

The 1986 tax law requires anyone applying for a U.S. passport (original or renewal) and aliens applying for permanent residence status (green cards) to provide certain tax information with their applications (IRC Sect. 6039E). This information is then passed on to the IRS. This requirement went into effect in January 1988.

All applicants are required to provide their taxpayer identification numbers (social security numbers). In the case of passport applications people must list any foreign country in which they currently reside. Aliens applying for permanent residence must disclose information about whether they were required to file tax returns in the previous three years. (The law also requires applicants to provide "such other information" as the IRS may prescribe. As of October 1991 no regulations have been adopted under this provision of the law.)

Failure to provide this information could result

Tom Wilson of Massachusetts lost his license to practice dentistry because of his resistance. Nevertheless, he continues his resistance and his dental practice today.

---

times we have observed that the collectors remain calm and polite while the "intelligence" men resemble tough cops or "bulls," who seem to feel it is a personal affront when someone refuses to cooperate with questioning.

The tall driver was writing busily, and when he finished he asked, "And what is your name?"

"I don't care to give you that information," I said. "It is a long-standing policy of ours not to give any cooperation to the Revenue Service because so much of the money they collect is used in the war effort."

"Do you own this house?" cut in the "intelligence" man.

"No, I don't."

Coming a few steps closer he began a rapid-fire questioning. "Who does own it? . . . Do you rent? . . . Who do you rent from?"

"I'm not going to answer your question," I said.

"Well, that's all a matter of public record," the driver said. "We can find out . . . That's all right."

The two men got in the car and backed down the drive in silence.

We were not surprised to have a call two days later from two revenue men asking for me. I had the feeling that if "Shorty" could spur anybody to do something about "That Woman" he would do so. These two were calm, they didn't seem surprised to learn that we did not cooperate with tax men. They accepted us, apparently, as noncooperators, and though they tried hard to get us so interested in conversation that we would start answering questions, there was no shock.

(*Handbook on the Nonpayment of War Taxes*, pp. 28-29, 1981)

in a penalty of $500 unless reasonable cause is shown for not providing it. The law also requires the agency collecting the information to give the IRS the names of the people failing to provide it.

There is no indication in the statute that applications for passports and green cards will be denied for failure to disclose the tax information. In fact, the inclusion of a monetary penalty suggests otherwise. If the government did try to deny passports on this ground, it would be possible to argue that this would violate the constitutional right to travel. (See *Kent v. Dulles*, 357 U.S. 116 (1958); *Aptheker v. Secretary of State*, 378 U.S. 500 (1964).)

Some war tax resisters wonder whether they can be denied passports if they disclose tax information with their applications. This can happen only if the resister is subject to an outstanding federal arrest warrant for a felony or subject to a criminal court order or condition of probation or parole which forbids foreign travel (22 C.F.R. Sect. 51.70 (a)(1),(2)). Given the rarity of the criminal prosecution of war tax resisters, this should not be a concern. (At any rate resisters will undoubtedly know if they are subject to an arrest warrant or criminal court order before they apply.)

People also wonder whether they can claim the Fifth Amendment as a basis for refusing to provide tax information with passport applications. The requirement to provide taxpayer identification numbers and country of residence certainly doesn't violate the privilege against self-incrimination. However, depending upon what "other information" the IRS may require, there may well be questions that would call for an incriminating response. In order to claim the privilege, people would need to fill out the form and claim the privilege in response to the specific questions that called for an incriminating answer. A good faith claim of the privilege should not subject an applicant to the $500 penalty (or denial of the application). As of October 1991 we have no information indicating that war tax resisters are encountering difficulties because of this law.

This chapter was updated and revised by Vicki Metcalf. For more information see NWTRCC's War Tax Manual for Counselors and Lawyers.

---

1 The nonpayment penalty starts out at 0.5% per month and is increased to 1% per month starting ten days after Notice and Demand for Payment.
2 Since April 1, 1991 the interest rate has been set at 10% compounded daily. This rate is subject to change quarterly, depending on the prime interest rate. The interest rate has ranged between 9% and 12% since 1987.
3 For tax returns not filed within 60 days after the due date, there is a minimum nonfiling penalty of $100 or 100% of the unpaid tax, whichever is less. Under the 1990 tax law, if the nonfiling was fraudulent, the nonfiling penalty is 15% per month up to a maximum of 75%.
4 *Handbook on Nonpayment of War Taxes,* Peacemakers, p. 27, 1981.
5 *Insight on the News,* April 19, 1988.
6 A legal right to hold property or to have it sold or applied for payment of a claim.
7 *Parade,* April 12, 1981.
8 ibid
9 *Money,* Oct. 1990, p. 80.
10 *Network News,* March 1990.
11 *National Law Journal,* August 11, 1980.
12 *People Pay for Peace,* p. 62, 1984.
13 *Washington Post,* p. 8, September 20, 1981.

Resisting Collection

At any point in the IRS collection process a war tax resister can end the proceedings by paying what the IRS wants. Nancy Moore of Austin, Texas had been resisting her telephone tax for some years and received notices from the IRS which she basically ignored. Coming home one day in 1972 she noticed a tow truck hooking up to her car, supervised by an IRS agent. She rushed over with her checkbook and paid the money owed plus towing costs; the tow truck unhitched and her car was spared.

Sometimes the IRS is willing to allow payment through installments (unless they have reason to believe you will not uphold the deal) or even make a deal, such as to drop or reduce the penalties. Some resisters have been able to stall the IRS by sending in partial payments of a dollar with each collection notice. However, that may work only for so long.

Resisters have used other tactics to frustrate collection. Filing an amended return (1040X) with a claim (such as a charitable contribution) not made in the original return (1040) has sometimes worked to stop collection. In these instances cases are sent back to the Examination Division *temporarily*. Be careful that new claims are not false, or this tactic may backfire. Some resisters have taken the IRS to court, always in a losing effort so far. (This tactic can also backfire because resisters *and their attorneys* may be fined for bringing a "frivolous" case before the court. See Chapter 5.) Some have sent their taxes directly to other government agencies, such as the U.S. Arms Control and Disarmament Agency, or to their Congressperson, asking that none of the money be spent on the military. However, the check is usually returned. Even if cashed by the government, a check written to any government agency can be drawn on by any other agency. So the value of this tactic is limited to that of protest. John Ed Croft, a homeless artist living in New York City, offered to pay his taxes with recyclable cans, the "currency" of the homeless. The IRS response: "There is no provision for paying taxes with cans."

Some resisters ignore all IRS notices and procedures. In a few cases, however, this has so angered collection agents that they overstepped their authority in order to harass a resister. Whatever tactic is used, war tax resisters should take every advantage of circumstances to *organize*. Never let a levy, seizure, lien, indictment, auction, etc., pass without taking the opportunity to publicize opposition. The IRS is very sensitive to adverse public opinion. It is one of the most disliked agencies of the government. You may be surprised at the amount of support and sympathy you will get from the general public and media when struggling against the IRS—if you take care to organize properly.

This chapter lists several methods of resisting collection, such as placing a bank account, car or house in someone else's name. There is no requirement to make it easy for the IRS to find your property, but an *affirmative act of deception* could be construed as criminal concealment, criminal obstruction of tax administration, or tax evasion (IRC Sects. 7201, 7206(4), 7212(a)). The line between legal noncooperation and criminal deception is fuzzy. No war tax resister has been criminally charged for such actions and the likelihood of future prosecutions seems small, but people should be aware of the possibility.

IRS Already Has Your Money

- File an amended return claiming a refund. This can be done up to three years past the original filing date.
- Go to court. As mentioned above there is virtually no chance of a legal victory in a court setting. (Only about 4% of the annual tax court cases are decided in favor of any taxpayer. War tax resisters can hardly expect better.) If you are seriously considering a court challenge, make sure to contact a national war tax resistance organization for the latest information and legal advice.
- If your state owes you a refund, file early. The IRS is known to seize state refunds for federal taxes. Adjust state withholding allowances to avoid refunds.

IRS About to Levy Bank Account

- Contact the bank and explain your position. Ask them not to honor the levy. They are unlikely to agree but it is a good consciousness-raising opportunity.
- Change banks. Choose an account that does not bear interest so that the IRS does not receive an annual statement. Move your account to a bank away from where you work or live to thwart or delay IRS collection efforts. Putting your account in a Canadian bank (that pays in U.S. or Canadian dollars) and banking by mail and Automatic Teller Machine (ATM) will make a levy unlikely.
- Put your money into the account of a family member or friend who is not currently in danger of being levied. Look for a noninterest

John-Ed Croft is a homeless artist in New York City being pursued by the IRS for back taxes. In October 1987 he called a "Can the IRS Rally," protesting skewed budget priorities. He offered his payment in cans, the "currency of the homeless," but the IRS refused to accept them. Photo by Ed Hedemann.

bearing checking account, or your friend or family member will be liable for taxes on your interest earnings. Since the advent of ATM's and bank machines, this practice has become very convenient since you can use a bank card to make your own withdrawals from the account.

- Put your funds into a collective bank account. To insure against charges of fraud, the group may want to write and publicize a charter stating that the purpose of the group is to provide a means for citizens to regain control over their own money and prevent illegitimate use of taxes by the government. To avoid the necessity of providing any one person's Social Security number, the group can apply for a Federal Taxpayer ID number on IRS form SS-4.
- Eliminate your bank account and place your reserve money in an alternative fund which makes loans to community groups. If you do not normally write a large number of checks, you can get by with money orders and cash.

Bank Adds Service Charge on Levy

- Protest the service charge and threaten to change banks if they do not refund it. Some resisters have even taken the bank to small claims court and won.
- If you have reason to doubt the uniform application or amount of the service charge, complain to the banking commission.
- Savings accounts are usually not subjected to a service charge, whereas checking accounts are. Also, most savings and loan associations do not add a service charge for a levy.

IRS About to Levy Your Wages

- Ask your employer to consider refusing compliance with the levy. It is not recommended that you ask an employer to *ignore* a levy notice, but if you have an open and friendly relationship, you may suggest that an employer return the notice to the IRS asking that it be "released." Possible reasons for requesting a release might include a statement by your employer that, "I believe this is a matter between the IRS and my employee. I do not think I should be required to compromise her/his position." Or, if you are an independent contractor, the company for which you are providing services might state that you are not owed any compensation at this time.
- Ask your employer to pay you in advance. According to section 6331 of the Internal Revenue Code "a levy shall extend *only to property possessed and obligation existing at the time thereof*" (emphasis added). So if an employer never owes an employee a salary (by paying in advance) the employer has nothing of the employee's which can be levied. However, in the case of Wally Nelson, his employer (Antioch Bookplate Company) stopped paying him in advance until the levy on his salary was honored. So he quit. Also, if the IRS can prove that payments in advance were deliberately made to frustrate collection, they might fine the employer.
- Become a contract worker (see page 34) and sign written agreements with companies and organizations that you are not owed payment

until such time as you complete all assigned work and present an invoice for services rendered. If a levy is imminent, withhold presentation of your invoice. Companies can then return the levy notice to the IRS stating that they do not owe you anything.
- Contract your labor to your employer through an "employment agency" set up by you and tax resisting friends. This employment agency is your official employer and as such is responsible for withholding taxes and honoring levies. However, you may find your employer reluctant to accept your labor through this agency (see page 35).
- Quit, reduce your hours and wages below the threshold of the amount exempt from levy, or become a volunteer. This is an extreme move but some resisters have done this to avoid a levy. An important consideration at this point will be whether your work is a vocation or merely the means to make ends meet.

IRS About to Seize Property

- Do not let an IRS revenue officer (collection agent) into your house, garage, etc. They have been known to seize anything in sight. The IRS legally needs a warrant in order to enter your premises without your permission.
- Use a post office box, or join with other resisters in your community to establish a "sanctuary address" (as suggested by Karl Meyer) which can be used for the address on your tax return. Mail received at a sanctuary address can be forwarded to you. Obviously, these measures must be taken well in advance of collection but may make it difficult for the IRS to find out where you live.
- When not driving your car, keep it locked either inside a garage or away from where you work and live.
- Trade cars with a friend for a little while. If there are several cars in the trade this may be confusing enough to cause the IRS to give up.
- Well in advance of any possible seizure or lien, transfer title on the car with someone not vulnerable to a seizure, such as a family member or friend. If you are purchasing a car, have the title transferred directly from the seller to someone other than yourself. Lease a car, or co-own one. Common ownership may not totally preclude seizure, but it will make it less likely.
- Prepare to block your car with bodies of friends. At times one person doing this has been successful, and other times even several people have not been successful. Car seizures are likely to occur on very short notice during working hours, so a mechanism needs to be set up which can

STATUTES OF LIMITATIONS FOR CIVIL AND CRIMINAL CASES

A statute of limitations determines the time at the end of which the IRS cannot bring a legal action against you or collect taxes for a particular year.

CIVIL CASES

ASSESSMENT (often made on form 4188). *Must Be Made Within Three Years After the Return Was Filed.* (IRS Code, section 6501(a)).

Assessment is the act of the IRS recording one's liability in its offices. The IRS sometimes does not give people notice when it assesses taxes, but it must give you a copy of your assessments if you request it. IRS Code Section 6203. If a tax return is filed early, the three-year time limit for assessing the tax does not begin to run until the last date the return is due (usually April 15). Section 6501(b).

COLLECTION. *Must Be Made by Levy or Court Proceeding Within Ten Years After the Date of Assessment.* IRS Code, section 6502(a)(1))

(Exceptions: Liens filed before November 5, 1984, have a six-year statute of limitations. Assessment of tax or a proceeding in court for collection without assessment may be made *at any time* where there is either no return filed (section 6501(c)(3)), or a false or fraudulent return with the intent to evade tax has been filed (section 6501(c)(1)). The three-year time limit for assessment is extended in certain situations, such as when a Tax Court case is brought. Section 6503.)

CRIMINAL CASES

PROSECUTION. *Must Be Within Three Years of the Offense* (6531).

(Exceptions: Prosecution must be within six years of the offense in certain cases, including the following:

1. Offense involving the defrauding or attempting to defraud the U.S. Government (section 6531(1)).
2. Offense of willfully attempting to evade or defeat the tax (section 6531(2)).
3. Offense of willfully failing to pay any tax or make any return at the time required (section 6531(4)).
4. Offense of declaring under penalty of perjury that statement is true which is not believed to be true (section 6531(5)).
5. Offense of willful delivery of false return or any other document (section 6531(5)).)

The time limit for criminal prosecution begins to run when the crime is committed. Where the crime involves a failure to do something (such as pay tax or file a return), the time limit begins when the act is required to be done (such as April 15 of the relevant year), assuming that the failure to act is "willful" at that time. In the case of an affirmative act (such as willfully filing a fraudulent tax return), the time limit begins to run when the act is committed.

Prepared by Vicki Metcalf. For more information see NWTRCC's War Tax Manual for Counselors and Lawyers.

respond quickly. It is possible the IRS would consider such actions "forcible interference with administration of Internal Revenue laws (§7212(a)) or "forcible rescue of seized property" (§7212(b)). However, those laws are means for violent responses to IRS collection, rather than the nonviolent resistance suggested above. People should be aware that the IRS has (on rare occasions not involving war tax resisters) obtained convictions for forcible rescue of seized property and corrupt obstruction of tax administration in cases not involving physical force.

Do not let IRS collection agents into your home.

Transfer title to your car, or at least keep it away from where you work or live if a seizure is imminent.

- The title to your house (and any other seizable property) can be transferred or held jointly with others. Again, joint ownership does not preclude seizure, but does make it less likely. However, you and your co-owners need to consider that your war tax resistance may place everyone's investment in the property at risk. One community house, set up by some people within the Peacemaker movement, was seized and sold in 1975 by the IRS for taxes of certain individuals and for a legally separate organization, Peacemakers. Through public pressure and agitation, the IRS voided the sale and returned the house (see page 101).
- A car still being paid for may deter the IRS from seizure since the seller or finance company must be paid off first (after an auction). In most (if not all) states, however, the IRS can seize a car even if the title is still held by the finance company.

IRS Has Seized Property

If a seizure occurs, organize a counter-auction. Be vocal and visible.

- Organize a demonstration or counter-auction around the seizure. Submit "creative" bids on the IRS form 2222 (see Chapter 12).
- Have a friend buy back the property for you (assuming he/she will be reimbursed).
- Organize a boycott of the auction. However, even if there are no bidders, the IRS will probably buy the item.
- If your property is auctioned off, you have a right to redeem it within 180 days from the purchaser at the price he/she paid for it plus interest. In other words you can buy it back from the purchaser, and he/she won't be able to make a profit except for the IRS-imposed interest rate. When the IRS auctions property, they first take your total tax obligation (including interest and penalties) from the proceeds, next pay themselves for the costs of the auction, and then refund any left-over proceeds to you. You can then use that refunded money, plus the amount of your total tax obligation plus interest to redeem the property from the purchaser. If you have set aside the amount of your resisted taxes in an escrow fund or in savings, you can redeem property without too great a financial hardship. You can also fundraise if you need assistance with a redemption.
- Be vocal and visible about the seizure. This is not just for educational purposes, but to increase the ranks of resisters. It may even have a chilling effect on such IRS tactics. Arnold Cuba, an Austin, Texas telephone tax resister, had his car returned as a result of the outcry after it was seized in 1972. However, his bank account was levied instead. During the Indochina War a community of people in New England promoted the concept of resistance communities responding to each seizure by several more people pledging to refuse a similar amount, thereby multiplying the effect.

IRS Has Indicted You

- Immediately contact a sympathetic lawyer. Get in touch with the National War Tax Resistance Coordinating Committee if you have no lawyer. Or you could ignore the whole proceeding, refuse to contact a lawyer, and go about business as usual. This, however, would increase the chances of incarceration.
- Alert movement and sympathetic community groups to help organize a response. The wider the publicity, the more likely the IRS will ease up. Also, knowledge of your stand will give courage to others, as well as provide a means to educate. We have often found that the amount of support a resister gets increases with the amount of repression from the government.
- Since a number of war tax resisters have been jailed on contempt for refusal to produce records, it is worth noting that there are cases where war tax resisters have succeeded in avoiding contempt by citing the Fifth Amendment (see page 42).

IRS Still in Existence by April 15

- Train war tax resistance counselors.
- Organize demonstrations outside the IRS.
- Leaflet in waiting and forms areas of IRS.
- Speak on radio and TV talk shows.
- Write articles and other literature.

This chapter was updated by Carolyn Stevens.

Alternative Funds

BY STEVE GULICK

War tax resistance alternative funds, which come under a variety of names, are part of the communities of resistance. Such communities are positive and cooperative alternatives to the materialistic, patriarchal, racist, and otherwise oppressive forms of the dominant social organization in the United States today.

Alternative funds began to grow in the late 1960s as a way of dealing with hundreds of thousands of federal tax dollars resisted because of the Indochina War. The alternative funds also provided some security from seizure by the IRS. They helped to emphasize that resisters were not simply keeping the money for themselves. Moreover, the funds enabled resisters to aid community self-help, social change, peace, and human service programs through interest-free loans and/or grants. Some funds were established primarily to hold money in escrow pending the the passage of the Peace Tax Fund Act (see p. 110), but most funds are of the first type.

Starting a Fund

Establishing a fund can be easy, perhaps deceptively so. Most alternative funds are informal—operating on trust and on a shoestring. There is certainly no need to become an official nonprofit organization, to incorporate, to have a charter or by-laws, or whatever. Some organizers of alternative funds don't institutionalize out of principle. On the other hand, being somewhat more formal might permit the fund to attract the interest and active support (and perhaps deposits) of a broader cross section of people.

Some funds have made special provisions along these lines, getting help from a sympathetic lawyer or accountant in drawing up by-laws, incorporating, and being recognized as a nonprofit organization by the state. As no fund pays interest to depositors, it is hard to attract deposits from sympathetic groups with money to invest, or individuals who aren't resisters, or any others. In any case, what is most important for keeping a fund going is a sustained commitment from enough people so as not to overburden a few.

Building the Fund

While some funds accept only contributions and/or only resisted war taxes, most offer a number of options. Several accept deposits of resisted war taxes which can be withdrawn by the resister "after collection by the IRS, if collection is imminent, or to pay legal fees" (Northern California People's Life Fund). In some cases it is clearly specified that such deposits become the property of the fund if the IRS has not seized the amount from the individual resister in a certain period of time. The Philadelphia Alternative Fund encourages long-term deposits, but permits withdrawals on demand. New England War Tax Resistance has set up separate funds for returnable and non-returnable deposits.

Alternative funds have generally been secure from IRS levy simply because of the amount of hassle the IRS would have to go through, including the publicity boost such a levy would give war tax resistance. In this context, an informal association has some advantage over a formal nonprofit organization. In January 1986 the IRS seized the funds of a war tax resister in a Vermont escrow account, which used the Social Security number of the resister. In setting up the account, make sure that it is not identified by the Social Security number of any resister. Even without formal structure, it is easy to get an organizational identification number from the IRS for use on any accounts.

Members of New England War Tax Resistance prepare for an action. Photo courtesy of New England WTR.

Banks and Where to Deposit the Money

The next major issue is how to handle and where to keep the money.

The People's Life Fund (Northern California) "strives to deposit contributions in alternative financial institutions, such as credit unions and socially responsible funds, whose goals are compatible with those of the members of the Fund."

The guidelines for New England War Tax Resistance state: "We are always seeking truly 'socially responsible' uses of the money entrusted to us, and ways to minimize rather than maximize interest. While part of our assets remain in com-

---

Alternative Funds provide an effective complement to war tax resistance. Not only is money resisted from war, but it is rechanneled into more peaceful, life-affirming activities.
—Tom and Francine Wall

Hundreds of thousands of tax resisted dollars have been diverted to community groups.

What is most important for keeping a fund going is a sustained commitment from enough people so as not to burden a few.

Philadelphia War Tax Resistance
2208 South St., Philadelphia, PA 19146

ALTERNATIVE FUND LOAN APPLICATION

Philadelphia War Tax Resistance/War Resisters League lends money at no interest to projects directly struggling for a society free from sexism, racism, imperialism, and militarism and/or for improved health, education, and well-being in the community. We give priority to groups or projects which:

1. Are working in the Philadelphia community;
2. Fill or attempt to fill a community need consistent with WTR/WRL goals;
3. Work to provide basic social needs in alternative ways (outside of "establishment" institutions);
4. Don't have access to power within establishment institutions.

Our fund is composed of resisted war taxes and the savings of a number of people who are not wealthy and who will need their money back. In the case of resisted war taxes, the money will be needed if and when the government attaches wages or seizes property of the tax resisters.

For as long as we are able to keep this money from the war machine, it should be used in the community, where it is most needed. That is why we formed the Fund. We hope we can keep it going and growing. To do this, we must minimize the risk of loan defaults; therefore, we have certain questions of each applicant.

Please answer these ten points on another sheet and return to Philadelphia WTR/WRL at least one week before the indicated meeting date. (We would appreciate 8 copies of your application.)

1. Name of organization, address, and phone.
2. Amount requested (generally for no more than $1,500).
3. Reasons for loan request. Please be specific about: a) why Philadelphia WTR/WRL is an appropriate source of funding—is a loan really what is needed; b) how the money will be used; c) why the money is not otherwise available; and, d) the overall expenses of the project.
4. Description of the organization and people involved—brief but specific! (A current brochure may be helpful, especially if the group has not borrowed from Phil. WTR/WRL before.)
5. Basis of repayment: if from receipts, attach prior and projected financial reports. If from ongoing fundraising, describe method and basis for predicting success. If from grants, indicate source and status of applications.
6. Proposed repayment schedule (we prefer repayment in installments completed within a year—please indicate dates and sizes of installments).
7. Name, address, and phone of person(s) who personally guarantee repayment of the loan and will take responsibility for it should other plans fail.
8. Because of our "political" objectives, we want to let people know how resisted war taxes are being used. How can the organization help us publicize this loan?
9. Name, address, and phone of person(s) whom we can contact about this application and who will attend the Fund meeting to present the request and answer any questions. (We hope this process will help foster openness and trust with each group to whom we make a loan!)

If you have any questions or concerns, please call us. In peace,_____
On_____ we will consider the loan request from _____.

a local affiliate of the War Resisters League and the National War Tax Resistance Coordinating Committee

---

mercial banks, we are turning more and more to alternative investment, such as revolving loans to food and housing coops, progressive publications, and socially responsible businesses. How far we go in these experiments in alternative economics depends upon the enthusiasm of our members."

"The Pioneer Valley (Massachusetts) fund will not put its money into interest-gathering or speculative investments. The feeling among members of the tax resistance group is that this

Philadelphia War Tax Resistance
2208 South St., Philadelphia, PA 19146

LOAN FUND AGREEMENT SHEET

This is an agreement between _____ and
(name of group)

Philadelphia WTR/WRL for repayment of a loan of _____
(amount)

made by Philadelphia WTR/WRL to _____ on _____.
(group)   (date)

_____ commits itself to repay the loan in
(name of group)

_____ installments of _____ each, with the
(# and frequency)   (dollar amount)

initial payment of _____ due on _____ and the final payment
(amount)   (date)

of _____ due on _____.
(amount)   (date)

Signed for Phil. WTR/WRL   Group Receiving Loan

_____   _____
Signature   Signature

Name_____   _____
Address_____   _____
Phone_____   _____

This loan is secured by a *Personal Pledge* of repayment by

Signature_____
Name_____
Address_____
Phone_____

a local affiliate of the War Resisters League and the National War Tax Resistance Coordinating Committee

---

fund should not invest its capital in banks or other mainstream economic institutions that are invariably related to the war economy. Our intention is to make grants and loans within short periods of time so as not to stockpile money... At present we have a checking account. This is seen as a concession to the pragmatics of handling money, cashing checks, mailing grants, etc., and it will not be used as a place to accumulate money."

The Philadelphia Alternative Fund lends up to

59

ESCROW ACCOUNTS

People sometimes use the term "escrow" to refer to funds which hold redirected taxes, but will return the respective amount to a resister if the IRS collects from him/her. The Conscience and Military Tax Campaign (CMTC), based in Seattle, maintains an Escrow Account to support passage of the Peace Tax Fund Bill. The Escrow Account was established in 1980 to collect resisted tax dollars, payable to the government on passage of the Peace Tax Fund Bill.

The CMTC Escrow Account most closely resembles escrow in the legal sense. Holding money *in escrow* means that the money is held "in the keeping of a third person for delivery to a given party upon the fulfillment of some condition." *(Webster's Encyclopedic Unabridged Dictionary)* The contract is binding on all parties.

With the CMTC account, CMTC acts as the third party, holding an individual's funds until the bill passes. The account itself is legal. However, if an individual puts resisted taxes into the account, the difference from legal escrow is that the government does not accept that deposit in lieu of tax payment to the IRS. The government does not subscribe to the war tax resister's conditions.

The use of the term "escrow" for alternative fund accounts that will return the money to the resister on request is not really escrow at all, since the funds may keep the money or return it to the depositor, not a third party. Nevertheless, an alternative fund account is legal. Again, it is the act of resisting tax payment to the IRS that the government deems illegal.

Many alternative funds make interest free loans and avoid investing in banks and other mainstream economic institutions.

Most funds operate through consensus decision of steering committees made up of members of the funds.

$1,500 per loan interest-free to community groups working for community improvement, education, peace, justice, nonviolent social change, etc. These loans can total as much as one-third of the fund. Another third is lent in larger amounts at low interest to similar community groups for long-term projects. The remaining amount is in credit unions, available should depositors need access quickly. Over the years discussions have altered the collective position about whether to accept interest, how clean any money can be, and so forth.

By and large alternative funds do earn some interest on money deposited with or contributed to them, but in no case is the interest returned to those who deposit the money. It is used variously for grants, for operating expenses, and/or for covering loans that are not repaid.

Making Decisions

In all cases decisions are arrived at by some form of consensus of the members of each Fund.

Grant and loan decisions at the Lutheran Peace Fund in Wisconsin are made by representatives appointed by the Lutheran Peace Fellowship Coordinator and Board of Directors. "Any depositor to the Lutheran Peace Fund who wishes to assist in making grant decisions may be appointed as a Fund representative by contacting the Lutheran Peace Fellowship office."

The guidelines of the Northern California People's Life Fund (PLF) state: "Applications are screened and grants are made by any members of the PLF who choose to attend the meetings for these purposes in January and February of each year. Decisions are made by consensus of the members involved." In addition, the PLF allows resisters "to earmark a contribution for a group of the resister's choice—in this case the PLF acts as a channel only."

The Philadelphia Alternative Fund and the New York City People's Life Fund both have steering committees. The New York group reports: "Our decisions have usually been, if not in total agreement, then with no strong objection by any single member. We have a PLF Board elected annually and seven have been considered a quorum. In years where active interest has dropped, we have had to lower the quorum."

In Philadelphia, the steering committee model was adopted some years ago when three consecutive monthly meetings had only two members present! The quarterly meetings are open to all members, but the steering committee members make a more overt commitment to attend.

The Atlanta Tax Conversion Fund for Peace and Human Needs makes decisions "by consensus of those who have put money in the Fund and those who have received grants recently."

Some funds have monthly meetings to consider loan or grant requests. Others consider loan or grant requests quarterly, and still others award grants only once or twice a year. The frequency of meetings often depends on the amount of money available and the number of people involved. The cycles often center around tax day, the time when war tax resisters, like others, figure their "taxes" and redirect their monies.

Groups which have chosen to make loans accept some risks. Sometimes the recipient cannot repay the loan or takes a very long time to do so. Some funds therefore limit the maximum size of loans to guard against losses or tying up too much money at a time. The Philadelphia and New England funds both make written loan agreements and repayment schedules with loan recipients.

The New York City People's Life Fund reports: "In the early days of the Fund, when resources were quite limited, we gave only loans. Our thinking was that monies coming into the Fund should be recycled; after getting a booster loan, one group repays it, making it possible for another group to benefit. We found, however, that loans were turning into grants by default. Many of these groups were strapped for funds so it was difficult for them to pay the loan back. In the late 1970s we changed the policy and decided to award grants."

Guideline Priorities

Whether the funds give grants or loans, they offer war tax resisters (and sympathizers) a positive and relatively pure use for resisted war taxes—in a rather impure system. Most funds have written guidelines for choosing the recipients of grants and loans. A general survey of recipients from around the country shows the choices to be fairly similar. One variance is that the size of the fund and the locality of contributors may determine whether they give on the local, state, regional, or national level. Most funds focus on humans needs and peace groups within their communities.

The Wisconsin Alternative Fund states: "There will be an attempt to balance grants and loans between social service organizations and social change organizations. It is important that we do not fund only white, middle class groups."

New England War Tax Resistance "distributes refused tax money to a broad range of groups that request our aid." They give to many peace, justice, and human needs groups in the New England region as well as to some national organizations or projects.

The Northern California People's Life Fund has detailed priorities for distributing their grants "to groups in Northern California whose work falls within one of the following areas:

First Priority: Provision of essential, day-to-day human services (food, health, childcare, housing, etc.) which the government is not adequately furnishing, together with educational or other work aimed at pointing out and changing the root causes of whatever problems the group is addressing.

Second Priority: Provision of essential, day-to-day human services without an explicit, conscious attempt to deal with an analysis or eradication of the problem.

Third Priority: Education or action, in a spirit of nonviolence aimed at social, economic, or political change.

In addition, the PLF gives up to 25% of its "give away" fund and the interest earned on all deposits "to support the work of war tax resistance, both locally and nationally."

The size of a fund clearly determines how much it will be able to do. This is especially true of those funds which allow depositors to withdraw their deposits at any time. These funds have to keep some amount in reserve, although such reserves can be "doing good" in a credit union or other life-affirming investment."

Related Activities

Besides the lending and grant-making functions, alternative funds can provide the basis for other activities. Fund meetings can be times for resisters to share information about their personal resistance efforts and seek advice and/or support for audits, tax court appearances, and other problems or pressures presented to them by their resistance.

Many alternative funds publicly award their grants or loans by holding a ceremony or rally, or issuing a press release. This can provide public education about war tax resistance and the work of the groups receiving money. Similarly, some funds help finance their own actions, which may be complementary but not directly related to the operation of the fund. For example, in Philadelphia, some of the interest earned by the alternative fund helps maintain a War Resisters League action group, which has done coalition projects and projects on its own, such as organizing house meetings and forming war resisters' affinity groups.

In Conclusion

Setting up and running an alternative fund takes a relatively large commitment by a small group of activists, but for war tax resisters, the benefits often outweigh the problems. The Northern California, New York City, New England, and Philadelphia funds have all been active for more than twenty years. The hundreds of thousands of dollars redirected by these and other funds have benefited countless small, grassroots groups around the country.

At the end of this book is a listing which includes alternative funds nationwide. The National War Tax Resistance Coordinating Committee (NWTRCC) has a resource packet entitled "Alternative Funds: How to Start and Maintain Them" for $5. Write to NWTRCC, PO Box 774, Monroe, ME 04951.

Steve Gulick works with the Philadelphia War Tax Resistance Alternative Fund and WRL. This chapter is based on a survey he did of alternative funds around the country in 1981 with a 1991 update.

Some funds limit the maximum size of loans to guard against losses.

Most funds make loans or grants to human service and peace and justice groups which do not have access to funding from establishment sources.

Fund meetings can be times for resisters to share information, seek advice, and get support.

9 History of War Tax Resistance in the United States

A CHRONOLOGICAL HISTORY OF WAR TAX RESISTANCE IN THE UNITED STATES

1637
Algonquin Indians oppose taxation by the Dutch to help improve a local Dutch fort.

1755
John Woolman and a number of other prominent Quakers try unsuccessfully to persuade the Society of Friends to refuse payment of a £60,000 tax levied by the Pennsylvania colony for war purposes.

1816
William Lloyd Garrison and others founded the New England Non-Resistance Society which favored war tax resistance.

1847
Henry David Thoreau refuses to pay the Massachusetts poll tax levied for the Mexican War. He spent a night in jail. The experience was recorded in his essay, "On the Duty of Civil Disobedience."

1913
Sixteenth Amendment establishes income tax.

Up until World War II, war tax resistance in the U.S. primarily manifested itself among members of the historic peace churches: Society of Friends (Quakers), Mennonite Church, and Church of the Brethren. And as a rule, it was only among a *few* members of these religious groups and usually only during time of war.[1]

The Quakers were the most active tax resisters of the three groups, though their resistance was generally in the form of personal witness. Those Mennonites who refused payment of war taxes did so primarily as a means for personal salvation and purity. The number of Brethren who resisted taxes was much smaller than among the Quakers or Mennonites.

Colonial America

One of the earliest known instances of war tax refusal took place in 1637 when the relatively peaceable Algonquin Indians opposed taxation by the Dutch to help improve a local Dutch fort.[2]

Shortly after the Quakers arrived in America (1656) there were a number of *individual* instances of war tax resistance. For example some Quakers refused payment of taxes for the repair of fortifications of New York at the beginning of the Anglo-Dutch War in 1672. However, all but a few Quakers were willing to pay war taxes when they were mixed with other expenditures. Their greatest problems came when an explicit war tax was levied.

In 1689 the Quaker Assembly in charge of the Pennsylvania Colony was resistant to appeals for funds to aid in King William's War. But they reluctantly turned over money after being persuaded it would only be spent on humanitarian efforts.

However, in 1709 the Quaker Assembly refused a request of £4,000 for an expedition into Canada, replying "it was contrary to their religious principles to hire men to kill one another." (Governor's letter of that year) Eventually £500 was voted with the proviso that it would not be used for war. A couple of years later the Quaker Assembly agreed to another request from England. Although most Quakers went along, some refused to pay the tax and several were imprisoned or had their property levied.

At the beginning of the French and Indian War in 1755, John Woolman and a number of other prominent Quakers tried to persuade the Society of Friends to refuse payment of the £60,000 tax levied by the Pennsylvania colony, primarily for war purposes. Unlike past efforts, this war resistance sought to go beyond individual protest and make pacifism more socially relevant. Though small, this appears to be the first significant group effort among Quakers against the collection of "mixed taxes" (taxes for nonwar programs). However, the Society of Friends was not persuaded.

A few Dunkards (Brethren) and Mennonites joined in opposition to the war by refusing to pay taxes. But their number was even smaller than that of the Quaker refusers.

American Revolution
(1775-1783)

Secular war tax resistance during the American War of Independence was limited to those who were loyal to the British Crown, rather than out of opposition to all war. Similarly, many Mennonites opposed payment of taxes for the war more out of loyalty to Britain than because of their pacifism. With the exception of a few members, the Brethren did not resist taxes for this war.

However, *most Quakers* were opposed to those taxes designated specifically for military purposes. Though the official position of the Society of Friends was against any payment of war taxes, this issue stirred up much debate. Property was seized and auctioned, and many Quakers were jailed for their war tax resistance. A number of Quakers even refused the "mixed taxes." Some Quakers, like Moses Brown, pledged tax resistance after the war in order to oppose war preparation. Up to 500 Quakers were disowned *for paying war taxes* or joining the army.

Following the war many Quakers continued to refuse because these taxes were being used to pay the war debt, and therefore were essentially war taxes.

War of 1812
(1812-1815)

Although this was a very unpopular war, most Brethren appear to have paid taxes. Many Quakers did refuse taxes and several were jailed or had property seized. Secular war tax resistance, again, was of a selective nature. Massive tax resistance was threatened by Federalists, shipowners, and bankers who thought the issues were not important enough to go to war over.

Following the war a small nonsectarian peace movement was formed. William Lloyd Garrison and others founded the New England Non-Resistance Society, which favored war tax resistance, but whose members seldom practiced it. However, a handful of them refused to pay and were jailed. The Shakers in New Hampshire

62

pledged to resist taxes for war, no matter what the consequences.[3]

Mexican War
(1846-1848)

The Quakers reacted more strongly to this war because of its aggressive nature and the threatened spread of slavery posed by the war. Many, again, refused to pay war taxes.

However, the most famous instance of war tax resistance was that of Henry David Thoreau. Although not a pacifist he was opposed to slavery and the imperialist and unjust nature of the war. His refusal to pay the Massachusetts poll tax levied for the war resulted in a night in jail. This whole experience was recorded in his essay, "On the Duty of Civil Disobedience," which has had a profound influence on many people. As opposed to most war tax resisters before him, Thoreau's action was aimed more at social change than personal removal from the war efforts.

Civil War
(1861-1865)

During the Civil War many who had previously refused taxes decided that paying war taxes was more of an effort to free slaves, than to kill people. Secular resistance to war taxes was minimal. There are records of a few individuals who were jailed for their refusal. Unlike the Mennonites and Brethren, the Quakers remained officially opposed to the payment of taxes for military exemption (offered by both the Union and the Confederacy to the peace churches). However, the Society of Friends was more tolerant of those who paid war taxes than before. The official Quaker position on mixed taxes was that they should be paid—and cheerfully. A few Quakers continued to refuse payment of even mixed taxes.

Right after the war the Universal Peace Union was formed, which called for immediate disarmament, denounced imperialism, and advocated a boycott of war taxes. A number of its members were jailed or had property seized for their war tax resistance.

For the next seventy-five years after the Civil War there were scattered incidents of Quaker war tax resistance, followed by levies. But effectively, promotion of war tax resistance by the three peace churches had come to an end.

Spanish-American War
(1898)

War tax resistance was virtually nonexistent. Mennonites and Brethren paid their taxes willingly. Some Mennonites even made clothes for soldiers. Quakers began to focus more on causes of war rather than on resistance to war. Secular war tax resistance was limited to a few individual cases.

World War I
(1917-1919)

There were some who resisted the sale of War Bonds or Liberty Loans, usually the historic peace churches and a few political resisters. Though the income tax was established by the Sixteenth Amendment in 1913, there is no record of income tax refusal. War bond drives were designed more to foster patriotism than to finance the war. The strongest stand by a group against the bonds was taken by the Hutterian Brethren.

World War II
(1941-1945)

Until World War II the individual income tax was a minor part of the federal government receipts. In fact, in 1939 only four million people (3% of the population) paid income taxes. However, by 1945 that figure jumped to fifty million (36% of the population). This was aided by the introduction of the employee withholding tax in

---

1942
Ernest Bromley refuses payment of $7.09 for a "defense tax stamp" required for all cars. He is arrested and jailed for sixty days.

1943
Introduction of the employee withholding tax.

1948
The founding conference of Peacemakers, the first organization to promote war tax resistance.

1949
Peacemakers issues "41 Refuse to Pay Income Tax" press release. War tax refusal receives nationwide publicity.

1959
Juanita Nelson is first U.S. woman jailed for war tax resistance. She was released the same day. IRS never collected the money.

The first article to appear on war tax refusal, by Ernest Bromley in Fellowship Magazine, *November 1947.*

1963
The first war tax refusal book, *Handbook on Nonpayment of War Taxes,* is published.

Maurice McCrackin is removed from the ministry of the United Presbyterian Church for his refusal to pay war taxes.

1965
Ken Knudson suggests inflating the W-4 form to stop withholding. As a result of this tactic, thousands join the war tax resistance movement.

1965

Peacemakers begin No Tax for War in Vietnam Committee and ask people to sign the pledge "I am not going to pay taxes on 1964 income."

1966

Karl Meyer writes, "Hang Up On War," initiating mass resistance to paying the 10% telephone tax which subsidizes the war effort.

370 people sign ad in *The Washington Post* announcing refusal to pay part or all of their 1965 income tax. Signers include A.J. Muste, Joan Baez, Lawrence Ferlinghetti, Noam Chomsky, and Staughton Lynd.

1967

Writers and Editors War Tax Protest is organized by Gerald Walker of the *New York Times Magazine*. 528 pledge to refuse at least the 10% war surtax added onto income taxes for the war.

1968

Telephone tax resistance case of Martha Tranquilli leads to clarifying decision that phone service may not be disconnected for nonpayment of federal tax.

New England War Tax Resistance alternative fund begins.

1969

National War Tax Resistance is founded to devote all its energies to promote tax refusal. Local groups form around the country.

Cover of an early 1950s war tax resistance flier. Peacemakers.

1943. In addition, 1941 income tax returns had a 10% "Defense Tax" tagged on. The unprecedented amount of money being raised and spent for World War II suddenly touched the consciousness of many pacifists, who up until the war were not required to pay taxes.

A number of organizations, such as Women's International League for Peace and Freedom (WILPF) and American Friends Service Committee (AFSC), protested this tax but did not resist its payment. A strategy meeting was held in January of 1941 to discuss protesting the tax and to urge government recognition of a conscientious objector status for taxpayers. A few people did not pay the tax.

In 1942 Ernest Bromley refused payment of $7.09 for a "defense tax stamp" required for all cars. He was arrested and eventually jailed for sixty days (see p. 78). On the day of his sentencing, courthouse personnel pointed out some cars parked in front of the building that were without these stamps. By 1944, so many cars were being driven without the stamps that the law was declared unenforceable and was dropped. Bromley and a few other pacifists did not pay income taxes during

WHY we REFUSE to pay TAXES for WAR

If a thousand men were not to pay their tax bills this year, that would not be a violent and bloody measure, as it would be to pay them and enable the state to commit violence and shed innocent blood.
—Henry David Thoreau

World War II, but there was no movement of war tax refusal, nor much interest in the subject.[4]

In April of 1948 a conference on "More Disciplined and Revolutionary Pacifist Activity" was held in Chicago, attended by over 300 people. The Call to the Conference (signed by A.J. Muste, Dave Dellinger, Harrop Freeman, George Houser, Dwight Macdonald, Ernest Bromley, and Marion Bromley, among others) expressed a need for a more revolutionary pacifist program and action techniques, and the use of the cell structure of organization.[5] Out of this conference grew a new organization, calling itself the Peacemakers. Their newsletter was titled *Peacemaker*.

About forty people who attended the conference stated their intention to refuse part or all of their federal income taxes, forming a Tax Refusal Committee. This Committee began almost immediately to publish news bulletins, independent of the *Peacemaker*. The bulletins were instrumental in engendering concern and giving information on tax refusal. The Tax Refusal Committee operated within the Peacemakers, but was somewhat separate, partly because this group came to the founding conference pretty much ready to operate by itself anyway.

War tax refusal succeeded in achieving nationwide publicity for the first time with the issuance of a Peacemaker press release on March 14, 1949, titled "Forty-one Refuse to Pay Income Tax." For almost twenty years Peacemakers was virtually the only consistent source of information and support for war tax resisters. *The Catholic Worker*, the *Progressive*, *Fellowship*, and a few other movement newsletters and magazines, would occasionally print sympathetic articles on war tax resistance.[6]

Korean War
(1950-1953)

Following World War II and up to the start of the Vietnam War only six people were imprisoned for war tax resistance: James Otsuka, Maurice McCrackin, Juanita Nelson, Eroseanna Robinson, Walter Gormly, and Arthur Evans. All had been found in contempt of court for refusing to cooperate in one way or another with the proceedings. War tax resistance and peace movement activities in general dropped off considerably during the Korean War and through the hysteria of the Cold War and/or McCarthyism.

In 1963 the Peacemakers published the first handbook on war tax resistance, appropriately titled *Handbook on Nonpayment of War Taxes*. This handbook was actually formed on the basis of a three-part series of memos issued by the Tax Refusal Committee in 1948—fifteen years earlier.[7]

Indochina War
(1964-1975)

War tax resistance gained nationwide publicity when Joan Baez announced in April of 1964 her refusal to pay 60% of her 1963 income taxes because of the war in Vietnam. Early in 1965 the Peacemakers formed the "No Tax for War in Vietnam Committee," obtaining signers to the pledge "I am not going to pay taxes on 1964 income." By 1967 about 500 people had signed the pledge.

Then in 1965-1966, three events occurred making this a pivotal period for the war resistance movement, signaling a shift in war tax resistance from a couple hundred to eventually tens of thousands of refusers.

First, a committee led by A.J. Muste obtained 370 signatures from the lists of the Committee for Nonviolent Action (CNVA) and the WRL for an ad in *The Washington Post*, which proclaimed their intention not to pay all or part of their 1965 income taxes. Among the signers were Joan Baez, Lawrence Ferlinghetti, David Dellinger, Dorothy Day, Noam Chomsky, Nobel Prize winner Albert Szent-Gyorgyi, publisher Lyle Stuart, and Staughton Lynd. According to a subsequent IRS analysis, one quarter of the signers had no taxable income.[8]

Second, a suggestion to form a mass movement around the refusal to pay the 10% telephone tax was given an initial boost by Chicago tax resister Karl Meyer, who wrote "Hang Up on War." Though promoted by Peacemakers, CNVA, AFSC, WILPF, among other national organizations, it was the WRL which succeeded in effectively developing its national appeal.

And third, in a letter to the *Peacemaker*[9] Ken Knudson suggested that inflating the W-4 form would stop withholding. Again, Karl Meyer with the aid of groups like the Catholic Worker, Peacemaker, WRL, and eventually National War Tax Resistance promoted this idea in the late 1960s. As a result, the number of known income tax resisters grew from 275 in 1966, to 375 in 1967, to 533 in 1968, to 848 in 1969.[10] According to the IRS there were 2,000 income tax resisters in 1971.[11] These figures continued to grow,[12] perhaps to an estimated 20,000. This method also brought a new wave of indictments and jailings by the government—sixteen were indicted for claiming too many dependents; of those, six were actually jailed.

In the summer of 1967, Gerald Walker of The New York Times Magazine began the organizing of Writers and Editors War Tax Protest. The 528 writers and editors (including Gloria Steinem and Kirkpatrick Sale) pledged themselves to refuse the 10% war surtax (which had just been added to income taxes) and possibly the 23% of their income tax allocated for the war. Most daily newspapers refused to sell space for the ad. Only the *New York Post, Ramparts,* and the *New York Review of Books* carried it.[13]

The popularity of war tax resistance grew to such an extent that the WRL could no longer handle the volume of requests. So in December 1969 a press conference was held in New York City by Allen Ginsberg, Pete Seeger, Bradford Lyttle, and Kennett Love to announce the founding of the National War Tax Resistance (WTR). Bradford Lyttle was the first coordinator, followed by Robert Calvert and Angie O'Gorman Calvert. Local WTR chapters blossomed around the country. By 1972

Cover of an early telephone tax brochure. WRL.

1971
Philadelphia War Tax Resistance alternative fund, Northern California and New York City Peoples Life Funds are founded.

1972
Telephone tax resisters reach an estimated 200,000–500,000. Estimated numbers of income tax resisters reaches 20,000.

Congressman Ronald Dellums (CA) introduced the World Peace Tax Fund in Congress.

1975
National War Tax Resistance folds. Interest in war tax resistance drops, but thousands continue to refuse.

1978
The Center on Law and Pacifism is formed to assist war tax resistance efforts.

1980
Conscience and Military Tax Campaign establishes an Escrow Account to hold refused tax dollars until passage of the Peace Tax Fund Bill in Congress.

1981
Roman Catholic Archbishop Raymond Hunthausen of Seattle urges citizens to refuse to pay 50% of their income taxes to protest spending on nuclear weapons.

A SERIES OF PROSECUTIONS

From 1970 to early 1973 there were fifteen to twenty war tax resisters who were indicted for "inflating" their W-4 forms by claiming excessive dependents. As far as we know, only six were ultimately jailed. The IRS has backed off on criminal prosecutions since then and focused more on technical changes in the W-4 system to control resistance. Brief accounts of some of those indicted follow. Related stories (Karl Meyer and Paul Monsky) appear in Chapter 11.

Jim Shea, a college instructor at George Mason College in Fairfax, Virginia, was the first war tax resister to be indicted (July 1970) and convicted (September 1970) for altering his W-4 form. He had claimed twenty dependents on his W-4 as an act of solidarity with the Vietnamese revolutionaries and millions of oppressed people. He was sentenced to one year.

Sally Buckley of St. Paul, Minnesota, was indicted in September 1970. She claimed "other members of the human family as dependents" and was sentenced to thirty days or payment of the $200 owed. While she herself refused to pay, the fine was paid anonymously (to her displeasure).

Others who were indicted, fined, or jailed during this period include Bill Himmelbauer and Mike Fowler of Chicago; Mark Riley, California; James Smith, Springfield, Missouri; Ellis Rece, Augusta, Georgia; Henry Braun and Donald Callahan, Philadelphia; Dennis Richter, Minneapolis; and Ron Mitchell and Roy Schenk, Madison, Wisconsin. Jack Malinowski of Philadelphia spent three months in jail. The next year (1972) he again claimed fifteen dependents and filed for money previously withheld. Several months later he received a check for almost $500.

John Leininger filed an inflated W-4 form while doing civilian alternative service during the Vietnam War at a Dayton, Ohio hospital. It wasn't until 1972 that he was indicted for filing a false W-4, filing a false income tax return, and failing to file. Eventually he pleaded no contest and was sentenced to time served.

The case of Lyle Snider was one of the most visible and widely supported; CBS network news carried the story during his trial. Snider had claimed *three billion* dependents on his 1971 W-4 form. He submitted a letter explaining that he felt the population of the earth depended on him (and others) to refuse to pay their war taxes.

In December 1972 Snider was arrested in Greensboro, North Carolina on charges of filing a false and fraudulent withholding statement. A trial was held in June 1973, and the judge handed down a surprisingly harsh eight-month prison sentence (plus thirty days for Sue Snider, who along with her husband had refused to stand for the judge). The next year, however, the Court of appeals (*U.S. v. Snider*, 502 F. 2d 645 (1974)) reversed the decisions and acquitted Lyle. In a sixty-page opinion, the Court ruled that in making a false statement there must be an "attempt to deceive," and that fraud "implies bad faith, intentional wrongdoing, and a sinister motive." It said that Snider's claim of three billion dependents was obviously a hyperbole, legally providing no information to the IRS.

there were 192 such groups. The number of telephone tax resisters was estimated to be between 200,000 and 500,000 (the IRS claims the numbers were short of 100,000 at their peak), while income tax resisters may have been around 20,000. WTR published a comprehensive handbook on tax resistance, *Ain't Gonna Pay for War No More* (edited by Robert Calvert), and put out a monthly newsletter, *Tax Talk*.

Radical members of the historic peace churches began to urge their constituencies to refuse war taxes. The Church of the Brethren, though supportive of individual war tax resisters, did not advocate nonpayment. The resisters among the Brethren viewed tax refusal as more than a personal witness; they saw it as a means to influence government policy. Similarly, though the Mennonite Church did not endorse tax resistance, many within the Church refused to pay and urged others not to. Many Quakers became war tax resisters and were supported by the AFSC and many yearly meetings.

In 1972 Congressman Ronald Dellums (CA) introduced the World Peace Tax Fund Act in Congress, which was designed to create a conscientious objector status for taxpayers. The National Council for a World Peace Tax Fund was formed to promote this legislation (later changed to National Campaign for a Peace Tax Fund, see Chapter 14). The bill has been introduced into each Congress since, with introduction in the 102nd Congress (1991) by Representative Andy Jacobs (IN) in the House and Senator Mark Hatfield (OR) in the Senate.

During the Indochina War, war tax resistance gained its greatest strength ever in the history of the United States, and on a secular basis rather than as a result of the historic peace churches, who played a very minor role this time. The government did its best to stop this increase in tax resistance, but was hamstrung by telephone tax resisters. There were so many resisters and so little tax owed per person, that the IRS lost every time they made a collection. The cost of bank levies, garnished wages, automobile and property seizures, and even the simplest IRS paperwork was simply too expensive to be worth it.

The Reagan Military Escalation

National WTR folded in 1975 with the end of the Indochina War. By 1977 interest in war tax resistance dropped off to the point of about 20,000 telephone tax resisters and a few thousand income tax resisters. Then in 1978 some radical members of the three historic peace churches got together to issue a "New Call to Peacemaking." The Call was in reaction to the growing nuclear arms race and military budget; it suggested war tax resistance was one way to oppose the arms race. This resurgence in interest in war tax resistance by the peace churches was joined by members of other churches, particularly Catholics. Tax resisters began to go to court in order to establish the right of exemption to taxes for people conscientiously opposed to war. The Center on Law and Pacifism was formed in 1978 to assist these and other war tax resistance efforts, issuing the book *People Pay for Peace* (written by William Durland) in 1979.

With the election of Ronald Reagan as President in 1980 and his call to rearm the U.S., many more people began to resist war taxes. The IRS admitted the number of war tax resisters tripled between 1978 and 1981. Like Joan Baez's tax refusal announcement seventeen years before, a national stir was created in 1981 when Roman Catholic Archbishop Raymond Hunthausen of Seattle urged citizens to refuse to pay 50% of their income taxes to protest spending on nuclear weapons. Letters of endorsement of his stand were made by other religious leaders in Seattle and elsewhere around the country.

This renewed interest in war tax resistance, spurred on by the unprecedented increase in military spending during peacetime, appears to have stimulated an escalated response by the government. After several years of no prosecutions for war tax resistance, three were indicted and convicted: Richard Catlett (1979), Bruce Chrisman (1979), and Paul Monsky (1980). Catlett served sixty days in jail; Chrisman and Monsky received "public service" sentences. Though there have not been additional criminal prosecutions of war tax resisters since, the IRS shifted tactics and began seizing property. In 1984 and 1985 after almost ten years of very few seizures, about a half dozen automobiles and a similar number of houses were seized from war tax resisters.

Furthermore, in 1982 the government came up with a clever new civil penalty which was specifically aimed at war tax resisters. Called the "frivolous" fine, it charged a $500 penalty against anyone who altered their 1040 forms (e.g., by claiming a war tax deduction). The IRS has the authority to tag on this penalty instantly without any due process. Several dozen war tax resisters stung by the penalty appealed to the courts with little success.

In an effort to coordinate the growing interest in war tax resistance, a National Action Conference was called by WRL and the Center on Law and Pacifism in September 1982. Out of this conference the National War Tax Resistance Coordinating Committee (NWTRCC) was formed. A year later an office was established and staff hired. NWTRCC has grown into a network of eighty national and local affiliates. Every year a conference of war tax resisters is held in order to share information and plan future activities. (See Chapter 16.)

The End of the "Cold War"

Historically, the level of activity of the war tax resistance movement, as with that of the peace movement in general, rises and falls with national and international events.

As the Berlin Wall fell and Eastern European countries demanded independence from the Soviet Union in 1989, war tax resisters looked for ways to work in coalition with groups calling for a "peace dividend." Six months later, George Bush sent U.S. troops to the Persian Gulf region, and war tax resistance groups were flooded with calls from people saying that they'd "had enough!"

The second edition of the National War Tax Resistance manual, issued in 1972.

1982
Government establishes the "frivolous" fine with a $500 penalty against anyone who alters their 1040.

April 15: As a result of a 1981 federal court decision, the IRS is forced for the first time to allow leafletting inside the IRS building waiting area (NYC).

The National War Tax Resistance Coordinating Committee (NWTRCC) is founded.

1984
Karl Meyer calls for "Cabbage Patch" resistance and files 365 returns—one-a-day—to protest the frivolous fine.

1985
Court rules in favor of war tax resister Larry Bassett on Fifth Amendment grounds. He could not be required to give financial information to the IRS.

1989
In Greenfield, Massachusetts IRS auctions the home of Randy Kehler and Betsy Corner. A few months later the home of their neighbors Bob Bady and Pat Morse is auctioned. The case receives national publicity for war tax resistance and an outpouring of support for the resisters.

1989
Don Mosley and Max Rice are jailed for contempt of court for refusing to give the IRS income information. They served 40 days of 60-day sentences. The IRS did not get the information it sought. First jailings since Richard Catlett in 1979. Total number of war tax resisters jailed since WWII: 19.

1990-1991
Alternative Revenue Service Campaign begins. Hundreds of activists participate in the ARS by circulating the EZ Peace Form, a parody of the IRS 1040 EZ.

1991
Northern California War Tax Resistance holds a conference "Lives of Resistance: Communities of Support" during the Gulf War. Over 300 attend.

This list prepared by Judy Kowalok.

War tax resisters and other political activists continue to evaluate and adjust to the changing political climate.

Over the years, a solid core of resisters have kept numerous groups going. Many local groups have celebrated more than twenty years of activism. The New England War Tax Resistance Fund, Philadelphia Alternative Fund, New York City Peoples' Life Fund, and Northern California Peoples' Life Fund are among the alternative funds that have supported hundreds of community groups with grants and loans since the late 1960s.

When resistance is strongest the IRS often escalates its attacks, and then there is a corresponding response by resisters. For example, the strong phone tax campaign during the Vietnam War era led the IRS to seize property for small amounts of phone tax. The movement responded by organizing actions around auctions to reap its own publicity, sometimes causing the IRS to back down. W-4 resistance to overcome automatic withholding from paychecks led the IRS to limit the number of allowances that could be claimed. The movement responded by inventing the war tax deduction and credit methods; with the imposition of frivolous fines resisters dropped those methods and emphasized others. IRS actions and creative counter-actions by resisters are a continuing cycle.

In the 1980s the IRS put into place an "Automated Collection System" which appeared to allow them to match social security numbers with bank accounts, job locations, and filing history more quickly than in the past. People who had been nonfilers for years began to notice new contact from the IRS. The national war tax resistance network has been an important venue for creating new tactics and activities to help the resistance community continue to grow despite IRS activity.

The circumstances of a particular case can also bring new attention to war tax resistance and set an example of principled resistance despite the risks. In 1989 the IRS seized the home of Randy Kehler and Betsy Corner and their daughter Lillian. Randy, a Vietnam War draft resister, had gained some notice in the early 1980s as Director of the National Freeze (the Arms Race) Campaign, and the press was drawn to their story. Significant articles appeared in *The New York Times, Philadelphia Inquirer, Boston Globe, Washington Post,* and other major newspapers. (See their story in Chapter 11.)

Local war tax resistance actions have continued unabated over the years. Press clippings from small and large cities around the country prove that tax day actions invariably receive good coverage in local papers. Newspaper photos of leafletters, street theatre performers, speakers, and vigilers flood national offices during the height of tax season. Reaching out individual-to-individual on the local level is the heart of the war tax resistance movement.

---

1 Except where noted, this section up through World War II draws largely from Barbara Andrews' undergraduate thesis, *Tax Resistance in American History,* Goddard College, 1976.
2 *The Tax Dilemma: Praying for Peace, Paying for War,* Donald Kaufman, p. 29, Herald Press, 1978.
3 Kaufman, op. cit., p. 34.
4 Communication from Ernest Bromley, October 11, 1981.
5 *WRL News,* March 8 and May 10, 1948.
6 Ernest Bromley, op. cit.
7 Ernest Bromley, op. cit.
8 *The Washington Monthly,* Kennett Love, p. 62, December 1969.
9 September 11, 1965
10 Love, op. cit.
11 Andrews, op. cit., p. 251.
12 Figures based on IRS counting include only those that the IRS has direct contact with, excluding many people the IRS is not aware of as well as many people not clearly identified as war tax resisters. So IRS figures represent only the tip of the iceberg.
13 Love, op.cit.

Global War Tax Resistance

Individual war tax resistance has probably been around since the first taxes were levied for war. Mass war tax resistance may be almost as old. There are reports of collective tax refusal as far back as the second century, A.D., in Egypt.* In fact, it is not too far-fetched to assume that there have been instances of war tax resistance sometime or other in every country of the world.

The system of tax collection varies from country to country and thus, to some extent, defines the style of war tax resistance. In the U.S. it is easier to control withholding than in most other countries. In Germany there is greater emphasis on resisting excise taxes. In England there is a strong campaign for a law allowing conscientious objector status for those who wish to refuse military taxes. An international network has developed over the last few years for information sharing and support.

The first international conference on war tax resistance was held in Tubingen, West Germany, in September 1986. About 100 people from thirteen countries participated in the conference, which was sponsored by Ohne Rustung Leben (Live Without Weapons). The second international conference met in the Netherlands in October 1988, sponsored by Beweging Weigering Defensiebelasting (War Tax Resistance Movement). A third meeting was held in Italy in September 1990. The meetings continue to be held every-other-year. These meetings serve to connect the network of war tax resisters and peace tax fund campaigns around the world.

These meetings also sparked the idea for choosing an international project to which war tax resisters and alternative funds around the world could all contribute. In 1990 support for the struggle of the Innu living in the Quebec-Labrador Peninsula of Canada was suggested. The Innu are fighting a NATO base on their land.

Angola

In 1966 twelve village chiefs refused to cooperate with the Portuguese attempt to collect taxes. Portuguese military officials tried to convince the chiefs, to no avail, that refusal was hopeless, since the Portuguese military was far superior to anything the Angolans had. Eventually, they were released even though they pledged to continue tax refusal.
(Source: *Strategy for a Living Revolution*, George Lakey, pp. 123-4, 1973.)

Australia

Resistance to military spending (estimated to be at least 10% of the budget) has been ongoing since 1980. In 1983 the Peace Tax Campaign was formed and has received financial support from the Quakers. Though small, war tax resistance has been on the rise due to opposition to the joint U.S.-Australian military facilities, U.S. nuclear ships visiting Australian harbors, and because of Australia's significant arms exports (ranked 12th in the world).

In 1988 Senator Jo Vallentine redirected 10% of her taxes to Melbourne's Peace and Development Foundation. She explained to the Senate that she would do so "as long as Australia is involved in a military alliance with the U.S. government and in mining and export of uranium . . . I hope this action will encourage people to think of security in nonmilitary terms." Senator Vallentine has also introduced a Peace Trust Fund Bill into the Australian Senate.

In another well-publicized case, long-time resister Robert Burrowes along with Brendan Condon dumped a trailer-load of Aboriginal "land" at the Australian Taxation Office in partial payment of their tax bills for 1988-89. They wanted the land returned to its Aboriginal owners, and they also protested the military policies of the government. Burrowes has offered other "alternative payments" in the past: 104 trees in 1987, 94 shovels in 1986.

Government response to resisters has been to seize bank accounts, as happened to Robert Burrowes in a well-publicized case.

For more information, contact **Peace Tax Campaign** (PTC), 5/26 East Crescent St., McMahon's Point, NSW 2060.
(Sources: *War Resisters' International (WRI) Newsletter*, June 1990; 1985 correspondence with Margaret Bailey of PTC, Robert Burrowes, and Roger Sawkins of Religious Society of Friends.)

Belgium

Because Belgium is a country of two languages, it is not surprising to find two war tax resistance groups: Vredes Akti (for the Flemish, or Dutch-speaking) and Contribuables pour la Paix (for the Walloon, or French-speaking). The Flemish campaign began in 1983 under the theme "Geen geld woor geweld" (no money for violence), and is asking supporters to refuse a symbolic amount of 500 BF ($12), only a small fraction of the per capita amount that is spent on the military. These refusals have led to some seizures of furniture (or salary)

The Politics of Nonviolent Action, Gene Sharp, p. 241, 1973.

> Collective tax resistance has been reported as far back as the second century in Egypt.

> In Australia Senator Jo Vallentine redirected 10% of her taxes to a peace foundation.

> About 14% of all taxes in Britain go to for military spending.

> The Peace Pledge Union, Society of Friends, and Peace Tax Campaign are all active on war tax issues in Britain.

and public sales with very good publicity for the case. The Walloon group began in 1984, stimulated largely by the refusal of the government to hold a referendum on the deployment of the U.S. missiles.

Since 1985 bills for the recognition of conscientious objection to military spending and the establishment of a peace tax fund have been introduced in parliament. A petition was also sent to the King asking him to make a law allowing for conscientious objection to taxation.

For more information, contact **VRAK** (Aktie Vredesbelasting), van Elewijckstraat 35, 1050 Brussels; and **Contribuables pour la Paix**, Avenue des Allies 11, 6000 Charleroi.

(Source: *Paying for Peace*, 1985; update 1991, Dirk Panhuis.)

Britain

In 1197 A.D. St. Hugh of Lincoln refused to pay a tax levied to fund Richard the Lionhearted's war against the King of France. Subsequently, all his property was seized.

Almost eight centuries later (around 1977), the Peace Pledge Union (PPU) and Quaker Peace Committee began a legislative effort to create a conscientious objector status to military taxation. It is estimated that at least 14% of all taxes go to the military. In 1980 the Peace Tax Campaign was formed. In 1981 the *Manchester Guardian* printed a letter signed by parliamentary and religious leaders calling for a peace tax fund. Currently, there are approximately 20,000 who have signed the Statement of Support. A bill for a peace tax fund has been introduced in parliament, and in 1990 it was supported by eighty-six members of Parliament (MPs) from five parties and sixteen Labour MPs.

Actual resistance is small, but at times very creative. For example, in 1984 a group in Wales went to the Inland Revenue office (their IRS) with tax payments in a bucket of blood. When the officials refused to accept the payment, the protesters poured it down the front steps of the building.

In 1990 baker Nigel Wild served twenty-eight days in jail for refusing to pay £182 income tax to Inland Revenue. During a court appearance he offered 182 bread buns in lieu of pounds. "I am being sent to prison for refusing to pay income tax until I am given an assurance that none of it will be used for military expenditure. I am quite prepared to pay an equivalent amount in bread as I am a baker, and people are in need of bread not bombs." A headline from the *Daily Mirror* at the time read: "'Hand over the Dough' Tax Row Baker Told ... But Bun Fight is On!"

Tax resistance is very difficult because of the British equivalent of our withholding system, called pay-as-you-earn (PAYE). Unless you have a sympathetic employer or you are self-employed, you have no alternative. The PPU has been refusing to turn over 45% of its staff's PAYE contributions since 1982. In 1985 the PPU took tax resistance a step further by refusing £450 of its £1,100 corporation tax as a protest to military spending, the first organization in Britain to do so. Inland Revenue has taken them to court for both areas of resistance but has yet to collect the full amount. In 1983 the Society of Friends refused PAYE contributions from thirty-three of its employees. In 1985 a London judge ordered them to turn over £2,700 to Inland Revenue. An appeal was made of that decision.

In November 1985 the Peace Tax Campaign joined PPU by withholding 14% of its corporate tax, and the Campaign has continued its protest over the years. In 1990 the Peace Tax Campaign

Graphic from Britain's Peace Tax Campaign Annual Report, 1990.

sent a check for £386.52 (withheld taxes from staff wages) to Margaret Thatcher along with a letter asking that she spend it without violating their consciences. The check was returned. They then received a letter threatening immediate action if they didn't pay in full. The Campaign refused to pay, but said they wouldn't prevent a Tax Collector from personally collecting a check for the withheld tax from the Peace Tax offices, a process they went through the year before. Inland Revenue eventually picked up the check, although the Collector at first refused to enter the office.

Lawyers for Nuclear Disarmament have produced a fifty-page booklet called "A Tax on Peace—Conscientious Objection and the Taxpayer." It explains how to calculate the military percentage of taxes and what is likely to happen to a tax resister. Government reaction to tax resisters usually takes the form of fines and seizure of bank accounts; they can also seize property or jail the resister.

For more information, contact **Peace Tax Campaign**, 1A Hollybush Place, London E2 9QX; **Peace Pledge Union**, 6 Endsleigh St., London WC1H 0DX; **Lawyers for Nuclear Disarmament**, 2 Garden Court, Middle Temple, London EC4.
(Sources: *Conscience,* Newsletter of the Peace Tax Campaign, December 1990; *The Pacifist,* PPU, June 1985; *People Pay for Peace,* page ii, William Durland, 1984; *Paying for Peace,* 1985; *Peace News,* p. 16, February 7, 1986; Conscience and Military Tax Campaign newsletter, Fall 1991.)

Canada

In 1978 the Peace Tax Fund Committee was established by the Quakers in Victoria to promote a conscientious objector status for taxpayers. This movement was given a boost by the 1982 Canadian Constitution, which proclaimed the Freedom of Conscience as its first freedom. Seeing in this clause an opportunity to legally redirect the military portion of taxes, a Peace Tax Fund in Trust was set up to collect redirected taxes from those Canadians with some control over their tax dollars. In 1983 the campaign was incorporated under Conscience Canada, Inc.

Military spending amounts to approximately 8.6% of federal expenditures. Because 75% of all taxpayers have taxes withheld from their salaries, only 25% are able to resist taxes. In 1982 there were sixty resisters redirecting some percent of the taxes; by 1990, 500 people were redirecting tax dollars to the Peace Tax Fund in Trust.

Based on the new constitution, a number of war tax resisters have appealed to the federal tax court for legal recognition and lost, the most publicized case being that of Dr. Jerilynn Prior. In 1983 Dr. Prior and her attorney appealed to the federal tax court saying that the Income Tax Act violated her religious and conscientious beliefs. The judge ruled against her, and she appealed to the federal court where the judge ruled that she had no case, based largely on the court not recognizing a connection between the payment of taxes and government expenditures.

Dr. Prior and her lawyer appealed to the Canadian Supreme Court, which refused to hear her case in 1990. In February 1991 Prior and her lawyer, Thomas Berger, appealed the case to the United Nations Human Rights Commission in Geneva, Switzerland; in the spring of 1991 the Commission agreed to hear her case. The process could take two years. Through the 1980s Revenue Canada generally avoided collections on those paying into the Peace Tax Fund until the courts made a decision. This is the first time the U.N. Human Rights Commission has agreed to hear a case related to conscientious objection to military taxation. In cases of conscientious objection to military service they have asked states to provide alternative service.

For more information, contact **Conscience Canada, Inc.,** Box 601, Station E., Victoria, B.C. V8W 2P3.
(Sources: Communication with Edith Adamson, 1985; *Conscience Canada Newsletter,* Winter 1989, Spring 1990, Autumn 1990, Winter 1990-1991, Spring 1991, Summer 1991.)

France

In 1789 during the French Revolution, the National Assembly (constituted by the people and some clergy) encouraged refusal to pay all past taxes to the King. Only the payment of future taxes (to be spent by the National Assembly) to the assembly was approved.

In 1966 the Tax Refusal Movement began as a protest to the first French atomic tests at Moruroa in the Pacific. A few individuals refused 20% of their tax. The money was redistributed to peace groups. Then it was realized that if the refused amounts were dropped to 4%, more people could participate. The Inland Revenue reacted by confiscating goods.

Beginning in 1973 the Tax Refusal Movement shifted to support the "battle" of Larzac. The Larzac is a region of France occupied by sheep farmers. The government made plans in 1970 to

The U.N. Human Rights Commission will hear the case of Dr. Jerilynn Prior, a conscientious objector to war taxes in Canada.

During the battle of Larzac, hundreds of French citizens refused some of their taxes.

"War Tax Boycott" graphic from the German movement's Handbuch fur Rüstungssteuer boykott/protest.

German tax resisters include an emphasis on protesting value added taxes on gasoline or restaurant meals.

expand their military base in the region to five or six times its original size. The peasants began organizing immediately to stop this expansion which would have taken away a lot of their land. "Tax refusal" groups eventually counted as many as 3,000 resisters. In 1981 this nonviolent struggle by the peasants came to an end with the election of Socialist François Mitterand as President, who cancelled plans for expansion.

In October 1981 the Mouvement pour une Alternative Non-violente (MAN) initiated a campaign to encourage its members and others to refuse 3% of their taxes. This campaign was in reaction to the French government's decision to build a seventh nuclear submarine. Then in 1983 the national campaign evolved into Contribuables pour la Paix, which proposed that 3% be withheld in protest to spending on nuclear weapons and testing in the Pacific. About 18% of the budget goes to the military.

There are approximately twenty war tax resistance groups throughout France. In 1984 about 100,000 francs were withheld and reinvested. The government usually seizes resisted money plus a 10% penalty from a bank account or post office account, rarely from salaries or through seizure of property. However, the government considers signing petitions advocating resistance worthy of a very hefty fine and possible jail sentence. In 1987 there were approximately 700 people who refused some portion of their taxes and redirected that money to peaceful uses.

For more information, contact **Contribuables pour la Paix**, C.C.O., 39 rue Courteline, 69100 Villeurbanne.

(Sources: *The Politics of Nonviolent Action*, Gene Sharp, pp. 241-2, 1973; *The Battle of Larzac*, Roger Rawlinson, pp. 35-36, 1976; IFOR Report, October 1982; *Paying for Peace*, 1985; *Let's Empty the Arsenals and Fill the Granaries*, a selection of articles on war tax resistance and peace tax campaigns from the *WRI Newsletter*, 1988.)

Germany

A movement to resist war taxes began in 1981 in what was then the Federal Republic of Germany. Modeled somewhat after the one in the Netherlands, the campaign was initiated to oppose the introduction of the 572 U.S. land-based Pershing II and cruise missiles. Resisters were also concerned about the size of the military budget, estimated to be anywhere from 20%-30% of the federal budget.

The war tax resistance movement grew quickly in the 1980s. There were about thirty groups promoting war tax resistance. An estimated 100 or 200 people refused a substantial part of their income, and another 500 to 1,000 refused a symbolic 5.72 DM on the car tax, representing the 572 missiles. As in many other countries, income tax resistance is very difficult because of withholding. The government has seized goods and money from resisters.

In 1984 the Arbeitskreis Kriegssteuer-boycott Koln published a 55-page handbook on a war tax boycott called *Zum Frieden Bei-Steuern* (meaning either "to peace by tax" or "to steer toward peace").

In 1988 the Friedenssteuerinitiative (peace tax initiative) launched a campaign under the slogan, "Not with my taxes! Disarmament from below." The campaign focuses on symbolic actions to raise public awareness of individual involvement in the militarization of society. They printed stickers with the slogan to attach to money that circulates to others, and they printed forms for resisters to hand to people each time they pay for something that is taxed, like gasoline or a restaurant meal. The form notified the receiver that the individual is paying the tax under protest because 25% of it goes to the arms race.

In 1991 twelve small alternative companies and institutes in Wupportal started a war tax boycott. The companies wanted to take into account the conscientious objection of their workers not to finance the Gulf War. They planned to give appropriate tax records to the Internal Revenue offices, but transfer the money to a special account.

The Threshold Foundation (Fischerhude) edited a 1991 book, *The Right of Refusing to Pay Taxes Based on Conscientious Objection*. It looks at the philosophy, practice, and legality of war tax resistance. (Available in German from Lubrecht and Cramer, Forestburg, N.Y.)

For more information contact **Netwerk Friedensteuer Initiative**, Pfr-Dorn-Strasse 18, 6500 Mainz 32; **Steuern zu Pflugscharen**, Neissestrasse 4, 4300 Essen 1; **Rüstungssteuerboykott**, Bliednerweg 21, 4800 Bielefeld 11.
(Sources: Several groups and 1982 correspondence with Sophie Behr, plus Christa Nichels office of the Green Party; *Paying for Peace*, 1985; *WRI Newsletter*, Aug/Sept. 1988; *Transcontinental Peace Newsletters*, July and Nov. 1991.)

Hungary

Hundreds of Hungarians stopped paying taxes in 1861 to the Austrian Emperor, who needed more money to fight Napoleon III. When an Austrian tax collector would come, the Hungarians told him he was acting illegally and refused to pay. When property was seized for the unpaid taxes, Hungarian auctioneers refused to auction it. When Austrian auctioneers were brought in, Hungarians refused to bid. It was costing more to collect than what was ultimately collected.
(Source: *Strategy for a Living Revolution*, George Lakey, p. 94, 1973.)

India

There were a number of instances of mass tax resistance during the Indian Campaign for independence from Britain. Bardoli peasants in 1928 met revenue collectors with closed doors or tried to argue with them against collecting. Then when police began to seize equipment, peasants dismantled their carts, etc., and hid the parts in different places. Again in 1930 during the Salt Campaign, there were pockets of tax resistance, as well as the boycott of the salt tax by illegally making salt.
(Source: *Conquest of Violence*, Joan Bondurant, pp. 57, 95, 1965.)

Ireland

Quakers during the Irish rebellion of 1798 refused to pay military taxes. The Protestants viewed them with suspicion because they did not help fight the insurgents. And the Catholics thought they should be killed because they did not fight for Irish freedom.

In 1987, one known war tax resister was active in Ireland. Mike Garde had been resisting for seven years. Garde refused to pay about 4% of his tax, based on his calculation of military spending.
(Source: *The Tax Dilemma*, Donald Kaufman, p. 33, 1978; *WRI Newsletter*, July/August 1987.)

Italy

In 1981 the National Campaign for War Tax Resistance was organized by four pacifist groups. There are now over 100 groups nationwide promoting war tax resistance. The number of war tax resisters grew from 400 in 1982, to 10,000 in 1991. Objectors either withhold 5.5% of their taxes (the percentage represented by the Ministry of Defense part of the budget), or they ask for a refund of that amount if the tax money has already been collected by the employer. Many actually double-tax themselves: since the 5.5% is rarely refunded, they pay that amount into a special peace fund anyway. The redirected money has been used to buy property for a peace camp near the cruise missile site at Comiso, for projects in the Third World, for alternative technology projects, to fund nonviolent civilian defense projects, etc.

The Campaign's hard work over the years finally received high-level attention in 1990. A delegation has made annual visits to the office of the President to deliver a check of withheld war taxes and ask that the money be used for peaceful purposes. For the first time, they were greeted by a dignitary—the Head of the Office of the General Secretariat of the President. They handed over a check totaling 182,102,758 lire (about US $144,000)

During the Indian campaign for independence from Britain, tax resistance played a crucial role.

from 4,404 resisters and were told that the President would be personally informed of the matter. In 1991 thirty-eight representatives to the Italian Parliament were objectors themselves, and the entire municipal council of Calcinato passed a resolution in favor of the peace tax bill. The council asked parliament to put the proposed bill on their agenda.

In 1983 fourteen people who had refused to pay the 5.5% of their taxes were tried by the Court in Sondrio for inciting to tax resistance. They were all acquitted. The government appealed, and they were acquitted again. Since then, similar cases have been tried, also ending in acquittal. In these cases, the courts have ruled that publicizing tax refusal and distributing information about their campaign is not an offense.

The Campaign publishes a war tax resistance handbook titled *Obiezione Fiscale Alle Spese Militari—Guida Pratica*. A monthly publication *Azione nonviolenta* (Nonviolent Action) carries updates on the campaign.

For more information, contact Campagna **Nazionale di Obiezione**, via Milano 65, 25128 Brescia.

(Sources: *WRI Newsletter*, March/April 1985; *Paying for Peace*, 1985; letter from Vincento Rocca of *Azione nonviolenta*, October 7, 1983, July/August 1991; *Nonviolent Activist/WRI Newsletter*, April/May 1990; *Peace News*, November 1991.)

> In 1991, 38 representatives to the Italian Parliament were war tax objectors.

Japan

Military tax resistance can be documented as early as 1903 during the Russo-Japanese War. There is also a case of a person who withheld all his income taxes in 1959 because the money was being spent for Japan's so-called Self-Defense Forces. The government seized his telephone.

Today an estimated 5% of federal taxes go to military expenditures (although the Japanese constitution does not permit military expenditures to exceed 1% of the GNP, military spending has surpassed that limit).

Modern war tax resistance has been spearheaded by Conscientious Objection to Military Tax (COMIT), organized in 1974 largely through the efforts of Michio Ohno and seventy others. Today about one-third of COMIT's 500 members are Christian. In 1975 eleven members of COMIT withheld the part of their taxes which they believed to have been allotted to the Self-Defense Forces. COMIT has pursued two approaches in their campaign: war tax resistance and suing the government to recover their withheld (or seized) war taxes. The government reaction to war tax resistance has been to disconnect telephone service and seize money from bank accounts.

Members of COMIT have been to court numerous times accusing the government and tax office chiefs of collecting and spending tax money for the unconstitutional preparation of wars and of neglecting and offending taxpayers' consciences. In September 1991 such a case was dismissed by the Tokyo High Court. The courts have held that the tax office collects money without specifying what it is used for. Parliament makes the decisions about military spending.

For more information, contact **COMIT**, 1789-14 Toko-Cho, Chiba-Shi, 299-31.

(Sources: *God and Caesar*, March 1985; *Paying for Peace*, 1985; *Let's Empty the Arsenals and Fill the Granaries*, WRI, 1988; *Japan Times*, September 19, 1991.)

Luxembourg

Officially Luxembourg has no army, but it is a member of NATO for which it provides about 500 soldiers per year. Military expenditure is about 1.14% of the budget. In 1988 Franco Perna became the first known war tax resister there, paying 1.14% of his income tax to a state-administered development fund for economically deprived countries. Perna is self-employed; otherwise it is nearly impossible to resist. Tax authorities did not accept the alternative payment, even though Perna offered to pay the same amount again as long as it would not be used for military purposes.

(Source: *WRI Newsletter*, Oct/Nov, 1988.)

The Netherlands

War tax resistance has a long history in the Netherlands. It goes back as far as the 16th century when in different regions people refused to pay a special war tax imposed on the Dutch to finance the wars of Philip II, King of Spain and Duke of Holland.

In the mid-seventeenth century, Jacob Klaasz and a group of religious humanists, who acknowledged neither the Church nor the State, refused to pay taxes because of their opposition to violence. Since the 1930s there have always been some people who have refused to pay taxes for the military. But until recently, war tax resistance was limited to a few scattered religious pacifists. Most opponents of war have urged parliamentary means to achieve peace. Then in about 1976 the government added a 3% energy tax to pay for a fast-breeder nuclear reactor. Anti-nuclear activists, enraged by this, began a movement to refuse payment. Because so many refused (about 10,000) the government created an alternative energy fund for those who opposed nuclear power to take their resisted money. However, agitation continued and the government was forced to eliminate the tax.

Then another movement developed in opposition to an environment tax which collected additional tax money to clean an increasingly polluted sewage system. Some 50,000 people refused this tax, saying they would not pay the tax until the real polluters paid first.

In December 1979 after the announcement that 572 Pershing II and cruise missiles were to be stationed in Europe, a few peace organizations came together to form the Beweging Weigering Defensiebelasting (BWD), or the War Tax Resistance Movement. The BWD has agitated for conscientious objector status for taxpayers. The BWD initiated Betaal Niet Mee aan Cruise en Pershing II (Don't Pay for Cruise and Pershing II) to encourage objectors to refuse either 5.72 guilders (symbolizing the 572 missiles) of their Value Added Tax on gas bills, or 950 guilders ($500) of their income tax, which represents the military's share of the budget.

In 1982 the Dutch Peace Fund was established. As an independent foundation it has its own board and administration. This was done to avoid any suspicion of fraud. War tax resisters deposit the money they withhold in the Peace Fund until the Revenue Service (RS) succeeds in collecting it in another way. Then it can be returned. With the interest the deposits produce and with gifts the fund receives, peace projects are subsidized. At the high point in 1986, the fund contained about 100,000 guilders ($50,000) and about 18,000 guilders ($6,000) was spent on peace projects. In 1990 about 16,000 guilders ($8,000) was available for peace projects.

With the INF treaty the "5.72 action" ended and many people left the war tax resistance movement. BWD then reworked its campaign to focus on military spending. They encouraged total resisters to continue resisting; suggested a new symbolic amount of 9.70 guilders to symbolize the 97% of nuclear weapons still threatening the world (less the cruise and Pershing); or withholding 2% of any tax, tying in with the Thorsson report to the United Nations calling for a fund to be established from 2% of each country's military budget to pay for development in the Third World.

In 1988 a group of people (from several churches) presented a bill in parliament containing regulations with respect to taxpayers who have conscientious objections against the military destination of tax money (the COMDTM Act). The bill asks that every citizen be able to indicate on their tax forms that they want the military amount diverted to a special peace fund. After introduction in parliament, the bill was sent to the Council of State for advice. The bill was discussed in parliament in November 1991.

Tying in with the recent developments in Eastern Europe, the BWD started a new action in 1990 called: "One golden peace" (in Dutch the word "golden" means guilder as well). People were asked to write to the Minister of Defense offering him one guilder to use for a positive peace policy. They would send the Peace Fund one guilder as well, to be used for peace projects immediately. Some 2,000 people took part in this action.

BWD celebrated its tenth anniversary in 1990. The BWD publishes a quarterly newsletter and has produced several handbooks on war tax resistance and civil disobedience.

For more information, contact **BWD**, Oosterkade 13, 3582 AT Utrecht.
(Sources: 1981 communication from the BWD to Lori Nessel, translated by Elaine Lilly; *Paying for Peace*, 1985; *WPTF Newsletter*, February 1983; 1991 correspondence from Trix van Vugt, BWD staff.)

War tax resistance has a long history in the Netherlands dating back to the 16th century.

New Zealand

The Peace Tax Campaign began in New Zealand in 1982 and consists of two working groups and about 200 individuals. Only a few people actually resist taxes. The withholding system makes resistance very difficult. Initially, the government responded to resisters by taking them to court. More recently, bank account levies and property seizures have been more likely. In 1984 the New Zealand Labour Party passed a motion supporting the idea of a peace tax. It is estimated that 5% to 6% of the government's budget is for direct military spending. The Peace Tax Campaign is working for legislative change and is not advocating resistance at this time.

For more information, contact **Peace Tax Campaign**, McLeod Street, Upper Hutt.
(Sources: Dudley Mander communication, 1985; *Paying for Peace*, 1985.)

Norway

In 1515 Norwegian peasants refused payment of tax increases levied by the Danish king to support his war against Sweden. They also killed the tax

Global War Tax Resistance

Graphic from "Desarma Tus Impuestos" published by Spain's Campana Objecion Fiscal.

collectors. In the 1630s there was another widespread movement against paying taxes. Then in 1764-65, as a protest to the high taxes and corruption, another major tax rebellion occurred. In some areas peasants absolutely refused to pay and drove tax collectors away. Tax collection was reduced to one half of the assessment.

Folkereisning Mot Krig, a section of War Resisters' International, has published an article about war taxes. Norwegian Quakers support the idea of a peace tax. However, because of withholding, tax resistance is almost impossible.

For more information, contact **Folkereisning**, Rosenkrantzgate 18, 0160 Oslo 1.
(Sources: *The Politics of Nonviolent Action*, Gene Sharp, 1973; *Paying for Peace*, 1985.)

Palestine

One of the actions of the *intifada*, the mass resistance of Palestinians against the Israeli occupation, has been tax resistance. It was chosen as a tactic to separate Palestinians from the Israeli economy and administration. In 1989 the mostly Christian Palestinian village of Beit Sahour unanimously decided to withhold taxes from the regime. "We will not finance the bullets that kill our children, the growing number of prisons, the expenses of the occupying army. We want no more than what you have: freedom and our own representatives to pay taxes to," read part of a statement from the town on October 19, 1989.

Before long the Israeli government responded by declaring the town a "closed military zone." Telephone lines were cut, entry into the area was prohibited, and a curfew was imposed from evening until morning. During this time property was seized from individuals and businesses. Tax collectors confiscated truckloads of personal belongings, and many citizens were fined or jailed. International support was drawn to Beit Sahour, and the solidarity of its citizens continued despite the harassment. Beit Sahour was nominated by the Nobel Committee for the 1990 Nobel Peace Prize, and received the annual award of the Danish Peace Foundation in 1990.
(Source: *Conscience*, Winter 1990; NWTRCC *Network News*, July 1990; *Al Fajr*, June 4, 1990.)

Russia

In 1820 Russia became the first country to establish legislation exempting pacifists from paying war taxes. Thirty British citizens were invited by Czar Alexander I to establish a cotton mill. Because some of the employees were Quakers, a petition was submitted to the Czar from the employees asking for freedom of conscience and an exemption from military service, church taxes for war, etc. The Czar issued a certificate which read "His Imperial Majesty has given his gracious assent to this petition ... all ... shall be exempted from all civil and military taxes ... the sect of Quakers may now and in future be freed from war taxes for the support of the Military. ..." Two English Quakers visiting Russia in 1856 found these provisions still in effect.
(Source: *Conscience Canada Newsletter*, Autumn 1985.)

Spain

The Campaign for Tax Refusal was launched in 1980 by the Asamblea Andaluza de Nonviolencia

(AANV). Military spending is officially listed as 11% of the budget, but the real figure is closer to 25%. Although employer withholding prevents effective tax resistance during the year, citizens are required to pay an additional income tax at the end of the year. The Campaign suggested that resisters refuse 11% of this additional tax. Then in 1983 the Campaign decided that resisters should refuse 11% of the total income tax. But because the fines imposed by the government were so great, this tactic did not receive widespread support. Therefore in 1984 the AANV decided to return to the first tactic of refusing 11% of the additional tax. In 1989 a fund of withheld taxes amounted to 8,565,528 Spanish pesetas deposited by some 1,500 resisters. The government was again cracking down on resisters.

For more information, contact **AANV**, c/o Gonzalo Arias, Casatuya-El Zabal, La Linea (Cadiz); **Movimiento de Objecion de Conciencia**, Desengano 13-1' izq., Madrid 13; **Grupo de objecion fiscal**, Apartado de correos 61034, 28080 Madrid.
(Sources: *Paying for Peace*, 1985; *Peace News Bulletin*, World Peace Council, No. 11/90.)

Sweden

In 1988 Krigsskattevagrargruppen, a new war tax resistance group, began organizing in Sweden. About 8% of the national budget goes toward military expenses. As in much of Europe taxes are taken directly by the employer. Resisters must fill out a form asking for a correction to the amount of income tax they have to pay. They also state an alternative receiver to show that they aren't going to keep the money themselves. The group ties its appeal not to pay for the military to the state acceptance of conscientious objection to military service. By 1990 the group had about sixty members and two volunteer staff.

For more information, contact **Krigsskattevagrargruppen**, Kvakargarden, Box 9166, 102 72 Stockholm.
(Source: *WRI Newsletter*, Aug./Sept. 1988.)

Switzerland

Modern war tax resistance in Switzerland has been going on since 1972, when thirty-two churchmen refused all participation in the military. In 1978 Pour une Politique de Paix Active/Fur eine Aktive Friedenspolitik (For an Active Peace Policy) began a campaign to refuse the 20% of the federal budget devoted to military spending and to work for nonviolent civilian defense.

In 1983 a three-year Campaign was begun to gather about 500 people who would withhold 20% or 100% of the military tax (imposed on men excused from participation in the military) and/or 20% of direct federal taxes (imposed on all citizens). They also sought to divert .1% of the military budget into the creation of a Peace Research Fund.

In 1984 about 200 people signed a common declaration about war tax refusal. Gathering in Aktion Friedenzonen, some individuals have proclaimed that they will refrain from any organized defense of the state and will pay no federal direct taxes. All people who refused taxes eventually have been forced to pay. They also run the risk of being sent to jail for ten days for every year of refusal.

For more information contact **Pour une Politique de Paix Active**, Centre Martin Luther King, Avenue de Bethusy 56, 1012 Lausanne.
(Source: *Paying for Peace*, Quaker Council for European Affairs, 1985.)

Research for this chapter was done largely through the efforts of Kate Renner (1985) and Lori Nessel (1981) and Paying for Peace, Lobbying for Legislation: An Overview of Peace Tax Bills throughout the World, 24 p. 1991, Quaker Council for European Affairs, Brussels, Belgium. Thanks to Dirk Panhuis and Veronica Kelly for 1991 help.

Drawing by Len Munnik, The Netherlands.

11 Personal Histories

This chapter recounts the history of some of the people who have been longtime war tax resisters or who have been prosecuted for their war tax resistance. The purpose of this chapter is to demonstrate that despite government attempts to intimidate them, these resisters have, by and large, succeeded in frustrating collection by the IRS. The reader should recognize that these histories, in one sense, are very unusual: most were jailed for their resistance. Only about twenty (that we are aware of) of the tens of thousands of income war tax resisters have been jailed in the past fifty years.

For those who want additional personal accounts, the Peacemakers' *Handbook on the Nonpayment of War Taxes* contains some forty histories. Several edited versions of these histories come from the *Handbook*. Those accounts which do not acknowledge a source were sent to WRL directly by the resister.

Ernest Bromley, 1939.

Ernest Bromley was the only person to be prosecuted for not buying a "defense tax stamp" for his car during World War II.

Ernest Bromley

After the Pearl Harbor attack in December 1941 every automobile was required to have a "defense tax stamp" on its windshield. Motorists were given until January 31, 1942 to display this $2.09 tax stamp which would be in effect until June 30. Then they would have to buy a $5.00 stamp good for a whole year.

Ernest Bromley, then a Methodist minister in North Carolina, felt this tax to be a direct financing of the war the U.S. had just entered. One February morning after leaving the local post office, the county police (working with the FBI) intercepted him, saying they noticed his car did not bear the defense stamp. He said that he had sent the $2.09 to the Methodist Commission for Overseas Relief instead. A few days later an IRS agent came to his parsonage, beginning a long series of visits that alternated between threats and persuasion. By the time July 1 had rolled around, he had refused to buy the second defense stamp. A letter was sent by the prosecuting attorney of the district. Pressure was brought by the district superintendent, bishop, and other church members. "You are young," they said. "This is your first church. Take advice from us who are older and who know."

Bromley wrote to pacifists around the country, but was unable to learn of anyone who had not bought the stamps and displayed them on their windshields. He later discovered that there were other pacifists who refused to buy the stamp, but they were not prosecuted.

On October 5 he pleaded not guilty in Federal Court, explaining that he was not evading the tax but refusing to pay it on principle. Defending himself without an attorney, he presented vouchers for $7.09 from the Methodist Commission for Overseas Relief. "Under law," he said, "it seems to be criminal not to support war." Later he said: "If, in time of war, when taxes are increased many times over for the sole purpose of financing the war machine, no attempt is made by those in authority to distinguish between war taxes and the common federal taxes, then it is left to the individual to make his own distinction." He went on to quote Thoreau and John Woolman, pointing out that war tax resistance had a long and honorable history in the U.S.

The judge listened attentively, interrupting twice because the defendant, having never been in a courtroom before and being unfamiliar with the procedures, had inadvertently turned away from the judge and spoke to the people in the well-filled courtroom. At the conclusion the judge, looking up the law on this new tax, said there was a mandatory fine of $25 on each of two counts. When Ernest Bromley would not pay the fine, the judge said there was a mandatory sentence of thirty days on each count.

The following morning, the Raleigh *News and Observer* carried the full statement with the story. Other state papers carried at least part of it. The *Christian Century* also reported the case but opposed it editorially, titling the editorial: "Reductio ad Absurdum." Bromley served the sixty days in Wake County Jail, Raleigh.

Though he lost his church, enough support came his way as a result of the ensuing struggle on nonpayment of taxes and rights of conscience to sustain him in conference membership, and he held other churches. The first year for which he owed an income tax was 1944. He filed, but refused payment. He continued to file and refuse payment each year up to 1950. That year he stopped filing as a result of the Korean War and the worsening world situation. He could not cooperate at all with the system which taxed heavily for war. Although revenue agents came occasionally to see him, he answered no request to go see them. They have never collected any of his taxes.

In 1947 he wrote letters to many people, attempting to find individuals who had also refused to pay taxes. The result enabled him and Marion Coddington to publish the experiences and views of a few people who had also independently made a tax refusal. Among them were Walter Gormly, Ammon Hennacy, Max Sandin, Valerie and Francis Riggs, and Mary Bacon Mason. The following year (1948) at the founding conference of the Peacemakers, considerable interest was expressed in tax resistance. A committee formed to further the effort was joined by Ernest Bromley, Marion (Coddington) Bromley, Walter Gormly, Valerie Riggs, Caroline Urie, and Ralph Templin.
(*Handbook on the Nonpayment of War Taxes*, pp. 25-26. The story of an auction involving the Bromleys appears on page 102 in this book.)

James Otsuka

James Otsuka, a student at Earlham College, began refusing taxes in 1949. According to the Assistant U.S. Attorney, his decision to refuse 29% of his tax ($4.50) was made after attending a Quaker meeting in Richmond, Indiana. Also there seemed to be several others around the U.S. who were declining to pay.

On August 19, 1949 Otsuka appeared in Indianapolis District Court. At one point the judge looked at the American-born young man of Japanese ancestry and asked, "How would you like to go back where you came from?" Upon getting a negative answer, the judge said "I give you until September 1 to pay it or face serious consequences."

The following is a portion of the dialogue between the judge and Otsuka on September 1:

Judge: Why didn't you pay your tax? I gave you all this time to do so.
Otsuka: My reason stems from certain moral and religious principles in which I believe.
Judge: How do you know where your taxes go?
Otsuka: Many sources... show that a certain proportion of taxes goes toward military purposes.
Judge: Have you ever paid any kind of taxes?
Otsuka: Yes, income taxes, and others.
Judge: How did you know where they went? The government has the right to allocate those taxes.
Otsuka: It does, but it is not consistent with my religious principles to help support war.
Judge: I don't care. You refuse to pay your tax? Well then, you will be sentenced to jail for ninety days, with a fine of $100.
Otsuka: I am willing to accept the jail sentence. ...
Judge: It doesn't matter if you aren't.
Otsuka: I am willing to accept the jail sentence, but I am concerned about where the fine will go.
Judge: I don't know.
Otsuka: Then I will have to refuse to pay it.
Judge: All right. I will give you a longer sentence.
Otsuka: If it will please your Honor. I would like to make a final statement.
Judge: Were you naturalized, or born here?
Otsuka: I was born in San Francisco.
Judge: What about your parents—were they naturalized, or born here?
Otsuka: They cannot be naturalized and were not born here. May I make my statement?
Judge: I don't know. What is it?
Otsuka read his statement referring to his belief in the "ultimate goodness" of all people, nonviolence, and the need "to apply love and mutual aid between individuals and among people of every race, creed and color."
Judge: What does that mean?
Otsuka gave some interpretation saying that he had written it before entering prison in World War II.
Judge: What? You weren't a soldier, were you?
Otsuka: No, I was in prison as a conscientious objector.
Judge: And that didn't teach you anything?
Otsuka: Only that I am even more convinced of this stand.

After Otsuka was led out to jail, the judge turned to Otsuka's lawyer and said, "I don't see how you can represent him. It is a terrible thing for a young fellow to take all the advantages of living here and then refuse to pay his taxes."

Bromley was jailed for 60 days in 1942 for refusing to pay the court assessed fine.

James Otsuka was indicted for refusing to pay $4.50 in income taxes.

Personal Histories

Otsuka served 136 days in jail though he paid no fine and no tax.

Because the fine was not paid, he served an additional thirty days. Though due to be released from the federal prison in Ashland, Kentucky on December 28, the U.S. Commissioner ordered that he be kept in prison indefinitely until he paid the fine. This caused a stir among pacifists and others around the country. So on January 15, 1950 Otsuka was unconditionally released, after serving 136 days though he paid no fine and no tax.

Two months later on "tax day" (then March 15), James Otsuka rode a bus into the restricted area of the atomic bomb plant at Oak Ridge, Tennessee. He passed out leaflets to workers, was arrested by the FBI, and while in custody burned 70% of a dollar bill, symbolizing what is happening to every tax dollar. This act, which had been announced in advance, made papers across the country. (*Handbook on the Nonpayment of War Taxes*, pp. 32-33.)

Maurice McCrackin at New England War Tax Resistance Gathering, October 1991. Photo by Ed Hedemann.

Maurice McCrackin

Maurice McCrackin began to refuse taxes for war in 1949 and was eventually jailed for 6 months in 1958.

In 1949 Presbyterian minister Maurice McCrackin of Cincinnati refused to pay 70% of his 1948 income tax. He said:

> That Jesus would participate in or lend his willful support to war and violence is to me unthinkable. Therefore, if I am loyal to him I will oppose war and the spirit that makes for war to the limit of my ability. To give financial support to war while at the same time preaching against it is to me no longer a tenable position.

Two months later he received a notice from the IRS to pay up. The following month he received a notice to visit the IRS. When he went the agent listened to his reasons for nonpayment and said, "Well, this is a free country. You can do what you want but we'll get the money some way." A few days later a lien was placed on his checking account.

Year after year the IRS levied his bank account. So in 1952 he stopped filing and closed his account. At that point McCrackin realized "how our government is now invading individual rights and privileges . . . [and] the violence done to the individual conscience. . . . Disobedience to a law is an act against government, but obedience to a law that is evil is an act against God."

At that point he began to noncooperate totally with the IRS. He didn't pay, he didn't file, and he refused to visit the IRS or give them any information. In 1958 the IRS came to his church and asked to see the church financial records. He refused, but the governing board of the church designated the treasurer to make the decision. The board set up an arrangement to pay McCrackin's rent, utility bills, other personal expenses, plus an honorarium at intervals instead of a salary.

A few months later the IRS asked him for the keys to his car. When he refused, they asked him to open his safety deposit box. Refusing again, a lien was placed on the box preventing him from opening it without the IRS present. The lien was lifted later after his sister opened the box in the presence of the IRS, only to discover that it contained nothing of value to the IRS.

In September 1958 he was served with a summons to appear with records and sources of earnings and assets. On September 12 federal marshals came and took him, without his cooperation, to a hearing in the federal building before the U.S. Commissioner. "If I had walked," he said later, "I would have felt I was in prison. But in not walking, I felt I was free." When the government tried to get him to obtain a lawyer, he replied, "God is my advocate." They tried to get him to agree to a date for a hearing, but he responded, "I have no control now over what happens. . . . According to the summons, you say you will bring the body. The body is here. I am trying to follow my conscience, and you fellows will have to do what your conscience leads you to do."

A personal recognizance bond of $1,000 was set, but McCrackin would not sign for it. He was placed in a cell for four hours and then released. He did not show for the September 26 hearing scheduled for him. A federal grand jury met on November 7 without him, though he was summoned to appear there, too. However, he was carried into District Court a week later. In refusing to cooperate with the proceedings he stated, "I would cooperate with making a plea where it did not involve me in cooperating with the government's attempt to force me to pay for war." The judge responded, "This refusal to step to the bar is more serious than your failure to answer the summons. I give you one last chance to step up here and plead. If you don't you may spend your life in a mental institution."

He was given a "mental test," released, then carried into court again on November 24. When asked to plea, he stated, "I have only this to say: that the government cease making materials to destroy the world and that it respect the conscience of those who do not want to support these efforts with their money. This is my only plea." He was jailed again.

On December 12 he was brought into court and sentenced to six months and a $250 fine. The judge added that McCrackin would "stand committed until the fine is paid." The sentence was for "neglecting to appear and testify and to produce books, records, and memoranda." Nothing was said about contempt. In pronouncing sentence the judge said, among other things,

> You have admitted giving your donations to the Fellowship of Reconciliation and the Peacemakers instead of paying taxes. These groups are notorious and have overwhelming Soviet sympathies. We won't go into whether you are a card-carrying Communist or not. Tax money is to provide the United States of America with a means of defending itself against Communist Russia.... And here is Mr. McCrackin saying he will not give taxes to the government because it is evil. I don't know of a more pious way to be called a traitor than that.

After spending six months in jail, Maurice McCrackin continued his refusal. There had been no further government action, except to try to get some money left him by his mother's estate. He disclaimed this money in favor of other heirs. IRS claimed he couldn't do that. But on November 8, 1960 a judge in the District Court in Dayton ruled that IRS had no claim to this money and that Maurice McCrackin, who had been charged with "fraud," was not guilty. Although summoned, he did not appear at the proceeding. IRS appealed the decision, but later withdrew the appeal.

As a result of his beliefs and actions, he was deposed from the ministry of the United Presbyterian Church by the Presbytery of Cincinnati on February 9, 1963. However, eighty members of the local church he had served for seventeen years withdrew membership, and with others established the Community Church of Cincinnati. They called him as their pastor.

At tax time in 1961 he said publicly, "Each trial, civil or ecclesiastical, serves but one purpose for me, and that is to strengthen my belief that to withdraw from the support of war, in refusing to contribute one's life or money, is not a negative action but potently positive, and never more needed than now." He has continued to serve the Community Church as pastor and to refuse to pay taxes.

In 1972 the FBI called McCrackin to talk about money they said he owed. He told them it would be a waste of their time because he wouldn't discuss it. A few days later a subpoena from the Justice Department was served ordering him to come in and pay the fine, but saying nothing about unpaid taxes. He didn't appear and never heard from them again.

On September 6, 1987 in the West Cincinnati Presbyterian Church, the Cincinnati Presbytery conducted a service to restore to its ministry the Rev. Maurice F. McCrackin, now age 87. McCrackin was reinstated to the ministry in the very church from which he had been removed. The Presbyterian Church apologized for its previous actions; over the years it has put new emphasis on peacemaking and raised questions about the assumption that the government is always right. Individuals in the church had lobbied for years for McCrackin's reinstatement.

In December 1990 Maurice McCrackin and Ernest Bromley were among those arrested in Washington, D.C., for climbing the White House fence to deliver a message to George Bush against war in the Persian Gulf.

(*Handbook on the Nonpayment of War Taxes,* pp. 36-38; letter to editor, October 26, 1981; "War Tax Resister Restored to Ministry" by William Yolton, *Peace Tax Fund Newsletter,* Winter 1988.)

Juanita and Wally Nelson

Soon after the Nelsons made their first refusal, they were called on by a revenue agent in July 1949 in Covington, Kentucky. The agent asked questions about the statement of refusal his office had received. He was so bewildered by the outright refusal to file and pay, the frankness and openness of the refusal, and the apparent fearlessness of this delinquent "taxpayer" that he asked Wally to go to the office to talk with the agent's superior. Wally

> "Disobedience to a law is an act against government, but obedience to a law that is evil is an act against God."

> In 1952 McCrackin began his noncooperation with the government. He would not pay, file, answer summons, or walk when in custody.

> Wally Nelson avoided withholding by self-employment and as a commission salesman.

Personal Histories

Wally and Juanita Nelson at New England War Tax Resistance Gathering, October 1991. Photo by Ed Hedemann.

Juanita Nelson would work shorter hours for the same pay rather than take raises in order to avoid withholding.

In 1959 Juanita became the first woman in modern times to be arrested for opposition to war taxes.

declined, and the next morning the superior came to see Wally. Nothing much resulted. Then the minister on whose church Wally had been doing some extensive repairs was called into the tax office. He refused to open the books on the church to the IRS or to give any verbal information about his employee's income.

Both Wally and Juanita were determined not to work where any taxes were withheld, and they continued through the years to be self-employed or in situations where the employer was not legally obligated to withhold. Besides working as a carpenter's helper and painter, Wally developed a fresh egg route and then added other food items. Later he became a commission salesman, where nothing was withheld by the company. Every year or two there was a visit by revenue agents, but they never found any money or property they could lay hands on. One agent retraced the egg route, asking questions of customers. Two of the unsuspecting people who had been buying one or two dozen eggs a week later told their "egg man" that the fellow he sent around to collect did not seem to want to take the money. Only a dollar or so was owed in each case. For eleven years Wally earned a good income by selling on consignment (e.g., bookplates and calendars). He left the job when it appeared that the company would yield to IRS pressure to pay the taxes it said Wally owed.

Juanita worked as a model at an art museum and as a typist. Because Wally had no occasion to sign a withholding slip, she signed for two exemptions on each job, enabling her to earn up to $26 on any one job with nothing withheld. Once she worked part-time as a librarian in an historical society and as an office worker for an anti-tuberculosis league. One difficulty was that pay raises would put her into a withholding category. So, on jobs which she kept for several months or more, she raised her wages by working fewer hours for the same pay. These part-time jobs were found by telephoning organizations and businesses listed in the yellow pages. It took several hours to do this, but didn't cost much. On one job she was able to have the checks made out to a letter service in which she was a partner. This made the letter service the employer which was loaning out her services, making her salary withholding-free. Later, she became a speech therapist and took private patients.

Soon after moving to Philadelphia from Cincinnati the Nelsons learned that the IRS was on Juanita's trail, apparently having tracked her from Ohio. One day in March 1959 revenue men delivered a summons and, when she did not accept it, left it on a table. It ordered her to appear with books and records on March 31; an order she did not honor. On April 15 the Nelsons made public another statement of refusal. It said in part,

> This year, as for the past ten years, we are not paying federal income taxes nor cooperating in their collection. ... We hope our action may have some effect. But, in any case, simply in order to justify our humanity, we must persist in our attempt to make action serve belief.

On June 16 Juanita became the first woman in modern times to be apprehended by the federal government for opposition to war and war preparations. Four red cars were sent to the Nelsons' house. The U.S. Commissioner did not know what to do, especially since she was wheeled into the courtroom in only a bathrobe, having been in bed when the authorities arrived. "You are guilty of contempt," the Commissioner finally said, "and I could sentence you to not more than a year in prison and/or a fine of not more than $10,000." He gave her until June 19 at 2 p.m. to supply information and sent her home.

June 19 came and went. On August 8 the U.S. Attorney announced that the charges against her had been dropped. "She is violating no income tax as far as we are concerned," the papers quoted him. He did not mention her refusal to obey the summons.

About 1973 when the Nelsons lived in a tiny New Mexico village, an attempt was made to tow away their two vehicles, one awaiting decent burial in a junk yard, to satisfy a lien of some $7,000. Each of them sat in front of a vehicle and the agents finally left. In 1979 an agent visited them in Deerfield, Massachusetts "to get information." He left with none. The Nelsons for some years have lived below taxable level but are still liable for all taxes charged with because they've never filed and still do not.

The Nelsons were two of the "Frivolous Five" from Western Massachusetts who, from January 15 to April 15 of 1985, filed weekly 1040 short forms with no information other than name, address, and magic marker messages on why they were not paying. (The action was inspired by Karl Meyer's year long "Cabbage Patch" resistance. See his story below.) All five members of Pioneer Valley War Tax Resisters were assessed frivolous fines of $500 per form, plus penalties, but were not hotly pursued. After a long silence from the IRS, both Wally and Juanita received bills in 1991 charging them for nine of the twelve fines ($4,500 for each individual), but with no penalties! The last IRS communique contained a general lien on the Nelsons. (*Handbook on the Nonpayment of War Taxes*, pp. 33-35; 1991 update by the Nelsons.)

Eroseanna Robinson

In the early fifties Eroseanna (Sis) Robinson began her tax refusal. Single and a social worker, she sought employment with several agencies, earning a withholding-free income at each. She filed no statements of income.

In 1959 she received notices from the IRS to appear with records. She declined. On September 22, 1959 she received a certified letter from the attorney of the Chicago division of IRS stating that a trial would be held on October 2. She ignored the matter. Chicago papers said a suit was being brought against her in district court "to make her pay or be cited for contempt of court." She was quoted as saying that she was "against her money being used for war," and that she had sent a sum larger than her tax to various "organizations working for the benefit of human beings." She maintained no bank account, owned no real estate, and her personal property was said to consist of an ironing board, a clock, a quilt, and clothes.

On January 26, 1960 federal marshals came to the Bethlehem Community Center in Chicago, where she was working, and asked her to go with them. When she declined they carried her out of the building and to the district court. Noncooperating with the proceedings, she was carried to the bench before the judge who tried to see that she was represented by legal counsel. When she refused to accept a lawyer's services, he said she must turn over records of her earnings or be cited for "contempt of court." He asked if she had anything to say. She said she would like to talk to him as woman to man but not as defendant to judge. When he told her to go ahead, she said,

> I have not filed income taxes because I know that a large part of the tax will be used for militarization. Much of the money is spent for atom and hydrogen bombs. These bombs have a deadly fallout that causes human destruction, as it has been proved. If I pay income tax, I am participating in that course. We have a duty to contribute constructively to life, and not destructively.

She was handcuffed and carried to jail in a wheelchair. The next day she was wheeled into court. When she declined again, the judge (a different one) called her attitude one of "contumacious criminal contempt." He said the issue was whether she obeyed the court's orders, and he

The Nelsons successfully blocked the seizure of their cars by sitting in front of them.

Social worker and amateur athlete, Sis Robinson spent 4 months in jail for refusal to cooperate with the government's attempt to collect war taxes.

She maintained no bank account, owned no real estate, and her personal property consisted of an ironing board, a clock, a quilt, and clothes.

ridiculed the around-the-clock vigil of support going on in front of the courthouse. He then committed her to jail until she should signify willingness to file a tax return and show records of her earnings.

She continued a fast begun on the previous day. On February 18 the judge had her brought before him again and sent her to jail for a year and a day for "criminal contempt." She was moved to the Alderson, West Virginia prison on March 1, where she continued to take no food. She ignored as far as possible the system into which she had been placed. She had contacts with officials and prisoners, and with those who came to do the force-feeding, but she was entirely alone for the rest of the time and did not attempt to send mail through the prison censorship.

On May 20 she was released unconditionally and without announcement. Nine Peacemakers who had been camping for a week at the gates of the prison welcomed her as she was taken to the railroad station in a vehicle. She stated that she would continue her nonpayment. On July 5, 1960 she received a statement from the IRS that she owed $380 for 1956-58, and that she must pay or face court action. She received reminders and demands for payments every couple of months for a while. Then in January 1962, a deputy collector tried to get her to pay, then sign a paper saying she didn't owe any tax. The IRS was not successful.

Eroseanna Robinson died October 9, 1976 in Toronto, Canada, where she had lived for five years. According to Juanita Nelson, "As far as I know, she never did pay anything to the IRS." (*Handbook on the Nonpayment of War Taxes*, pp. 45-46.)

Robin Harper

As a Korean War conscientious objector, Robin Harper was troubled by paying for war. So in 1958 after four years of paying income taxes, he began resisting. He eliminated withholding through self-employment in home construction, refused the whole income tax, and did not file a return. Each year he gave his refused taxes to programs that offered a constructive alternative to military expenditures.

Harper writes, "My two-fold sense of empowerment was profound! I was personally severing my major complicity in war by *cutting off the funds;* I was *affirming life* through my peace tax!" Robin's tax resistance is reflected in a personal pledge he has stated publicly on several occasions:

I renounce all war and will never support or sanction another. I shall do what I can to oppose preparations for war. I shall strive to make my daily life more loving, more nonviolent, and more truthful in thought, word, and deed. I shall devote my resources to creating conditions of peace.

His war tax resistance had been based on religious (Quaker), ethical, humanitarian, and legal (Nuremberg) principles. Harper refuses to pay all the tax, because there is no way to earmark it for peaceful purposes. He distributes the tax to constructive programs even though the IRS may eventually seize a "second" tax.

Until 1970 Robin Harper had only sporadic and perfunctory contact with the IRS. However, that year they billed him for $32,500 in alleged taxes, penalties, and interest for tax years 1958-67—over *four times* what it would have been had he filed. In order to protect his family from great financial hardship should the IRS seize such unwarranted sums, Robin set the record straight by filing returns for the years in question. At a four-hour conference with an IRS agent, "we established complete agreement on the figures (my figures) and complete disagreement that I should pay the IRS."

Then in 1973 with the guidance of lawyer and tax resister John Egnal, Harper took the IRS into Tax Court. This was the first war tax resistance Tax Court hearing of the Vietnam War era, and the only case to involve a period of ten years. The case was decided in favor of the government, and the court side-stepped the issues of the First Amendment, international treaties, and Nuremberg.

Later in 1973 and again in 1977, Robin was back in Tax Court to deal with four additional years. The dialogue was good but the results were the same. "It had become clear to me that the U.S. Tax Court . . . judges would continue to gloss over the real issues. I have therefore personally discontinued petitioning Tax Court, but I fully support resisters who are appealing their Tax Court decisions to Circuit and Supreme Court levels."

Harper had ended self-employment in 1966, and in 1972 used the W-4 resistance method to stop withholding, claiming a "war crimes" deduction when filing his 1040 form, accompanied by a letter of explanation.

Because of Pennsylvania laws, Robin's jointly owned bank account (held in the names of Marlies and Robin Harper, thus requiring two signatures for any check or withdrawal) and other assets have been immune from seizure (his wife does not resist taxes). When summoned by the IRS to appear with records, Harper has gone, but without records. He doesn't cooperate with the collection process. In 1975 the IRS took him into district court to enforce the summons. The judge issued a fifteen-page carefully reasoned opinion (*U.S. v. Harper*, 397 F. Supp. 983 (E.D. Pa. 1975)) ruling that Harper did not have to comply on Fifth Amendment grounds.

Then in a 1977 court action, his case ($11,000 owed in alleged taxes, penalties, and interest) was transferred from jurisdiction of the IRS to the Justice Department. And in August 1981 the Justice Department subpoenaed his financial records and ordered him to testify. A month later Harper and his lawyer filed a motion to quash the subpoena on First and Fifth Amendment grounds. After two preliminary hearings before a federal magistrate and a full hearing before a district judge, at which Harper gave lengthy testimony, the IRS failed to file a final brief and abruptly withdrew the subpoena.

However, the IRS initiated a second summary judgement action in 1983 and succeeded in transferring an additional alleged liability of $22,000 to Justice Department jurisdiction, thus circumventing the statute of limitations on collection. Also, in 1984 Harper lost his challenge of the $500 "frivolous" penalty for his 1982 tax return.

In 1983 the IRS placed a levy on Robin's salary for the alleged liability of $17,000. Harper promptly reduced his salary to the legally non-seizable level (at that time $75 a week plus $25 for each dependent), thus thwarting collection. He continues to refuse all federal income and telephone taxes and annually redirects the entire sums to a number of peace, environmental, and human aid organizations. He files a separate return each year showing zero taxes owed after deducting on page two of the 1040 all his alternative payments from the full tax figure. Photocopies of all the checks accompany his letter of conscience.

Harper writes, "I am happily married to Marlies; we have three grown children, and I am a member of Southampton Friends Meeting." After serving on the staff of Pendle Hill, the Quaker study center, for over a decade, he is once again a self-employed carpenter. Robin is active with the tax resistance movement in Philadelphia, and especially among Quakers.

When times have come to speak truth to power in an IRS office or federal courtroom, I have never lacked staunch and inspiring support

"It had become clear that Tax Court judges would continue to gloss over the real issues. I have personally discontinued petitioning Tax Court."

Harper distributes his tax to constructive programs even though the IRS may eventually seize a "second" tax.

Robin Harper, 1981. Photo by Sylvia Whitman.

Personal Histories

of friends and co-resisters. I have found my personal journey of war tax resistance/peace tax affirmation has led me toward a sense of planetary citizenship and a deeper commitment to help build the beloved community.

Karl Meyer, 1986. Photo by Ed Hedemann.

Karl Meyer was one of the earliest promoters of telephone tax resistance and inflating the W-4 form to avoid withholding.

Karl Meyer

I have successfully resisted payment of almost all federal income tax claimed from me since 1960. I began resisting in that year, responding to the examples of Eroseanna Robinson and Ammon Hennacy. I have used the W-4 resistance method and don't file returns.

From 1958 through 1971 I shared a very large part of my income with other people by operating and supporting a Catholic Worker "house of hospitality," providing food and lodging for unemployed and destitute men. In many cases I provided enough support through the year that I was legally entitled to claim them as dependents on my W-4 forms.

From 1960-66 the IRS did not contact me or take any action. In the spring of 1966 I was one of the 400 signers of the war tax resistance ad in the *Washington Post*. Shortly afterwards I was approached by IRS agents. They investigated my past income and filed tax returns for 1962, 1963, and 1965 without my cooperation or consent— claiming $1,100 in taxes, interest, and penalties. For 1960, 1961, and 1964 my income was below the taxable level.

In 1966 I began to refuse the telephone excise tax. I have paid no telephone tax since then, though the IRS managed to collect $8.00 from my wages in the first years. They have collected nothing since and haven't even tried the last few years. I was also an organizer of the first group of telephone tax resisters.

I resigned from three jobs in 1967, 1969, and 1970 specifically to forestall collection by wage levy. In 1969, however, one agent succeeded in collecting $46.60 from my employers.

In November 1969 and January 1970 the *Catholic Worker* published articles by me explaining and advocating the W-4 exemption method and the idea of alternative funds for resisted money. Distribution of these articles led to a great increase in effective income tax resistance.

In April 1970 I organized a tea party demonstration at the Chicago IRS headquarters and had a personal interview with the district director. An extended investigation of me followed. On April 15, 1971 I was charged in federal court on five counts of claiming extra exemptions on W-4 forms in 1968, 1969, and 1970. Bill Himmelbauer and Mike Fowler were charged with similar crimes at the same time. It is interesting to note that IRS actions against me have usually followed those public actions of mine which attracted special attention.

I pleaded "nolo contendre" on two counts for 1969 and 1970. The prosecutor dropped three counts, for seven and eight exemptions in 1968, when I stated that I was legally entitled to these exemptions for family and for guests in the house of hospitality. I chose to plead "nolo" rather than contest the charges at trial because, considering the needs of my family of five, I wished to expedite the case. I also believed that the court would be more lenient in sentencing if I did not contest the charges.

I was wrong in this expectation. At sentencing the prosecutor cited my long record of convictions of anti-war protests and read a prejudicial selection of excerpts from my *Catholic Worker* articles. I did not apologize, express repentance, or agree to pay taxes in the future. I was sentenced to the maximum penalty of one year and a $500 fine on each count, to be served consecutively for a total of two years and $1,000.

I was imprisoned at Sandstone, Minnesota, Federal Correctional Institution. Living conditions were austere and crowded, but the only aversive aspect for me was the imprisonment itself and the separation from my wife and three small children. They subsisted on public welfare payments and help from movement friends during my imprisonment. I was able to do valuable study in the fields of education and psychology; and the opportunity for extensive study, thought, and self-examination has proven very helpful in the development of my personal life since then.

When I went up for parole, I told the parole board that "my moral convictions against payment of Federal taxes... remain unchanged... but that it seemed "reasonable and necessary for me in the future to refrain from the violations of tax law which led to my imprisonment. This can be done by holding our family income below a level which would be legally subject to taxation." I was released on parole on February 16, 1972, having served nine months of the two-year sentence.

I went to work as a supervisor at a sheltered workshop for former inmates of mental institutions. Though I kept my salary below the taxable level, the IRS resumed efforts to collect taxes for 1966-67. A surprise levy of $114 was made on my wages. I quickly resigned to prevent further collections, but continued to work as unpaid staff. I appealed to fellow tax resisters and alternative funds for help. For nine months they provided generous support. After that time the IRS acknowledged that I couldn't afford to pay the back taxes. Presumably they were written off as uncollectible, for I have not heard from the Collection Division since concerning those taxes. I had conclusively demonstrated that the taxes were uncollectible, having served nine months in jail and worked nine months without pay to prevent collection.

While I was still on parole, the U.S. attorney's office also tried to collect the fine. I was subpoenaed to determine what income and property might be available for satisfaction of fines against me. Since I had no regular income and no significant property, he was compelled to conclude that the fines were uncollectible. Every couple of years the FBI calls to see if I can pay fines, which total $1,500 (going as far back as 1959). I have given them the same answer each time.

At the end of my parole in 1973 I returned to my old criminal ways, accepting a higher salary again and claiming complete exemption from withholding. In 1975 I became a carpenter and have worked ever since as a carpentry subcontractor outside the withholding system. I have continued as an active practitioner and proponent of war tax resistance by writing articles, counselling, and giving several public talks each year. I did not file returns or contact the IRS directly, until 1984. That year, as a protest against the "frivolous" penalty, I began to file *daily* tax returns—365 of them in all—on my 1983 income. I called this "Cabbage Patch" resistance. As a result I had a lot of contact with the IRS. In fact, they assessed me $140,000 in penalties during 1984. And in February of 1985 they seized my station wagon in an attempt to collect on the fines. It was sold for $1,020.

On July 3, 1981 the *National Catholic Reporter* described my tax resistance history and quoted me as saying that I hadn't heard from the IRS (at that time) since 1972. On August 13 a woman from the IRS called, asking for returns for 1974 through 1980. I said, "Well then, you must be familiar with my history and background?" "Oh," she gasped and hung up without another word. Though I never heard from her again, the IRS did contact my landlord to find out where I worked. They sent me notices to appear for appointments, then a summons to appear with my records, then gave up after I ignored them.

I have been told by a former IRS employee that I am well known in the Chicago office for my resistance activism, but they must regard me as a hopeless case, because they seem to have given up on any efforts to assess or collect taxes from me.

Martha Tranquilli

Martha Tranquilli achieved considerable notoriety in the peace movement for two instances of war tax resistance. The first she described as follows:

> When I first moved to Mississippi and had a phone installed, I withheld the excise tax as I had in Illinois. Each bill I received from the telephone company carried a long distance charge I had not made that equalled the amount of the previous month's withheld tax. All these additional charges I deducted along with the tax. After three months of this I received a letter from the company. My phone was disconnected while they still owed me a month's service.
>
> For almost two years I enjoyed the peace of no jangling phone calls (much inconvenience, too) until the extremely poor service we received at the all-Black hospital where I work was such as to endanger the lives of our patients because we could not use the phones to quickly summon doctors for emergencies. When I made the com-

"I had conclusively demonstrated that the taxes were uncollectible."

Karl filed 365 tax returns in 1984 to protest the "frivolous" penalty, thus accumulating $140,000 in fines.

Martha Tranquilli had her phone removed for telephone tax resistance. Two years later the FCC ordered her phone service restored, establishing a precedent which still stands.

Personal Histories

Martha Tranquilli. Photo by Crystal Burgstrum.

A few years later Tranquilli was convicted of fraud for claiming 6 peace organizations as dependents on her 1040 form.

Her case received nationwide publicity as the "63-year-old tax resisting grandmother" about to be sent to prison.

plaint to the FCC, I expected no response. Just vented my frustrations. With Dean Burch head of the FCC and Stennis and Eastland so powerful, who would expect action?

On December 22, 1969 my phone was hastily installed while I was out of state. They entered my home with a key I had left with my neighbor who cares for my pets. (See pp. 26–27 for details on the FCC ruling in this case.)

The other well-known instance of war tax resistance for Tranquilli stems from her refusal to pay 61% of her 1970 and 1971 income taxes ($1,100) as a protest against the Vietnam War. She did this by claiming WRL, WILPF, AFSC, and three other peace organizations as her dependents, while working as a supervising nurse at Mound Bayou Community Hospital in Mississippi. She was convicted of tax fraud in a federal court trial. On May 15, 1973, sentencing day, the judge offered her probation if she "would apologize and wouldn't do it again." She refused, later commenting, "That was ridiculous. How could I promise him something when I had already promised myself something else?" She was sentenced to nine months in prison and two years probation. She appealed with the help of the Mississippi Civil Liberties Union. While the appeal was pending, she moved to California.

The Supreme Court refused to hear the case. So on July 19, 1974, the day she was to begin serving her time, one hundred supporters turned out at 7:30 a.m. at the state capitol in Sacramento to participate in a Unitarian service and a short rally. Speaking at the rally Martha said, "I envision the day when scientists and workers will refuse to pay taxes or do war work.... I was very much afraid of going to prison, but I think I have overcome that fear. I plan to read, write letters, and meditate as much as possible. I'm going to try my best to make an adventure out of this thing." She was typically soft-spoken and calm during the whole affair. Those who went up to give her a hug of support noticed that she was visibly beaming and elated by all the support. Then after some singing and hand-clapping, people marched from the capitol to the federal building where she turned herself in to federal marshals. Her case received nationwide publicity—they could not resist the story of a "63-year-old tax resisting grandmother." All major TV networks and local stations, as well as many other sources, covered the event.

After beginning her nine months at Terminal Island Prison in San Pedro, California, she wrote in a letter,

> In my opinion everyone should spend a few weeks in a place like this for its education value. We would soon use our ingenuity to devise a more constructive way to handle those social problems. ... No chains can bind without the consent of the mind—so live with love. ...

She was elected to the Terminal Island Council, wrote for the prison paper, and took a course in Theater Arts. In another letter she wrote,

> But the staff is in even a sorrier condition of servitude. They have been trained to lie to us, to use the work program as a stick. ... Everything is geared to increase any sense of guilt the individual has and make her feel less than human. In such a program those who hold the power themselves become less than human. *And they think they are the free ones!*

Tranquilli received many letters from friends and sympathizers in the U.S. and around the world. She reported, "Three people who wrote to me whom I had never met are now being investigated by the IRS." And near the end of her term she wrote, "The College of Crime is graduating me March 3. I have learned much—how to rip-off welfare departments, the food stamp agency, a bank, and very colorful language to use when caught."

Martha was finally released March 3, 1975, after almost eight months in prison. "Be sure to say that I did not suffer in prison. It was a learning experience," she wrote. "By the time I got out, some of the guards referred to me as a political prisoner." She developed a friendship with Barbara Hutchinson that had a profound effect on both of them. Though Barbara was a right-wing tax resister, they were united by the spirit of opposition to the IRS and government policies.

She went back to the Sacramento area to live on land purchased by her three sons, worked as a nurse part-time, and was active with the Sacramento Peace Center and the Unitarian Church. Martha was called to the Pine Ridge Reservation as an observer from WILPF during the FBI invasion and subsequently became very involved in the Native American culture and struggle.

In 1977 she was requested to appear in a San Francisco court about her unpaid taxes. She refused to comply with orders to pay, and since she made little money, owned no property, and had no significant assets, the IRS could not collect. She received her last visit from an IRS collections agent a month before she died of cancer on September 2, 1981.

(*Ain't Gonna Pay for War No More*, Robert Calvert, p. 119, 1972; *WIN*, p. 12, May 31, 1973, p. 18, October 24, 1974, p. 19, March 13, 1975; *Peace and Freedom*, WILPF, p. 13, Aug-Sept. 1974 and p. 5, April 1975; *WRL News*, p. 6, Sept./Oct. 1974; *Handbook on the Nonpayment of War Taxes*, p. 50, 1981; letter from Vince Tranquilli, October 26, 1981.)

Paul Monsky

My first refusal to pay taxes for war was in 1966, shortly after I had come to Brandeis University to teach mathematics. I had been shaken by Jonathan Schell's accounts of the Vietnam War in the *New Yorker* which made plain that our bombings were deliberately planned to create refugees, and I was ready to take strong personal action. A talk by Howard Zinn on tax resistance convinced me to send a letter instead of a check with my tax return. A year later, after some correspondence, the IRS seized a couple of hundred dollars from my paycheck.

The same pattern continued for the next six years. Meanwhile, an alternative fund, the Roxbury War Tax Scholarship Fund (later to become New England War Tax Resistance, or NEWTR) started, and I joined it. In 1973 while speaking with other Fund members, I discovered that by claiming forty-two allowances on my W-4 form I was able to reduce the withholding taxes to zero. I then claimed a "war crimes" deduction on my return, and when the deduction was disallowed, I appealed through tax court. In this way an entire year's taxes of several thousand dollars could be kept from the government for years. In 1979 the IRS seized $15,000 in back taxes and interest for the years 1973-75 from my paychecks.

I had continued my tax protest after the war ended (claiming a "military deduction"), and I expected the IRS to continue collecting as before. But in the summer of 1979 two agents from the IRS criminal investigations division appeared on my doorstep. They told the lawyer I hurriedly consulted that they were going to report that there were grounds for prosecuting me.

I decided not to worry too much and went off to spend part of my sabbatical leave trekking in Nepal. On my return in January of 1980 I found myself charged with "willfully making a false statement on a W-4 form"—a misdemeanor punishable by up to one year in jail and $500 fine. A defense committee was set up by NEWTR and

"Everyone should spend a few weeks in a place like this for its educational value."

"I had been shaken by Jonathan Schell's accounts of the Vietnam War which made plain that our bombings were deliberately planned to create refugees."

Monsky's paychecks had been routinely levied for the taxes due.

Personal Histories

friends, and issues around the trial were publicized. Some conversations with sympathetic lawyers who saw things as lawyers do convinced me to represent myself in court, while getting advice from counsel. A jury was selected on March 12. My counsel and I had some hope of acquittal. We were relying on a similar case in which Lyle Snider had claimed three billion dependents (See p. 66).

The next day the prosecution presented its case before a courtroom filled with press and supporters. Since my tax returns were introduced as evidence, I was able to read to the jury the letters I had filed with the returns. During cross-examination of an IRS examiner, I was able to show that the IRS had known what I was doing since 1973, had ways short of criminal prosecution to collect the taxes, and had used these ways in the past.

The following day before I presented my defense, the judge outlined the instructions he was going to give the jury. He was going to ignore the Lyle Snider precedent and tell the jury that the government only needed to show that I used false, not deceitful, language in order to secure a conviction. At that point the verdict was clear.

As the major part of my defense I planned to call Randall Forsberg (Director of the Institute for Defense and Disarmament Studies). She would testify about the amount of tax money going to the military, the costs and consequences of our new nuclear weapons systems, the ease with which conventional war can slide into nuclear war, and the results of a nuclear war. The jury was not allowed to hear this testimony, but it was eloquently presented to the judge and the press. This was for me the key moment of the trial. But apart from one *Boston Globe* article there was little reporting on what Forsberg said.

The jury stayed out for a decent two-hour interval, but after the judge's instructions the verdict was certain. April 8 was sentencing day (the timing of this prosecution was plainly no accident). The prosecution called for a $500 fine and thirty days in prison with a year suspended. I asked the judge to discourage further political prosecutions by not imposing any penalties at all. The judge imposed no fine. He also suspended the entire one-year sentence on condition that I commit no crimes (particularly tax related crimes) during the year, and that I rehabilitate myself with eight hours a week of community service. I decided not to appeal the verdict or the sentence. The real issues seem likely to become blurred in higher courts.

I proposed to the probation department that I do my service at Rosie's Place, a shelter for women in Boston that draws some of its inspiration from Catholic Worker principles. This was accepted, and the probation officer left me pretty much alone.

Right after sentencing, I had decided to take the risk of once again enclosing no check with my return. Though I was harassed a little by the IRS, they returned to their past procedure of seizures.

My notoriety, such as it was (at one time I appeared on an all-night television show with the stripper Princess Cheyenne and Dr. Heimlich, inventor of the Heimlich maneuver), has faded by now. I am back teaching and a lot of my students seem not to have heard of Vietnam. I am no longer able to claim forty-two allowances. NEWTR continues the struggle, and the government builds ever more monstrous weapons.

Bruce Chrisman

Bruce Chrisman got an induction notice just before he graduated from college in 1971. After some thinking and discussions with a local Mennonite pastor, he defined himself as a self-taught Christian pacifist with no formal church membership or attendance. He applied to the draft board for conscientious objector status. He was turned down, but won on appeal. Bruce served two years alternative service in the Mennonite Voluntary Service.

Chrisman lived in voluntary poverty for the next three years to avoid having to pay income taxes or file. However, in 1974, he started working for a Mennonite Mental Health Center and had the

---

Paul was sentenced to a day a week alternative service for 1 year.

Paul Monsky, 1981.

"[Because of] my notoriety . . . I appeared on an all night television show with the stripper Princess Cheyenne . . . ."

withholding stopped from his paychecks. Then on tax day in 1975 he filed a blank return and attached a letter explaining his religious opposition to paying taxes for war, nuclear weapons, and power of destruction.

> I wanted to be part of the hope that nuclear war would not come to pass. I did this even though I trembled with fear at the slightest notice from the IRS. Out of this fear, I refused to talk to any IRS agents in person and became a total noncooperator. The IRS never tried to collect any taxes from me.

He and his wife left their city jobs in 1976 to try their hands at organic farming and raising a family in southern Illinois. He was not contacted by the IRS for two years. But in September 1979, while out of town visiting friends, he was called by his wife, Maryanne, who told him the IRS was prosecuting him for failure to file a return in 1975. An article had just appeared in their local paper detailing the charges against him. Chrisman pled not guilty at his October 1, 1979 arraignment and was given a week to get a lawyer. Trial was set for six weeks later. "As the legal process proceeded, it became quite clear that the IRS wanted to use my case to instill fear in others who believed as I did but had not yet acted on those beliefs."

The IRS set up the case so Chrisman would likely receive the maximum sentence of one year, to be served in Marion Federal Penitentiary. The IRS planned to publicize the case and sentence nationally to deter others. To ensure jail time a judge known for handing out jail time in tax cases and an expert prosecutor in tax protest cases (who had won 96 of his last 98 cases) were selected to handle his case. No time extension or change in venue from the isolated backwoods of southern Illinois was granted.

When the trial started, support developed out of nowhere—locally and nationally. The judge and prosecutor were totally caught by surprise. The trial lasted three days instead of the half-day originally scheduled. The government brought ten witnesses to testify against Chrisman, catching his lawyers by surprise.

Before the trial began the prosecutor threatened to tear apart Bruce's religious beliefs if he took the witness stand. Chrisman took the stand and was cross-examined from the Bible: "Render unto Caesar," etc. Chrisman responded,

> Today by being in this courtroom I am being subject to the ruling authorities, but only my body is subject not my conscience. As far as paying taxes to whom taxes are due, read further in the Bible it states, owe no one anything except love and that love is qualified in that it does not harm anyone. Therefore, I have no liability to pay taxes to the government for weapons which have the potential to harm people.

Then a "Bible bout" developed, which ended with Chrisman reading the definition of love from I Corinthians: "Love is patient and kind, it is not arrogant or rude. Love does not insist on its own way. Love bears all things, believes all things, hopes all things, endures all things. So faith, hope, love abide in these three but the greatest of these is love."

People in the courtroom started to break down in tears. The cross-examination ended. But a jury found Bruce Chrisman guilty in less than two hours of deliberation over lunch. His lawyer did not tell him that he thought Bruce would receive the maximum sentence of a year, $10,000, court costs, and all back taxes and penalties.

On sentencing day, January 2, 1980, the prosecutor attempted to trace Bruce's assets to his wife so they could seize her assets, too. Reacting to the unrelenting pressure of the prosecutor's attempts to put him in a bad light, Chrisman responded flippantly and even interrupted the judge at points, in violation of standard courtroom protocol. Chrisman commented, "Your honor I have no problem with paying more than my fair share of taxes. I just want to make sure every one of my tax dollars goes to relieving human suffering... and no tax dollars [should go] for nuclear weapons and other powers of destruction which have the potential to inflict a level of suffering beyond description." The judge responded that we would never use these weapons.

After a short recess the judge sentenced Bruce to serve a year in Mennonite Voluntary Service plus three years probation, and ordered him to file returns and pay back taxes. The prosecutor insisted the judge add $2,460.10 in court costs for travel expenses of three nongovernmental employees who were called to testify against Chrisman. The U.S. Attorney's office was infuriated at the sentence.

The case was appealed to the 7th Circuit Court of Appeals and denied. Then the U.S. Supreme Court denied *certiorari* in 1981. Bruce has since paid the back taxes and court costs. He and Maryanne, together with their children, Vanessa and Benjamin, continue to grow sprouts and vegetables as part of their Carbondale Mennonite Voluntary Service Unit. Bruce visits prisoners two days a week, as well, since the trial gave him a great deal of empathy for them.

Personal Histories

Richard Catlett

"One year, with sentence suspended except for sixty days to be served in a penal-type institution to be followed with three years probation," read the judge to Richard Catlett on April 14, 1978 after declaring he "must be as severe as possible."

Thus Catlett became the first war tax resister to be convicted of failure to file. Other nonfiling war tax resisters have been jailed, but for contempt of court, and for refusing to produce records, etc.—not failure to file.

After his appeal was denied later that year Richard spend January 5 to March 5, 1979 in Kansas City Municipal Correctional Institution.

Born in 1909, Catlett has been a pacifist his entire adult life. His father would not let him join the Boy Scouts because of their "militaristic tendencies." During World War II he performed alternative service as a conscientious objector in a civilian public service camp for three-and-a-half years.

Richard began his war tax resistance in 1947 by refusing to file his income tax return "because of the government's evident persistent preparation for war." He later declared, "It's immoral to pay someone to do what it would be immoral to do yourself.... War is immoral and I can't pay taxes that will buy war."

Richard Catlett is the first war tax resister to be jailed for "failure to file."

"It's immoral to pay someone to do what is would be immoral to do yourself."

Richard Catlett with his children Richard and Natalia on his 80th birthday.

The IRS did not notice his war tax resistance until 1966, when his union organizing activities among University of Missouri employees attracted their attention. But nothing came of this. In fact, later in the 1960s he received two refund checks from the IRS for taxes withheld, even though he never filed! (The union, however, eventually "redbaited" him out for his "pro-communist and treasonable activities," although today they are back on friendly terms.)

In the early 1970s the IRS Collection Division began to move against Catlett. In April 1974 the IRS seized a health food store owned jointly with his wife, Carol Kieninger. After being closed eight days, Carol borrowed $4,300 to pay the levy and assumed full ownership of the store.

The following year the IRS began a criminal investigation of his taxes. In 1977 the IRS transferred their files on Catlett to the Justice Department "for processing." And on October 25 he was indicted for willful failure to file for tax years 1971, 1972, and 1973. Since Richard agreed to a stipulation of the facts and waiver of jury trial, the government dropped two of the charges.

It was later discovered that some of the government's attorneys felt the IRS had abundant means to pursue civil collection within their own bureau. They also felt Catlett would get additional publicity from the prosecution, which could be counter-productive to the government. Also, Catlett's attorney made a "discovery" motion to examine government records, in particular a supplement to the IRS Field Manual. Though denied, if this motion had been upheld it would have "hit pay dirt," according to a confidential source.

At sentencing the judge asked Catlett if he intended to mend his errant ways or continue to flagrantly violate the law. Without a hint of repentance or admission of guilt, Richard responded, "I expect to continue under whatever circumstances I find myself to actively work for a more just and peaceful society."

Catlett, a member of the Columbia (MO) Friends Meeting since 1963, received broad local support as well as letters from Friends meetings throughout the country. His heavy legal expenses were paid in part by the Quakers.

After release from prison he filed a joint return to give his wife a reduction in her taxes, since his income was untaxable. In 1980, still trying to collect for 1971-73, the IRS demanded payment of $18,000 within ten days. Unemployed and owning no property except for "clothes, pocket items, magazines, and such ... I don't represent much of a prospect for lush collections." The IRS indicated a willingness to *consider* a settlement for $900, but first they wanted Catlett to sign a waiver of the statute of limitations, which he refused to do. In 1984 the IRS grabbed the $65 refund on Carol and Richard's joint return, but otherwise they have been unable to collect. The statute of limitations expired in 1986.

Richard and Carol have two children, Richard and Natalia. Besides being a Quaker peace activist, Catlett has worked for civil rights causes, against capital punishment, and has been a registered Socialist. He has spent most of his life since World War II in farming and construction work. In 1991 Richard turned 82.

My attitude toward supporting war is still adamant and at the present poses no tax problem as my economic base is a Social Security check. My consuming interest now is to produce and distribute safe, nutritious food. My immediate plans are for a modest garden to be in production in 1992. If that is successful and produces any significant income, I will have some careful planning to do to overcome the war tax collection threat.

I haven't been bored a day in my life, I've never been without plans for the future.... I realize one individual is not going to change society next month or next year. But I do believe a more just and equitable society is possible—otherwise I'd check out and try some other world.

Donna Johnson

Donna Johnson grew up in Colorado Springs, Colorado and has lived there most of her life. Area residents find employment with Peterson Air Force Base, Fort Carson Army Base, NORAD, SDI, Falcon Air Force Base, the U.S. Air Force Academy, or one of the many electronics companies that are dependent on defense department contracts. Donna Johnson and other Colorado Springs antiwar activists opposed the Vietnam War through creative actions at many of these sites. They still speak out against the war machine today.

In the late 1970s, Donna and many of her friends had low incomes and small amounts of tax to resist. Her direct encounters with the IRS began in 1973 when the IRS tacked a seizure notice onto the house she shared with others. The group owed about $7 in phone tax.

> We told them that taking the house was overkill. We had an old truck worth at least $7 that they could have taken and that would have been sufficient. So we said to the IRS, go ahead and take the house. We'll move out onto the sidewalk and make sure other people know you're taking our house for $7.

Within a few days the seizure notice disappeared from the door. Maybe federal agents were upset with some of the activists for plowing two acres of Air Force Academy land for a garden. They had planted vegetables, planning to sell them and send the money to the Vietnamese Children's Fund—the least the Air Force could do for the children whose parents had been killed.

Donna joins with other war tax resisters in Colorado Springs for annual tax day actions. For a number of years they called themselves Christian War Tax Resistance. Her scrapbook starts in 1979, when she was interviewed for the *Gazette Telegraph* at a protest outside the IRS. That year part of Donna's income tax was withheld, but she refused to pay to the IRS the additional $2,128 and redirected it to the Colorado American Friends Service Committee, which was seeking to close Rocky Flats. She was working as a clinical psychologist and told the reporter, "It is senseless to counsel someone at Fort Carson not to beat his wife while he is in a position to bomb someone else's wife."

The group's April actions from 1980-1983 always received a picture and special coverage in the local papers. During each of these years Donna and her friends tied $1,000 of her resisted taxes to helium filled balloons, and released them at a demonstration in front of the IRS office. Letting the money float away seemed a better use of $1,000 than allowing the IRS to give it to the military.

In September 1982 Donna was surprised by a call from a reporter in Yuma, Colorado. It had come to his attention that a farmer near Yuma found one of the balloons in his field—about 150 miles from Colorado Springs. Donna's father had grown up in Yuma, and the resulting article, "Protest Returns to Yuma Roots," told the story of her resistance action.

"This morning we are visiting the employment office in order to distribute some tax money that would otherwise be spent on war-making," began the group's 1984 flyer. Donna's annual $1,000 redirection was handed directly to individuals that year: a ten-dollar bill in an envelope with an explanation of her beliefs and resistance.

Donna has filed a complete and accurate 1040 form each year with the IRS. In the late 1970s she began a private practice in psychology and her income jumped. Around this time another war tax resister in Colorado told her about the Universal Life Church and how by setting up your own church you'd be able to use your income and a tax exemption for projects that did not benefit the military. Donna became a minister in the Universal Life Church and opened her own church called "Discussions for Peace." Donna gave half her income to Discussions for Peace, and the church bought a building in Colorado Springs and

"I expect to continue under whatever circumstances I find myself to actively work for a more just and peaceful society."

Donna Johnson grew up in Colorado Springs surrounded by military bases and military employers.

"It is senseless to counsel someone not to beat his wife while he is in a position to bomb someone else's wife."

Personal Histories

Living in community has been important to Donna's personal resistance and anti-militarism organizing.

ran a variety of community based programs.

In 1984 Donna went to Tax Court over her charitable contributions for Discussions for Peace in 1978. Because she had not incorporated her church in Colorado the IRS argued that the church was not a legal charity. The court ruled against Donna, saying that "The evidence... justified the inference that the organization known as Discussions for Peace was merely an extension of (Ms. Johnson's) personality and personal philosophy." An IRS representative termed tax protesters in Colorado Springs "a major problem," and Donna felt they used a technical error to stop other protesters. She said, "I don't have a gripe over technical decisions, but over funding the military."

By 1985 Donna was reducing her income to a nontaxable level, so the IRS has never been able to make the collections it desires. Revenue Officer Anita Jackson and two armed men posted a seizure notice on a house Donna was buying, but she stopped payments and the home reverted to the original owner. The Discussions for Peace building was also seized at one point. The building is now used to house several people and falls within an urban renewal area. It's still unclear what will happen when the city tries to pay for it!

In 1990 Donna received two bills from the IRS for tax years 1979-1984. It seems the Automated Collection System still has a few bugs, because the bills show different figures for the same years. "It doesn't matter," says Donna, "since I won't pay." The IRS is after more than $140,000.

Donna is still part of a community that works together on a variety of projects, such as hospitality houses, a soup kitchen, and a free clinic. They still put together creative actions against the military and military spending. "You have to be willing to do extraordinary things," says Donna, to live below the taxable income (about $5,300). "Living in community makes a big difference."

Randy Kehler and Betsy Corner

In 1988, Randy Kehler and Betsy Corner wrote the following explanation of their war tax resistance for the New England War Resisters' League newsletter:

Randy and Betsy have filed and refused to pay taxes to the federal government since 1978. They redirect the monies to groups serving people.

We have jointly withheld our federal taxes from the government for a decade, and Randy did so on his own for ten years before that. Throughout this period we have been deliberately self-employed so that our taxes would not be withheld by our employers.

Each year on April 15 we accurately fill out and send in an IRS 1040 form accompanied by a letter that explains our refusal to contribute voluntarily to such things as the construction of nuclear bombs and murderous interventions in other countries, which we believe to be criminal and immoral. We enclose no money.

For quite a few years we put our withheld tax money into a tax resisters' escrow account, the interest from which was distributed to community organizations serving people in need. This provided us with a kind of "insurance" account in the event of an IRS seizure of our money or property. A couple years ago, however, we concluded that other people's immediate needs were more important than our hypothetical future need, and thus we decided to take our money out of the escrow account and distribute all of it directly to worthy organizations. We have continued this practice on an annual basis since then. We have given half our withheld money to organizations that were assisting victims of the U.S. funded Contra war in Nicaragua, and the other half to local organizations serving people's needs in Franklin County, Massachusetts where we live. Some of these local groups are the Survival Center, Veterans' Outreach Center, a battered women's shelter, and Traprock Peace Center.

From time to time we put a letter in the newspaper explaining what we do with the money. We always felt it was important to make clear to our friends and neighbors that we are not tax "evaders" who are trying to avoid paying taxes for selfish reasons. We also try to make clear that we do pay our town and state taxes.

As a consequence of our actions, the IRS seized all the money we had in the bank in 1987 forcing us to do most of our business in cash and money orders. They also placed a lien on all of our property around the same time.

Shortly after this piece was published, Randy and Betsy found themselves in the middle of one of the most well-publicized war tax resistance cases in years.

On March 2, 1989 IRS agents personally delivered an official "Notice of Seizure" to Betsy and Randy. They said that their house would be advertised for sale at auction "for nonpayment of past due internal revenue taxes" of approximately $27,000 plus $6,000 in interest and penalties. In June 1989 the IRS informed the couple that their home would be put on the block at a sealed bid auction on July 19.

Randy and Betsy stood firm: "We're still not pay-

Personal Histories

Randy Kehler and Betsy Corner in front of their home in Colrain, Massachusetts, 1989.

ing, and we're definitely not moving—at least not under our own steam. ... How can we willingly hand over money to the federal government when we know it will cause so much suffering and deprivation." A support committee formed immediately and began plans with Randy and Betsy for a nonviolent occupation of their home if necessary, and for a strong presence at the IRS on July 19.

The IRS announced its auction through advertisements in area newspapers, so Randy and Betsy and the support committee took out their own ads. They asked people not to make monetary bids on the home, but to make creative bids for peace instead. In a sealed bid auction such as this, the IRS opens the envelopes publicly on the auction date announced and sets a minimum sale price. Complicating the sale was the fact that Randy and Betsy's home is on a land trust and cannot be sold in the future for profit.

On July 19 Randy, Betsy, and 400 supporters turned out at the IRS to listen to the announcement of the bids. As each envelope was opened and the contents read, cheers rose from the crowd.

There were bids of peace cranes, 100 Nicaraguan cordobas to mark the tenth anniversary of the overthrow of Somoza, a pledge of twelve pints of blood to be donated at the Red Cross, other pledges of community service, plus piles of donated food in response to a pre-auction call for donations to be made to the area food bank. The most humorous bid: ten toilet seats, which if priced according to Pentagon standards would cover the $5,100 minimum sale price. All-in-all the IRS rejected bids totalling nearly $6,000 in food and over $15,000 in pledged community service. They ended up quietly announcing that "the property has been purchased by the United States government for the minimum bid of $5,100."

The War Tax Refusers' Support Committee began planning and organizing for the January 19, 1990, date—the end of the six-month waiting period after which Randy, Betsy and their daughter Lillian could be evicted. Nonviolence trainings were held for individuals willing to participate in an occupation of the home should the government proceed with eviction. A rapid response phone tree included over 200 people

When the IRS seized their home, the couple stated, "We're still not paying and we're definitely not moving—at least not under our own steam."

400 supporters turned out at the IRS auction. The bids included offers of community service, canned food, and peace cranes.

Personal Histories

On December 3, 1991, federal marshalls arrested Randy and Betsy and padlocked their door.

Support groups took back the home and began a long-term occupation to prevent any future sale.

willing to risk arrest in such an occupation.

The January 19 deadline passed with no word from the IRS. Then on April 12 a federal marshal delivered a "summons" from the U.S. District Court in Springfield, MA. The U.S. government through the Department of Justice had filed a civil suit against Randy and Betsy complaining that they were illegally in possession of government property (their home).

The couple and members of the support committee discussed the pros and cons of responding or not responding to the summons. Randy and Betsy decided that they would answer the summons, hoping to "put the government on trial" by arguing that the government cannot legally force payment of taxes to support activities that are illegal (not to mention immoral). Their arguments would be based on the Nuremburg Principles and international law.

The date for a pretrial hearing was set by the court for January 18, 1991, and the support committee began plans for a rally in Springfield outside the court. However, as the date neared, the government postponed the hearing indefinitely.

In October 1991 Randy and Betsy learned that a Federal District Judge had made a summary judgement on their case. They had submitted a brief summary of their arguments for the pretrial hearing, and the judge used this overview to make a decision, denying all of their arguments. On November 18 the federal government handed Betsy and Randy an eviction notice for noon on November 22. Anyone remaining in the house past that deadline faced contempt of court, imprisonment, fines or both.

The Tax Refusers Support Committee swung into action again, and a long-term plan for re-occupying the home if the eviction took place was detailed. More than a dozen affinity groups signed up to take part in a reoccupation. On December 3 federal marshalls arrived and arrested Randy in his home. They also had orders to arrest Betsy—and did so even though she was in a neighbor's home at the time.

Taken before a federal judge in Springfield, Massachusetts that very day, Betsy agreed not to return to her home and was released, but Randy stated, "It is my intention neither to occupy or not occupy my house. It is my intention to oppose the use of my tax dollars for killing and preparations for war." The judge found Randy to be in civil contempt of the U.S. government and sentenced him to up to six months in prison or until such time as he agreed to comply with the court's order.

At this writing in December 1991, Randy is in jail, and Betsy and her daughter Lillian are staying with friends. On December 4 the "Morning After" affinity group (including eighty-three year old Wally Nelson) found their way back into the home, despite the court orders and new locks, and began the reoccupation. More than 150 people showed up for a rally that morning and support has poured in from around the country. The couple and supporters are determined to see that the home is not sold for the benefit of federal taxes and thus the military.

The foundation for Randy Kehler and Betsy Corner's resistance is expressed in the 1989 statement:

Are we nervous about the possibility of losing our home? Sure we are, to some degree. But we have to ask ourselves, is our home more important than the tens of thousands of homes that have been destroyed by U.S.-sponsored bombing in El Salvador, or by U.S.-sponsored terrorism in Nicaragua? More important than the hundreds of thousands of homes our country has denied to homeless people here in America? More important than the millions of homes here and around the world that will be incinerated in a flash if the nuclear arms race is not halted and reversed?

(Written in consultation with Randy Kehler. Some quotes and details taken from statements released by Randy Kehler and Betsy Corner; press releases issued by the War Tax Refusers' Support Committee 1989-1990; and *Peacework*, newsletter of the New England American Friends Service Committee, April 1989.)

Thomas A. Wilson, D.D.S.

In a dental school course called Practice Management, we aspiring dentists were told that the IRS audits self-employed individuals every seven years. For a few years I worked for others, but in March 1961, I began a solo dental practice in Shelburne Falls, Massachusetts.

In 1968 the IRS demanded an audit of my returns for the years 1964 and 1965. I cooperated with that audit, believing my figures were complete and correct. I taught myself the tax system and completed my own forms. I told myself that anyone with my education should be able to deal adequately with the tax laws. However, the revenue agent conducting the audit altered my figures and demanded an additional $800. He did his audit in my dining room, and when I offered him a cup of coffee, he acted as if it was a bribe.

Personal Histories

Tom Wilson at a support rally for Randy Kehler and Betsy Corner, December 1991. Photo by Ed Hedemann.

I ceased to cooperate with the audit at that point and asked him to leave my home. The additional tax had to be paid, but I was furious. A voice of resistance spoke within me. For the next four or five years I did not file or pay. The IRS eventually began proceedings against my wife and myself for failure to file. Threatened with property liens and a nonparticipating spouse, I capitulated.

I internalized my anger until 1977 when I met Wally Nelson and discovered other people refusing to cooperate with the IRS for reasons of conscience. It had never occurred to me to resist for reasons other than personal. We formed a support group and organized Pioneer Valley War Tax Resistance (PVWTR). My method of resistance became lowering income expectations and using loopholes in the tax laws to lower taxable income. I was preparing myself to be a conscientious objector to payment of federal income tax. At the same time, I became an anti-nuclear activist and could no longer support a government that promoted nuclear technology and threatened the world with future uses of nuclear weapons.

One tactic that I used in my resistance was to develop personal contact with individual revenue officers. I would pick up litter on streets and walk into the agents' offices to use the waste basket. I wanted them to know me personally as well as someone who carried a sign on the picket line that read, "Don't Pay War Tax." This method of humanizing the tax system was very empowering personally, but did little to change the IRS bureaucracy other than further entrenching the agents. (After we staged a sit-in at the IRS office in Greenfield during the Pledge of Resistance campaign, the IRS changed their security locks and access to the revenue agents' office space.)

In 1981 a revenue agent whom I made angry during a personal discussion audited my 1980 tax return. He disallowed my business deductions, increasing my income significantly, and sent an adjusted tax bill in an attempt to force me to supply records and information. I refused to cooperate. (The IRS mails threats and bills in official, sinister envelopes that usually arrive on Friday in an attempt to spoil the weekend.)

I began to identify myself as a war tax refuser and a noncooperator with the IRS and have not filed any income or tax information since 1981.

On two occasions the Commonwealth of Massachusetts cooperated with the collection efforts of the IRS. Each time they took $400 worth of checks made out to me for services rendered to low income patients on Medicaid. I stopped bill-

Personal Histories

> "I internalized my anger until I met Wally Nelson and discovered other people refusing to cooperate with the IRS for reasons of conscience."

> The IRS mails threats and bills in official, sinister envelopes that usually arrive on Friday in an attempt to spoil the weekend.

> In the past the money was taken from a bank account, but now I have no negotiable property or bank accounts.

> My decision of conscience put my license to practice dentistry in jeopardy.

ing the Commonwealth (with some exceptions), not wanting any money to go to the U.S. Treasury.

Aside from yearly updates on property liens, an occasional bill or similar mail, the federal collectors have been silent on my case. In 1991 I received a bill for an accumulation of federal taxes withheld from my phone bill. In the past that money was taken from a bank account, but now I have no negotiable property or bank accounts.

It appears that federal authorities pursued enforcement of my case through the Commonwealth. The Commonwealth Department of Revenue took the false figures from the punitive federal audit of my 1981 tax forms and adjusted my state income tax figures accordingly. When the Commonwealth sent me the revised bill, I went to an interview with a state agent and tried to explain what the IRS had done. The state revenue officer was not sympathetic. I refused to pay the Commonwealth and stopped filing state returns to circumvent their role in collection for the IRS.

Massachusetts has a state law requiring compliance to all state tax laws and liabilities before relicensure for any profession requiring a state license. My decision of conscience put my license to practice dentistry in jeopardy. I was called to two hearings in Boston designed to give me more time (and pressure) to change my mind. A number of people attended in support of my stand.

The magistrates recommended to the Board of Registration in Dentistry that my license be suspended. The other option was revocation. I chose to appear alone before my colleagues in dentistry on September 17, 1987. The common bonding among dentists is strong after the trials of dental school. The experience of telling my story in that setting and stating the reasons for my conscientious objection to paying for war was empowering. I named the organizations to which I donated withheld tax dollars. I said that I would continue to practice dentistry, serving my community as I have for the past thirty years, despite the outcome of their vote.

There was a spirited question and answer period with some strong statements on my behalf from the chairman and one other member of the board, all of whom I invited to be civilly disobedient and vote in my favor. They were mandated to abide by the magistrate's decision. The vote was five to two to suspend my license, one member arguing for revocation. Given another grace period, the suspension took effect November 9, 1987. Having my dental license suspended was a painful process, but it hurts a lot more knowing that our tax dollars pay for the murder and torture, displacement and terror of innocent people around the world.

The suspension of my license had nothing to do with dental ethics or competency. I have continued to serve my patients as an "illegal" practitioner. It is an act of civil disobedience for me to enter my office and work. In the interim one attempt was made to have the district attorney of Franklin/Hampshire counties take action against me. He declined to do this on the basis of jurisdiction and case priorities.

Clare Hanrahan

For over fifteen years I was a taxpaying wage earner, living mostly in the cities, struggling to survive with high rents and low wages.

I was raised in a large Catholic family, impoverished by alcoholism, and crowded in a small house in inner city Memphis, Tennessee. Though I was politically naive, I had been deeply affected by the Vietnam War and by the civil rights struggles that came to our city during the garbagemen's strike.

My two older brothers, seduced into joining the Marines out of high school, returned wounded in body and spirit. I volunteered with the USO, bidding farewell to countless young men and visiting the broken ones who were shipped back to the crowded Veterans' hospital. I also walked arm-in-arm with mourners in the silent memorial march through Memphis after Martin Luther King, Jr., was murdered. I was twenty then and had never before experienced such a tangible power in the midst of strangers. It left a deep and lasting impression.

During the last years of the Vietnam war, I was married to a Navy enlisted man I had met at the USO. I had little personal contact with anyone in the anti-war community. Most of the young men I knew were either conscripts or volunteers. But I could sense the growing discontent among the enlisted men and knew something was deeply wrong. After five years I was divorced and, as a single parent, again impoverished. I returned to school, finishing college on scholarship, and finding professional work with the deinstitutionalized mentally ill. It was then that I came to understand the systemic causes of the racism, poverty, homelessness, and economic oppression in my hometown and beyond. It was overwhelming.

My roots in Catholicism were deep, but as a

divorced mother, I felt estranged from that community of faith. My spiritual journey led me to study Buddhism, with its counsel of right livelihood, and to various aspects of yoga. I came to think of myself as a truth seeker of no particular dogma. I began experimenting then with a simple lifestyle, trying to find the right relationships with myself and with the earth that seemed imperative.

I was early into the third decade of my life and at a time of transition when I first read Leo Tolstoy's *The Kingdom of God is Within You*. His words seemed to reach out to me across time, resonating with a truth I knew, but that I had never heard so clearly articulated: the duty of non-cooperation with evil.

I was living then in Puget Sound with my daughter and a companion who had taught me many of the skills of living lightly on the earth. I had also become acquainted with some Friends who had a bookstore and a loan library. I attended my first Quaker Meeting. My political education began in earnest. By the time the tax forms arrived in my mailbox that year, 1981, simultaneous with the sight of a nuclear submarine surfacing in the nearby waters, my decision was clear. I could no longer remain complicit in war-making and war preparations financed with the fruit of my labors. This was a life-changing decision.

For most of the next decade my daughter and I lived a life of voluntary simplicity, forgoing the salaried and career opportunities that my education and professional skills could have provided. I simply could not cooperate with a system of taxation that used coerced monies in violation of my conscience. Our journey into voluntary poverty led us into soup lines and shelters. There we lived with those whose walk with poverty was not a choice but an imposition sustained by death-dealing government priorities. It was a demanding but empowering life. Together we established an emergency shelter and advocacy center for other single mothers; supported each other in and out of jail as we confronted the state with civil resistance; and found our voice to challenge the systemic oppression of our friends.

But life in inner city neighborhoods and shelters is dangerous and difficult, and the years of struggle took a toll. In 1989 we chose to avail ourselves of two opportunities in North Carolina, a scholarship for my daughter and a job editing a journal for myself.

Taking this job with an organization where W-4s are filed and taxes withheld involved much consideration. I realized that no matter how many exemptions I claimed, war taxes would be extracted under the guise of the "Social Security" tax, which is borrowed from for general federal spending. In addition, taxes from my wages would go to support North Carolina's death penalty through state tax withholdings. I needed the work, both to help with my daughter's education and to attend to our medical needs, but my conscience was troubled.

I accepted the part-time position, but requested the Board of Directors to honor my conscientious objection either by not withholding or by hiring me as an independent contractor. An important discussion resulted and the board was sympathetic yet unable to reach consensus regarding the withholding. I accepted the work of editing and producing the journal on a contractual basis and have worked for the past two years in that capacity. Being self-employed, I have chosen to not cooperate with the Internal Revenue Service. Acting in conscience has been a strong bulwark against the fear that these agents of death try to engender in those who resist.

In the fall of 1991 I again requested that I be hired as a regular employee and that my conscientious objection to war tax payments be respected. Again, sympathy was expressed, but consensus was not reached.

As a pacifist and a person convinced of the power of truth and nonviolence—Gandhi's *satyagraha*—I have no other course open to me but to continue noncooperation with the evil policies of our war-making government. My tax resistance has long been a personal and quiet one. I continue in resistance now, taking full responsibility for the consequences of my decision, and contributing what I can to life affirming projects.

While I work with others to build the positive alternatives that will bring about a just and sustainable future, I hope for the day when, as Gandhi said, we will make truth and nonviolence "not matters for mere individual practice, but for practice by groups, communities, and nations."

Clare Hanrahan watched her 2 brothers join the Marines and volunteered with the USO during the Vietnam War.

I came to understand the systemic causes of the racism, poverty, homelessness, and economic oppression in my hometown and beyond.

"By the time the tax forms arrived in my mailbox simultaneous with the sight of a nuclear submarine surfacing in nearby waters, my decision was clear."

"I have chosen not to cooperate with the IRS."

12 Resistance Actions

Tax resistance is a very personal action that can create feelings of isolation at times. But, war tax resistance takes on a collective aspect through demonstrations, support communities, alternative funds, etc. In many regions and localities around the country communities of support have been established. Such groups are critical to sustain and encourage resistance. Some groups meet together on a regular basis to discuss specific questions, and share successes and fears. An individual might keep a list of other war tax resisters in their area for someone to call when support is needed. Northern California War Tax Resistance has grown so much that they hold separate meetings on a regular basis—one for technical support and one for organizing actions and workshops.

1991 Tax Day march and rally at the Ukiah, California IRS office. Photo by Richard Bixby, Ukiah Daily Journal, Ukiah, CA.

Participating with other tax resisters in a public event dispels much of the sense of personal isolation, and the public expression of acts of conscience can have an impact on others that is impossible to measure. Your group may meet throughout the year or come together to organize events around "tax day" or an IRS seizure. War tax resistance lends itself to small, creative actions—you don't need thousands to get your message across. This chapter lists seven types of actions that have been taken to supplement and help publicize war tax resistance. Resources that you can adapt for local use are available from many of the groups listed in the back of this book.

April 15 is an ideal day to leaflet the IRS, not only because of all the people, but because the media is usually there.

Picketing and Leafletting

The most common actions are picketing and leafletting at the IRS the final day taxes are due—usually April 15. This is an excellent time to have a visible presence at the IRS, not only because of the large number of people you can reach, but also because media often do their annual "income tax deadline" stories on this day. Some groups leaflet during lunch hour for a week or a month preceding "tax day."

Also, a presence at the post office with leaflets and signs will catch a lot of people who need to have their returns postmarked before the day ends. Many post offices are open until midnight and offer a striking setting for candlelight vigils and other activities.

War tax resisters are often joined at tax day actions by many other peace and justice groups who also are making the connections between high military spending and federal budget cuts to human needs programs. Jobs with Peace, SANE/Freeze, ACT-UP, Women's International League for Peace and Freedom, Coalition for the Homeless, etc., are groups that war tax resisters might work with to plan public actions. In this way, resisters can also share their stand of conscience with many other peace activists.

Creative leaflets, such as those with tea bags stapled to them (e.g., to make historical connections with the tax revolt of 200 years ago), increase the likelihood that they are read by a high percentage of the takers. Some have used the 1040 form as the background for their leaflets or used a rubber stamp to put a short message on a stack of 1040 forms. The Alternative Revenue Service's EZ Peace Form was designed to resemble the IRS 1040; people notice the word "PEACE" on a "tax form" and grab it to see what it is about. Altered forms have been handed out or put alongside regular forms in the IRS office. Public burnings of 1040 forms have been done as a graphic call to resistance. But be careful that your tactics don't obscure your message.

Rallies and Marches

A noon rally at the IRS office often takes on the elements of street speaking, since the audience will be largely made up of people who work in the area plus taxpayers rushing by for last minute assistance. Further, it will be difficult to attract many sympathetic people in the middle of a work day. Props such as a stage, signs, banners, balloons, and an apple "tax" pie can help to attract attention. Guerrilla theater skits (e.g., a specter of death silently "haunting" the IRS) and music also are effective. Philadelphia War Tax Resistance rented a flatbed truck to use as their stage both outside the IRS and to travel to different sites around the city.

During the Indochina War a group of tax resisters in Pueblo, Colorado, went to the IRS with handcuffs and a warrant. They attempted to arrest the director of the IRS for collecting taxes used for illegal purposes. The director did not submit to arrest, so the group held a trial without him.

Broward Citizens for Peace and Justice in Fort Lauderdale, Florida, attracted lots of attention with their "Pentagon Potty caper" in 1991. People "flushed" dollars down the Pentagon potty, symbolic of the waste of U.S. tax dollars by the military.

At many of these rallies tax resisted money has been publicly donated to one or more community groups, thus dramatically making the connection between military spending and cutbacks in social spending.

Decorating the IRS

Some groups have hung banners above the entrance of the IRS, or pasted signs on the doors, all with appropriate messages. Also placing a "pie chart" (with the breakdown of federal spending) inside the IRS taxpayers' assistance area has achieved success in some cases. Demonstrators should, of course, be aware that these actions could lead to arrest, especially if the signs are pasted on IRS property.

Auctions

IRS auctions represent another ideal time to further publicity about war tax resistance. The most common item seized is an automobile, although bicycles, television sets, and even houses have been seized and sold at auctions. The number of such seizures against war tax resisters dropped after the Indochina War, but rose again in the mid-1980s. During the Vietnam War refusing to pay a telephone tax was sometimes enough to result in an auto seizure.

In addition to the standard organizing techniques (e.g., a news release) auctions provide further opportunities, such as holding counter-auctions (auction of appropriate items to raise money for the movement) and submitting politically relevant bids (e.g., a check made out to a community group, rather than to the IRS). Being an unusual event, auctions have great media potential for war tax resisters.

Sometimes an auction will cause significant financial hardship to the resister, requiring special

Gano Peacemakers, Inc. house, 1970. Photo by Ed Hedemann.

Decorating the IRS in Austin, Texas, 1970. Photo by Betty White.

LIBERATING THE POST OFFICE
BY WES NICKERSON

I am a war tax resister. On tax day, April 15, 1991, I was arrested for disseminating tax information at the Portland, Maine post office. I wore a name tag that read "AKA John Woolman." Woolman was an 18th century Quaker and war tax resister.

A plaque on the wall of the post office lobby reads, "This building is dedicated to public service." In order to be of service to postal patrons, I set up a table in the lobby with an array of flyers on war tax resistance and peace fund options.

No sooner had I set up service than the postal inspector demanded I leave the premises. In a courteous manner I explained the necessity of my presence. He continued to order me to take my leaflets outside and showed me a list of post office rules. I assured him of my right to be inside, in a public place, following my conscience and providing a public service. He carried my card table outside the building and I brought it back in. When he threatened to confiscate everything, I removed the card table, chair, my briefcase, and most of the flyers and began to distribute the leaflets by hand, announcing "Free Tax Information." Almost everyone took the information. Many people thanked me, and some offered words of support for what I was doing. I distributed hundreds of flyers in the space of two and one-half hours.

The inspector continued to make his demands, claiming to be the owner of the building. I shared with him the knowledge that all U.S. citizens own the federal building and that I had a moral obligation to provide this service on account of the increasing calamities of our nation's war economy. He threatened to physically remove me if I didn't leave. At one point he grabbed the flyers and pulled them from my hands. I asked him if he would help me to distribute them because I would hate to see them wasted. He seemed

Wes Nickerson distributes war tax information at Portland post office on April 16, 1991. Photo by Jeffrey Phillips.

organizing efforts. One such case involved a house owned by a community under the name of "Gano Peacemakers, Inc." where the Bromley family lived in Cincinnati. The IRS seized the property during January 1975 in a $30,000 claim against the corporation and the Bromleys. However, the assessment (made in 1972) was based entirely on a checking account belonging to the countrywide Peacemaker Movement. No connection existed among the funds of these three groups. The IRS claimed that many Peacemaker Movement checks written to individuals between 1966 and 1971 were wages, and that taxes and Social Security should have been withheld. However, these checks were sent to the families of imprisoned war resisters, not employees of the Peacemaker Movement, let alone employees of the corporation.

In April a Senate subcommittee report was published showing that Ernest Bromley and the Peacemaker Movement had been targeted for attack by the IRS "Special Services Staff" (see p. 51). Though the harassment became widely publicized, the IRS went ahead with a public auction in May 1975, selling the property for $25,000. During the period from the assessment through the sale, and after, the Bromleys and other Peacemakers acted in a manner that could not be interpreted by the IRS as official cooperation with its demands or procedures. They responded in an informal, personal, direct way, with emphasis on taking the whole story, including their tax refusal position, to the public. Support for the Bromleys and the Peacemakers was organized around the country in the form of letter-writing campaigns, demonstrations, and news stories. After the house was seized, but before sale, Ernest Bromley was arrested while leafletting, injured while in custody, and released after six days bringing more publicity to the case.

Though sold in May the new owner was not allowed to take possession until September. Through the summer a group went to Washington, D.C., to work for reversal of the sale. Their strategy was to leaflet, picket, argue with officials in the IRS and other parts of the government, and develop personal contacts. This was all to culminate in a civil disobedience at the IRS on the day the new owner was to take possession, September 3. Plans were also made for an occupation of the house should the new owner try to take possession. Then on August 29 the Bromleys were informed that the IRS would reverse the sale and cancel the lien. IRS Commissioner Donald Alexander told two of the organizers in Washington that the IRS felt that it was in a "no win position...and so they figured they might...just as well do what is right." (*Handbook on the Nonpayment of War Taxes,* pp. 50-51, 1981, and November 29, 1982 letter from Ernest Bromley.)

In 1984 there were an unusually large number of property seizures of war tax resisters (about a half dozen or so). In the case of a house seized in Chicago, the IRS cancelled the auction when about sixty supporters of the resister showed up for the sale. The IRS has not tried to sell the property since. Another auction of a seized house in Seattle was also cancelled by the IRS. In Colorado Springs the IRS released a seized house of a resister after five months because the title was not clear. However in Georgia and Kentucky seized property was auctioned, but bought by friends of the resisters involved. (*War Tax Manual for Counselors and Lawyers,* pp. v. 7-8 & 9, 1985.)

In 1989 two homes were seized in Western Massachusetts, and the support committee that developed around the seizures and auctions was well-organized and highly visible. The home of Randy Kehler and Betsy Corner was auctioned by the IRS on July 19, 1989; the support action is described in their story in Chapter 11. On November 30, 1989 a second auction took place in the small town of Greenfield, Massachusetts, after the IRS seized the home of Bob Bady and Pat Morse, neighbors of Kehler and Corner. The War Tax Refusers' Support Committee swung into action again, calling for a "Human Priorities Day" outside the Greenfield IRS offices the day of the auction. Area war tax refusers testified about their witnesses of conscience and distributed thousands of dollars withheld from the military to human service organizations. Although the house was sold to the only bidder, ninety-one people signed a public statement pledging to peacefully resist any eviction attempts. Efforts were made to contact the bidder, who never came forward publicly and has not made any move to take over the property.

Leafletting Inside the IRS

Though strictly speaking it is not civil disobedience, people have risked arrest by leafletting in the forms area or the taxpayer assistance area of the IRS.

For example, in New York City a few members of the War Resisters League leafletted inside the IRS, sometimes with a literature table, each tax day (April 15 or thereabout) for many years in the 1970s and '80s. Though permission was sought and routinely denied by the IRS, leafletters were not arrested until 1979. Leafletters were also ar-

startled, but refused to be of assistance. Even after he threatened to call the police and have me arrested, I held my ground.

Several media people came, interviewed me, and left.

And then the police arrived. After walking around me for a while, they confronted me and threatened to arrest me if I didn't go outside. With the inspector in front of me and a policeman on either side of me I was given a final warning. While the three men were trying to convince me to quit and go outside, I reached between them to hand a flyer to a man who was standing close by. He thanked me. The two police officers then took my arms and pulled me forward. I went limp and was dragged out of the post office and down the steps to the waiting police car. [Nickerson was held overnight in jail.]

On May 14, I appeared in District Court in Portland. With the help of a legal support team, I acted as my own attorney. Judge Jane Bradley took the issue of First Amendment rights very seriously. The state's prosecuting attorney and the postal inspector were very friendly. We were permitted to present our entire case just as we had planned it, including the Quaker Peace Testimony as it relates to war taxes and the need for educating the public on how the government spends taxpayers' money. Each party was asked to file a legal brief within thirty days.

[Editor's Note: Nickerson filed his brief, but the case was dismissed. The District Court judge said that since the post office was under federal jurisdiction, a district court couldn't decide such a case. Nickerson hoped to "liberate" the post office lobby as a legal site for tabling. Court rulings across the country have yet to guarantee such access for activists.]

Wes Nickerson is an educator in the Brunswick, Maine school system, and a Quaker. His action at the post office was supported by an ad hoc affinity group and endorsed by Food Not Bombs. His story was excerpted from a slightly longer piece in the Maine Progressive, June 1991.

Saunders Dixon and Bob Smith of Brandywine Peace Community, April 15, 1977.

Some groups have physically attempted to hamper the operations of IRS through civil disobedience.

ANATOMY OF AN ACTION
BY MARTHA CAIN

In the fall of 1990 amidst the build-up for the Gulf War, some of us at Northern California War Tax Resistance anxiously anticipated something else as well—IRS levies. As a result, we decided to make our resistance more public. We organized an action at the IRS calling for the institution of conscientious objector (CO) status for taxpayers. One member drafted a CO form for individuals to fill out. I secured an appointment for 1 p.m. on November 15 with my IRS collections officer in downtown Oakland to get us into the IRS.

The action began at noon across the street from the office. We carried a six-foot airplane wrapped in giant dollars bills. A local band started the program, followed by speakers including a Vietnam Vet and the mother of a soldier deployed in the Gulf. Five war tax resisters made personal statements while dollar bills were stripped from the airplane and transferred to a tree of life where the "fruits" of food, shelter, health care, education, jobs, etc., grew abundantly.

Marti Mogensen concluded her remarks by handing out $1, $5, and $20 bills (her redirected taxes) with suggestions that the recipients "take an elderly neighbor out for a piece of pie" or "buy a book for a daycare center" or "send vitamins to the Middle East." One recipient said, "I'm going to save it as a momento of what's going on here and get started doing something myself."

After the public event, we war tax resisters, a few supporters, and a television camera crew (totalling fifteen in all) made our way to my 1 p.m. appointment at the IRS office. We carried a stack of completed CO forms. The security guard outside the elevator didn't even blink an eye, let alone block our entrance into the building.

Fortunately, the IRS' reception room provided adequate standing room and access for the TV camera, since I had declined an invitation to discuss my case privately in the back room. It took the IRS officers a good fifteen minutes to decide how to respond to our entourage; they left the receptionist alone with us to fend for herself. Finally my collection officer came forward with her supervisor, and they nervously listened to our comments and accepted our CO forms. They refused, however, to accept Marti's offer of a $1 and $5 bill, saying they could not take cash!

Months later when I called my collections officer to check on the status of my account, I asked her if she remembered me. "How could I forget you?" she replied.

Martha Cain is a member of Northern California War Tax Resistance.

rested in 1980. But in 1981 twenty-four people were arrested during the week preceding April 15 with about four people going in each day to leaflet. A lot of publicity was generated by this effort, particularly on local TV stations. Defendants were acquitted in two separate trials (one in Federal Court and the other in City Court). The judges ruled the leafletters had a right to leaflet in the IRS waiting area (see the May/June 1982 *WRL News*, page 3, for more details). On April 15, 1982 as a result of this decision, the IRS was forced *for the first time* to allow leafletting inside the IRS waiting area. Since 1982 there have been no arrests of people leafletting inside the Manhattan IRS.

Civil Disobedience

Some groups have physically attempted to hamper, nonviolently, the operations of the IRS through civil disobedience. The Brandywine Peace Community in the Philadelphia area has used civil disobedience for a number of years to promote war tax resistance. On a few occasions people were arrested after they poured blood on 1040 forms in public recognition of the bloody consequence of a war economy. Another time a coffin containing torn 1040 forms and ashes, representing the devastation of a nuclearized world, was carried into the IRS office. On April 15, 1977 two Brandywine members chained themselves to the entrance of the IRS office before it opened for the day.

In Boston on February 17, 1972 twelve people waited with over a hundred others in the IRS taxpayer assistance area. They rose from their chairs and together slumped down to the floor. One of the demonstrators explained to the people that those on the floor represented Vietnamese dead and that "we choose this way to bring to your attention the use to which your tax dollars are being put. We urge you to refuse to finance America's crimes." The police dragged people out, but they kept going back in. Finally the police got everyone out and blocked the door. So some laid down in front of the police and were arrested.

In Ithaca, New York war tax resisters and antiwar activists staged a five-hour sit-in at their local IRS office in January 1991. Calling themselves the "Ithaca Resistance Service," the action was designed to protest the Persian Gulf war. "It is through our tax dollars that the fruits of our labor are turned into instruments of death," the group's statement read. Twenty people were carried from the offices at the end of the day.

Court Action

Court actions against resisters provide excellent opportunities to generate publicity on war tax resistance, while supporting the resister. Since these events are relatively rare, the media is more likely to give them good coverage if the organizing is done well. A defense committee should be established as soon as someone is indicted. News releases should be issued periodically, interview programs lined up, and complicity statements and pledges of resistance made. If there is to be an appeal or the resister goes to jail, substantial fundraising may be necessary. The fundraising will be most effective if begun early.

Even Tax Court cases, which the resister initiates against the IRS, publicity in the form of news releases, pickets, and supporters in the courtroom are useful in generating attention. Since these cases are always decided against the resister, they should be utilized for their propaganda value.

Marti Mogensen distributing her redirected war taxes in downtown Oakland, California, November 1990. Photo by John Jernegan.

Cartoon of NYC WRL leafletting inside the IRS, by Stan Mack, Village Voice, *April 15–21, 1981.*

13 Other Tax Resisters

War tax resisters are a small part of all those who refuse taxes on principle in this country. Most tax resisters come from a right-wing perspective, often fed up with having their paychecks eroded by more and more taxes. Others on the left and right of the political spectrum resist taxation in principle because they oppose the concept of a nation-state, or for feminists because they oppose the male power structure which both excludes and harms women.

Anarchist Tax Resisters

Anarchists, being opposed to the State and any form of government based on force, naturally oppose all taxes which support the State. Tax resisting anarchists roughly fall into one of two categories. The first is the "socialist-oriented" anarchist who sees the need to organize collectively for the benefit of all. The other is the libertarian or individualist-oriented type that sees the State as not only restricting personal liberty but protecting monopolies, which suffocate free enterprise (laissez-faire capitalism).

Most anarchists are also war resisters, agreeing with Randolph Bourne's famous observation: "War is the health of the State." In fact, a significant percentage of war tax resisters describe themselves as anarchists. There are probably few tax resisting anarchists who are not primarily motivated in their resistance by opposition to military expenditures. Some anarchists, who oppose all taxes, pay state and local while refusing federal taxes in order to focus on the most extreme manifestation of the state: war and militarism. Other anarchists refuse to pay all the taxes that they can.

This mixture of socialist-anarchist and pacifist politics is reflected in the following statement by Marion Bromley:

> Again this year I have refused to pay federal income taxes because I will not voluntarily contribute to the mass annihilation provided by the weapons these taxes buy. I do not want anyone killed in my name. The State has chosen an enemy, but I have no enemy. I do not accept the notion that the State can choose an enemy for me and force me to help annihilate the State's enemy. For I was born not of the State, but of woman, sired not by the State, but by a natural man. And I have not been conveyed to the State, neither body nor soul. Therefore I must decide the degree of allegiance I choose to offer the State. I offer no cooperation with the State's assumption of its right to kill. I hope the State will relinquish this evil death-power.[1]

Feminist Tax Resistance

The analysis of feminist tax resistance recognizes that violence exists in many forms besides war and in many spheres beyond the military. Our experiences as women oppressed by a (hetero)sexist society have taught us a great deal about the many forms of violence. "We know more about violence," Andrea Dworkin writes, "than any other people on the face of this earth. We have absorbed such quantities of it—as women, *and* as Jews, as Blacks, Vietnamese, Native Americans, etc...." And from our experiences we have come to understand that "nonviolence must begin for us in the refusal to be violated, in the refusal to be victimized."[2]

Women are especially targets of violence—of not only the violence of rape, battering, and pornography, but of the violence of budget cuts as well. A feminist analysis of racism, classism, ageism, sexism, and other institutionalized forms of oppression leads us to broaden our resistance to the social institutionalization of violence: the government does not represent us as women, as lesbians, as mothers, and therefore as feminists, we do not support the government. We refuse to pay for the violation and victimization of others.

Would you in daily life give money to people you knew to be dishonest and destructive? To someone who locks our sisters away in prisons, nursing homes and juvenile halls, who sterilizes them, who refuses them prenatal care or abortions? To someone who takes children away from their lesbian mothers, prosecutes women on reservations and in countries where "life is cheap"? Would you give money to someone who can afford $500 million a day for war in the Middle East, but who never seems to have enough money for daycare centers? To someone who spends $71 million for one F-14D fighter plane, but cannot even find enough loose change for adequate nutrition for women and children on welfare? Of course not.

Yet, this is exactly what we do when we pay income and telephone taxes. Our taxes support the military, Bureau of Indian Affairs, federal and state prisons, the "justice" system, the "welfare" system, the FBI, the CIA—all part of a destructive, women-hating government—to the exclusion of affirming, life-giving programs.

We do not have to turn over our hard-earned money to be used against us and our sisters. We can regain control of our money; we can refuse to pay these taxes.

Right-Wing Tax Rebels

"Right-wing" is used here in the broadest sense to include a variety of people and groups, who often use very different tactics. These resisters usually like to think of themselves as patriotic "rebels" in the tradition of the American revolutionaries.

Most of these people are not opposed to war or taxes which support war. Many even favor greater "defense" measures and favor cuts in federally funded welfare and education programs. The Constitution states that Congress shall "provide for the common Defense and general Welfare..." To this group that means spending on health, farms, churches, the "support of millions of illegitimate children" through the income tax is unconstitutional because it is not for the *general* welfare.[3]

Some contend that the income tax is a violation of God's Law, because Christian Americans must provide for their own and stand against the income tax which supports the welfare system. This is justified by 2 Timothy 5:8 which reads, "But if any provide not for his own, specially for those of his own house, he hath denied the faith, and is worse than an infidel."

Others oppose the income tax as a socialist plot to steal their private property. They argue that human beings have an absolute right to life, liberty, and justly acquired property. Therefore, since the income tax is designed to take this property from people without their consent it is theft, and redistributing it to others is socialism.[4]

Most right-wing tax resisters believe the income tax is unconstitutional. They contend that direct taxes, such as the income tax, violate the spirit of the Constitution. Originally, direct taxes were forbidden, then the Constitution was amended in 1913 to allow direct taxation (Sixteenth Amendment). Indirect taxes (e.g., customs duties, excise taxes, corporation taxes) do not infringe on human liberties because an individual can decide whether or not to buy items so taxed. These taxes do not give the government an opportunity to investigate taxpayers' affairs. Many of these tax rebels support the Liberty Amendment which seeks to repeal the Sixteenth Amendment.[5]

A relatively new approach to tax refusal is based on Article I, Section 10 of the Constitution which reads "no State shall...make anything but gold or silver coin as tender in payment of debts." Since 1968 citizens have been unable to get silver or gold for Federal Reserve Notes (i.e., paper currency); therefore, no one has had any real income to pay taxes on for over eighteen years. These tax rebels refer to existing money as *fiat currency*, because it is not backed by gold, silver, or anything of real value.[6]

Other tax rebels even charge that the withholding system is unconstitutional because it forces an employer to act as a tax collector without pay. This is seen as a violation of the Thirteenth Amendment, which prohibits slavery.

There are two basic methods used by these tax rebels: the *Fifth Amendment return* and the *ministerial exemption*. It has been well established, by the Fifth Amendment and subsequent court cases, that one is not compelled to bear witness against oneself in criminal cases. See page 29 for how this method is used.

The ministerial method is based on the First Amendment. A minister can take a vow of poverty and donate all possessions and earnings to the Church. The Church provides a home, car, clothes, and other living expenses. A person becomes a minister when ordained by another minister. Any minister can found a Church. This method created a flood of "mail order ministry" organizations. The Universal Life Church is probably the best known example. Some tax rebels do not view this as a radical tax revolt method because it is not a direct attack on the tax system. They feel that if enough people become ministers to avoid taxes, the government would simply clamp down on that exemption.[7]

Those who argue that they owe no taxes since they made no money (as defined by the Constitution), simply show no income on their return (or don't even file). Those few who do show some "real" income, pay in silver coin.

Another new tax avoidance method, similar to the ministerial exemption, is the *family trust*. The tax refusers assign all rights to their future services and earnings to this trust. Money sent to a trust is not taxable. However, courts have held that trusts which have no purpose other than tax avoidance are to be ignored.[8]

A lot of tax rebels engage in outright defiance of tax laws either by refusing to pay or refusing to file. The most extreme example of outright defiance is the Posse Comitatus. The organization was formed in 1969 in Oregon and has spread to Wisconsin, California, and Arkansas. They have ties to the Ministry of Christ Church, California Rangers, Tax Rebellion, National Association to Keep and Bear Arms, the Minutemen, the Ku Klux Klan, and the U.S. Labor Party.

Basically, the Posse Comitatus hold that the

> Most right-wing tax resisters are not opposed to taxes for the military.

> Some oppose the income tax as a socialist plot to steal their private property.

> Unlike other taxes, income taxes give the government an opportunity to investigate a taxpayers' affairs.

Other Tax Resisters

The Posse Comitatus has advocated public hangings of IRS agents.

county is the true seat of government for citizens according to the Constitution. They draw on the Bible, Constitution, and Federalist papers as proof that every able-bodied (white) male should take up arms and join the Posse.

In Wisconsin they carry guns and wear sheriff's deputy uniforms as well as star-shaped badges which read "Sheriff's Posse Comitatus." They present the Posse Comitatus as White Christian, America's last defense against the Communist Party, the "Jewish alien menace," and the "Black subhuman lumpenproletariat of the Devils Center" (urban America).

They are known for stopping citizens for speeding, filing liens against state and local officials, holding citizens' grand juries, using their own currency, stockpiling weapons, and manufacturing their own ammunition. They claim the Federal Reserve system is "fraudulent and illegal" and discourage people from paying taxes. They have advocated public hangings of IRS agents, judges, and other government officials.[9]

An estimated 5,000 auto workers in Michigan refused to pay their taxes.

The most well-publicized recent example of right-wing tax resistance was what has been labeled the "blue collar tax revolt." An estimated 5,000 auto and other workers in Michigan refused to pay taxes, by inflating their W-4 forms or claiming to be exempt. The organization which spearheaded this unusual movement was We the People—American Citizens Tribunal (ACT). The movement spread to Wisconsin, Ohio, and Washington state, with some interest in West Virginia, California, South Carolina, Illinois, and other states.

"We want to bring down the unlawful government of the United States."

They argued that the government constitutionally has no right to tax wages because wages are an equal exchange for labor and do not represent a profit or gain for workers. Some have stated "We want to bring down the unlawful government of the United States." Others stress more clearly right-wing reasons. The IRS was swamped with tax refusal cases stemming from this movement. So as a result the IRS changed its withholding rules (see (see p. 34) and sentenced a few tax rebels up to thirty months in prison.[10]

The feminist section was written by Betty Johanna with help from Jane Meyerding. An excellent resource is The Women's Budget *by Jane Midgley, published by Women's International League for Peace and Freedom, 1213 Race St., Philadelphia, PA 19107.*

---

1 *Handbook on the Nonpayment of War Taxes,* Peacemakers, p. 5, 1981.
2 "Redefining Nonviolence" in *Our Blood* by Andrea Dworkin, Harper and Row, 1976. Also published in *WIN,* July 17, 1975.
3 *Tax Revolt: U.S.A.!* by Martin Larson, Liberty Lobby, p. 165, 1973.
4 *Tax Resistance in American History,* by Barbara Andrews, Goddard College BA thesis, p. 48, 1976.
5 Ibid., pp. 49-50.
6 Ibid., pp. 65-66.
7 Ibid., pp. 51 ff.
8 *U.S. News & World Report,* p. 80, March 30, 1981.
9 *The Public Eye,* Citizens in Defense of Civil Liberties, pp. 17-25, vol. III, no. 1/2, 1981.
10 *Newsweek,* p. 33, March 9, 1981; *U.S. News & World Report,* p. 9, March 9, 1981.

National Campaigns and Legal War Tax Objection

Alternative Revenue Service

In 1988 war tax resisters at National War Tax Resistance Coordinating Committee meetings began to talk about developing a national campaign. Many resisters were looking for an action to unite the movement and bring more public attention to war tax resistance. Other goals included educating the public on "guns vs. butter" issues, increasing the number of war tax resisters, and reaching out to communities with whom we've had only limited contact.

As the concept for the campaign began to develop, Joel Taunton of Seattle suggested the name "*Alternative* Revenue Service (ARS)." The idea for a parody of the *Internal* Revenue Service had immediate appeal for its humorous and creative possibilities. The War Resisters League initiated the campaign because of its resources and solid national base. The National War Tax Resistance Coordinating Committee and the Conscience and Military Tax Campaign became co-sponsors, while many local war tax resistance groups, alternative funds, and peace organizations signed on as endorsers.

The EZ Peace Form

The centerpiece of the campaign is the "EZ Peace" form, a parody of the IRS's "1040 EZ." The 1991 form is pictured here, but the form, as with the ARS Campaign itself, is evolutionary and changes from year to year.

Resisted taxes that are returned to the ARS are redistributed geographically to established alternative funds and a report is sent to all participants. EZ Peace form "filers" may also choose to send their forms to the IRS with their 1040, to congresspeople, and to the president.

ARS coordinators tally the forms and redirected tax dollars and announce the totals to the press and at public events.

Is It Illegal to Use the EZ Peace Form?

There are legal ways to use the form *and* ways that involve you in an act of civil disobedience. One strength of the ARS Campaign lies in individual and group creativity—use the form to suit your needs.

One legal way to use the form is to give it to friends and relatives, to hand it out at rallies, and to leaflet it at the post office or IRS during the week before tax day. If you have not resisted before and are due a refund, you can still fill out the form and check off the line that allows you to pay "symbolic" taxes to the ARS. In addition, you can fill out the EZ Peace form and send it to the IRS with your correctly filed 1040 as a protest.

Primarily the EZ Peace form was designed to help people stop paying for war. Refusing to pay all or a portion of taxes owed to the IRS is an act of civil disobedience. If you were to file only the EZ Peace form with the IRS and the IRS chose to respond, they might tell you that you had not filed the "proper form." Other chapters of this book discuss the legal consequences of war tax resistance.

The First Year

During the 1991 Tax Season, over 70,000 EZ Peace forms were distributed around the country. By the end of April, 500 forms were returned to the ARS office, and countless others were sent directly to the IRS or elected officials. The Alternative Revenue Service collected over $13,000 in resisted taxes and redirected that money to areas

> Many resisters were looking for an action to unite the movement and bring more public attention to war tax resistance.

National Campaigns and Legal War Tax Objection

If you file only the EZ Peace form with the IRS, they would say you had not filed the "proper form."

Local groups and alternative funds reported a surge in requests for information.

Ralph DiGia (right front) leafletting at Alternative Revenue Service action, NYC IRS office, March 1991. Lisa Harper (ARS staff) is behind Ralph. David McReynolds is speaking with Leslie Cagan to his left. Photo by Ed Hedemann.

of human need. Another $53,000 in refused taxes was reported to the ARS but redirected by the individuals; and over $38,000 was sent directly to alternative funds by longtime resisters. This kind of annual tally helps connect the individual act of resistance to a collective effort.

For many people new to war tax resistance, the form provided them with the opportunity to turn their anger and frustration at military spending into positive action for social change. Local war tax resistance groups and alternative funds reported a surge in requests for information and increased membership.

How You Can Participate in the ARS

Individuals and groups can participate in the ARS Campaign. The national office produces an organizing packet along with the EZ Peace form and keeps a list of ARS organizers around the country. To order copies of the form and other materials or to register your group as part of the ARS network, contact:

Alternative Revenue Service
c/o War Resisters League
339 Lafayette St.
New York, NY 10012

National Campaign for a Peace Tax Fund

The United States Peace Tax Fund bill would amend the Internal Revenue Code to allow a taxpayer conscientiously opposed to participation in war to have her or his income, estate, and gift taxes spent for nonmilitary purposes. A Peace Tax Fund (PTF) would be established to receive the military portion of these taxes and distribute them to specifically designated peace-related activities.

Why PTF Bill is Needed

Since 1940 Congressional legislation has recognized that persons opposed to participation in war for reasons of conscience have a right to alternatives to military service. Similarly, people with deeply held religious, moral, or ethical beliefs against participation in war must have legal alternatives to paying for nuclear weapons and other elements of the war-making system.

All taxpayers participate in war and preparations for war. Because about one-third of every tax dollar is spent for current military purposes, taxpayers who are conscientiously opposed to such participation must either violate their beliefs or violate the law.

Under the PTF bill, taxpayers conscientiously

opposed to war would pay their full share of taxes. The current military portion, however, would perform "alternative service" through a government trust fund supporting peace-related projects.

Where PTF Money Would Go

Tax money received into the Fund could help finance peace-enhancing projects, such as:
- retraining of workers displaced by conversion from military production;
- disarmament efforts;
- international exchanges for peaceful purposes;
- research and study directed toward developing and evaluating nonmilitary and nonviolent solutions to international conflict, including selected projects of the U.S. Peace Institute;
- improvement of international health, education, and welfare;
- programs for providing public information and education about the above activities.

When Will the PTF Bill Become Law?

In World War I more than 400 conscientious objectors were imprisoned because there was an inadequate conscientious objector provision for their convictions. In 1940, when the nation was nearing war, some relief was granted as Congress passed legislation establishing alternative service for drafted conscientious objectors. Since World War II, at times of international conflict comparable provisions have been made.

In 1971 the current effort to obtain a legal alternative to military taxation began among a group of concerned citizens in Ann Arbor, Michigan. In 1972 the World Peace Tax Fund bill was introduced into the House of Representatives by ten members of Congress. In 1977 Mark Hatfield presented similar legislation in the Senate. In 1985 a revised and strengthened version of the bill was introduced into the 99th Congress, as the U.S. Peace Tax Fund bill.

The PTF bill will become law when our individual and united actions make clear to Congress how important its provisions are.

Commonly Asked Questions About the PTF Bill

Is it true that enactment of this bill still would not prevent the military from getting the money it wants?

The bill is primarily a civil liberties measure; it would not alter the need to work actively to decrease the military budget any more than legal recognition of conscientious objectors to the draft altered the need to work against military intervention; or any more than participation in war tax resistance alters the need for the war tax resister to work actively to expose the nation's misplaced budget priorities.

Wouldn't the fund allow COs to salve their consciences and drop out of other activities geared to changing national priorities?

As long as military activities endanger the lives of millions, a CO would have to have a very weak conscience to be content that his/her own money was not going for war, without doing anything actively to oppose the military system. Passage of the bill would release energies being expended in tax resistance to other protest activities and lobbying. Of course, conscientious objectors still have the choice of continuing their witness against current priorities by choosing not to register as a CO and refusing to pay war taxes.

Will the enactment of this bill open the "floodgates" for other groups to claim a tax exemption for their beliefs?

The Peace Tax Fund would not establish a precedent for other groups to demand legal alternatives for other issues such as public education, welfare, etc., nor would it undermine Congressional authority to determine how taxes are to be spent.

Opposition to war by a person of conscience holds a unique and established place in American tradition. Opposition to other kinds of government programs cannot claim such status, and it is invalid to carry to them an advantage given to religious conscience. The amount of money spent for those issues is almost infinitesimal when compared to military spending.

Present tax law contains many advantages for specific subgroups within the taxpaying population. Congress has not lost its power to decide which exemptions or advantages it considers worthy. It is the defined task of Congress to consider various citizen requests, including those of conscientious objectors, and to make proper legislative choices based on solid basic principles.

Legislators sometimes argue that paying taxes for military force does not implicate a person to the same degree as does military service, and therefore no "guilt" should be assumed in payment of taxes for military force. The federal government has, however, responded to citizens who felt implicated by the six-ten-thousandths (6/10,000) of one percent of their tax dollars for abortion and has disallowed almost all public funding for abortions.

Throughout our history the U.S. has recognized,

National Campaigns and Legal War Tax Objection

in varying degrees, the opposition of conscientious objectors to military activity. Such persons have been accorded unique status in our constitutional and legal system. The long-established tradition of recognizing those profoundly held views now offers sound precedent for proceeding with PTF legislation.

What You Can Do To Help the Peace Tax Fund

Through the efforts of the National Campaign for a Peace Tax Fund, the PTF bill has continued to gain strength in Congress. However, it still has far to go. To achieve enactment, your help is crucial. Here's how you can help:

- maintain personal correspondence with your Representative or Senators, urging them to co-sponsor the PTF bill. When writing, refer to the U.S. Peace Tax Fund bill (HR 1870, S689 in the 102nd Congress). Share copies of this correspondence with the NCPTF office;

Sen._____
Senate Office Building
Washington, DC 20510
Rep._____
House Office Building
Washington, DC 20515

- arrange individual and group visits to your Congressperson's district or Washington office;
- write letters to the editors of newspapers and other print media;
- contact the Peace Tax Fund for details and supporting materials (including a slide show) to present this issue to peace, religious, and civic groups.

National Campaign for a Peace Tax Fund
2121 Decatur Place NW
Washington, DC 20008

War Tax Resisters' Penalty Fund

The War Tax Resisters' Penalty Fund (WTRPF) was begun in 1982 by members and friends of the North Manchester Fellowship of Reconciliation. In the face of increasing numbers of resisters, the IRS has tried to make the protest very costly. For instance, the IRS enacted the $500 frivolous penalty in 1982 to intimidate tax protesters. Creative minds are continually inventing ways to carry on the witness despite these discouragements. The War Tax Resisters' Penalty Fund is part of this ongoing effort.

The Manchester group found that IRS interest and penalties kept many people from continuing their war tax resistance and prevented many more from even considering such a witness. The founders decided to invite sympathetic people to form a broad base that would help sustain and support war tax resisters. They hoped that with hundreds of supporters they could lighten the resisters' financial burdens and also actively involve larger numbers of people in the war tax resistance movement.

Since 1982 the Fund has sent out twenty-two appeals for assistance requesting from $2 to $30, and membership has grown during that time from 80 participants to 750, representing forty-four states plus the District of Columbia, Puerto Rico, and New Guinea. The fund has reimbursed over $115,000 to more than 188 war tax resisters in twenty-four states and the District of Columbia in that time.

How the Fund Works

Persons needing assistance with interest and penalties imposed by the IRS for war tax resistance make their requests to a committee, which reviews each resister's claim. (The WTRPF reimburses only interest and penalties already paid to IRS: it does not help with the original tax burden of the resister, nor does the Penalty Fund pay the IRS directly.) Resisters must provide documentation with their requests: a copy of the IRS collection forms, and a copy of their original "letter of conscience" to the IRS explaining their refusal to pay.

Persons interested in supporting war tax resisters are put on the WTRPF mailing list. Between two and four times a year the committee combines the requests for reimbursement and sends out an appeal to all names on the mailing list. If the requests total $1,000, for example, and the Fund has 500 names, each participant is asked to send in $2 which is used to reimburse the resisters who have requested help.

War Tax Resisters' Penalty Fund
PO Box 25
N. Manchester, IN 46962

Paying Under Protest

"Paying under protest" falls in the category of "legal war tax objection." Though not part of a national campaign, there have been some very creative actions which deserve attention. Of course, paying under protest can involve an action as simple as sending a letter protesting the use of tax dollars for killing with a tax payment. But this section mentions visible public actions that are designed to draw others into the movement against military spending. All of these actions received excellent local coverage and some national attention.

Cynthia Sharpe of Berkeley, California had been a war tax resister for eleven years when the IRS garnished her wages in 1988. Cynthia decided not to quit her job to avoid the levy, but was faced with a decision about future tax payments to the IRS. For the next tax year, she paid part of her taxes to the IRS, but found it impossible to quietly write out a check. Cynthia paid her portion of "taxes destined for the military budget" on a handmade wooden coffin. The coffin was both a symbol of military destruction and her desire to bury a death-oriented economy. Supporters from Northern California War Tax Resistance joined her on Tax Day 1990 in a funeral procession to the IRS office in San Francisco.

On the steps of the IRS Sharpe made a public statement about her repulsion that tax dollars support the military while so many human needs go unmet. She presented her coffin check for "One thousand dollars and no sense" to confused IRS agents who weren't sure if this was an acceptable payment. (Cynthia had arranged with her bank to honor the "check," and the IRS eventually removed the coffin lid and carried it away.) While the payment was painful, Sharpe said she felt "in control" and found that the well planned action offered a lot of publicity "for the cause." Over a year later Cynthia found out that the TV coverage from her action had brought a dedicated new member to the Northern California group.

In 1990 creative payments were made by longtime resisters Jo Kenny and Edward Van Valkenberg in Santa Cruz, California. Kenny wrote "checks" to cover tax bills on the bedpan of a deceased AIDS patient, a birth control diaphragm, a bag of rice, a map of Central America, and a cutout of a house. "I want them to get the message about what this money should be used for," said Kenny, who was executive director of the Santa Cruz AIDS Project. (Santa Cruz *Sentinel*, March 3, 1990) Edward Van Valkenberg handed the IRS a check written on a huge cardboard cutout of a nuclear missile. In his written statement Van Valkenberg said: "It sickens my heart to give this money, however involuntary, to this death machine; yet perhaps it would turn my heart to stone to give the lesser amount voluntarily."

Tax Day 1991 followed closely on the bloody U.S. war against Iraq. Ukiah, California, peace activist Susan Crane delivered to the IRS a check for $440.67 written on a bloody T-shirt. She resisted a token $10.40. Crane delivered the check in a "blood"-stained globe which also included figures of blood-stained people and animals. "Every minute fifteen children in the world die for want of essential food and inexpensive vaccines. And every minute the world's military machine takes another $1.9 million from the public treasury." (*The Willets News*, April 17, 1991.)

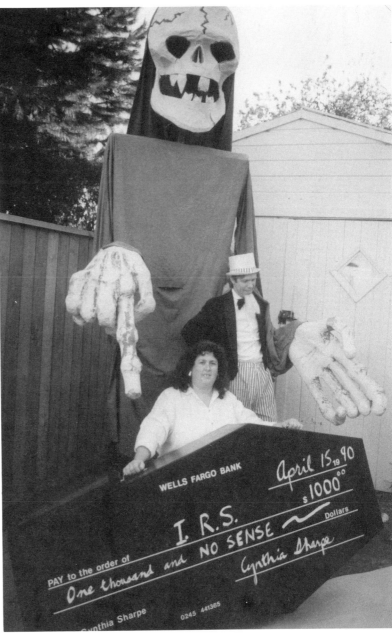

Cynthia Sharpe of Northern California War Tax Resistance with her coffin "check" to the IRS. Jim Best is standing behind. Susan Quinlan is in the death figure. Photo by Bob Van Scoy.

The Alternative Revenue Service section was prepared by Lisa Harper, ARS staffperson 1990-91.
The Peace Tax Fund section was prepared by Marion Franz, Executive Director of the National Campaign for a Peace Tax Fund.

15 Conducting a Session on Tax Resistance

It is clear that the peace movement needs many more war tax resistance counselors if it is to succeed in its efforts to build a large movement of war tax resisters. This brief outline is an encouragement for local organizers to set up war tax resistance training sessions. The sessions may form the basis of a resistance group. Such a group would be valuable as a community of support for resisters, as well as a pool of people who could organize and participate in April 15 actions.

Flier from Northern California War Tax Resistance announcing a workshop.

desirable but will not be sufficient to create a counselor where there once was none. Proper training of a counselor could involve several intense sessions, and an apprenticeship of sorts where the trainee does counseling with an experienced counselor. Also a thorough reading of key resources is indispensable.

Once the nature of the session has been decided, setting up the session involves the following: 1) advertising the session, 2) preparing the workshop presentation, and 3) obtaining appropriate materials for the participants.

Though a war tax resistance session can occur any time of year, the best time for a workshop is during the winter, when people are beginning to think about taxes. Therefore, February and March would be ideal months. For a March 1 workshop, notices should be sent February 1 to sympathetic organizations and people. Ads and posters should begin appearing in the first or second week of February. Make reminder calls to interested people a week before to ensure adequate attendance at the session.

If you have never made a presentation before, you may want to work with an experienced war tax resistance counselor. But if that is not possible, begin by reading "Notes on Public Speaking" in the War Resisters League *Organizer's Manual* (pp. 94-96). Also read the counselor's chapters in NWTRCC's *War Tax Manual for Counselors and Lawyers*.

Materials to bring to the workshop should include a copy of the following for each participant:

- Form 1040, 1040A, and EZ
- Instruction booklet for 1040
- Schedule A
- Form W-4
- Circular E
- War tax resistance materials (basic brochures, flyer on budget, etc.)

Other useful materials could include "The Collection Process" (IRS publication 586A), "Examination of Returns" (IRS publication 556), this guide, and the *War Tax Manual for Counselors and Lawyers*. Of course, the usual workshop implements (marking pens, chart paper, tape, etc.) should be bundled along.

Preparations

The preparation should begin by deciding what the purpose of your session will be. If it is to be an introduction to war tax resistance, then it should be short and less detailed. This introductory session could also be used as recruiting grounds for potential counselors. If it is to train potential counselors, then a longer session is

Section Outlines

The following is a sample outline for an introductory war tax resistance session.

5 min.
Introduction to session: describe the purpose of the workshop.

20 min.
Slide show: "More Than a Paycheck" available from NWTRCC or see other audio-visual resources listed in the back of this book.

30 min.
Introductions: each person introduce themselves, why they are at the session, and what their concerns are.

60 min.
Discussion: initially, respond to concerns raised during the introductions; then get into a question and answer session; try to avoid lengthy discussions with one or another individual on a very specific aspect of interest to no one else (suggest that you talk after the workshop).

60 min. (optional)
Small groups: if the group is large enough and time permits, divide into small groups (say, five to ten people in each); these groups may be able to encourage more participation, and begin the process of establishing a local support network, if one doesn't already exist.

The following is a three-hour workshop structured to deal more in depth with war tax resistance. Chapters of this book are noted that can be drawn on in preparing the workshop and dealing with discussions which may arise during the session.

30 min.
Introduction: describe the purpose of the workshop; have everyone introduce themselves and tell a little about why they are at the session and concerns they have.

10 min.
History: briefly review U.S. history of war tax resistance. (See Chapter 9)

10 min.
Why war tax resistance: this section is brief because it is assumed that most people coming are in basic agreement. (See Chapter 1)

10 min.
Which are war taxes? distinguish between trust funds and federal funds, excise and income taxes, local and federal taxes, etc. (See Chapter 3)

15 min.
The federal budget: show historical relation between wars and budget, and the current breakdown of the budget. (See Chapter 3)

5 min.
How much not to pay: from symbolic nonpayment to total nonpayment. (See Chapter 4)

25 min.
How not to pay: filing and not filing; the basic filing methods; dealing with withholding. (See Chapter 4)

5 min.
Break

25 min.
Consequences of resistance: briefly review appeal procedures; spend some time on what can happen; focus most of the time on what has happened to resisters and how to avoid collection. (See Chapters 6 and 7)

5 min.
Alternative funds: what they are, how they work. (See Chapter 8)

10 min.
Protest actions: demonstrations and other activities around April 15, and organizing around IRS seizures. (See Chapter 12)

20 min.
Common questions about war tax resistance (WTR): this is to deal with criticisms often raised about WTR. (See Chapter 2)

5 min.
Resources and follow-up: mention existing WTR literature, periodicals, the slide show (which should be shown to all participants at some point); try to get commitments for participation in WTR activities and possibly future meetings of resisters; participants should be encouraged to read this guide as well as the *Counselors' Manual;* another session should be on the techniques of counseling.

Proper training of a counselor could involve several intense sessions and an apprenticeship of sorts.

The best time for a workshop is during the winter when people are beginning to think about taxes.

16 The National Resistance Network

BY KATHY LEVINE

With the election of Ronald Reagan in 1980 and an increasing mood of militarism in the country, the number of people involved in war tax resistance grew significantly. This growing movement was characterized by national organizations supportive of particular areas of war tax resistance and local groups loyal to one or several war tax philosophies.

Seeing the need to bring these different groups working on war tax issues together into a unified effort, the War Resisters League and the Center on Law and Pacifism called a National Action Conference in September 1982. Besides bringing war tax activists together, the purpose of this conference was to discuss coordinated tax day actions the following year and to consider the possibility of organizing a national coalition. Following the conference, attended by over sixty war tax activists from around the country, a national coordinating body was established, later named the National War Tax Resistance Coordinating Committee (NWTRCC).

Members of NWTRCC were self-selected. The major national organizations involved in war tax resistance appointed representatives and an effort was made to have all sections of the country represented by local activists. NWTRCC members and groups volunteered time and labor to accomplish the goals set for the first year. These included producing an organizing packet; publicizing tax day actions held around the country in April 1983 with two national press releases and a press conference; organizing a national network of war tax activists, counselors, and lawyers; and holding a second National Action Conference.

By October 1983, because the work accomplished by NWTRCC was so well received but more than the volunteer members could manage, an office was opened and staff was hired. Much of the work continued to be done by volunteers, thus ensuring broad-based input. The staff person acted as a coordinator, handling the day-to-day operation of the Long Island (New York) office; communicating and consulting with the several task forces that had been formed to work on specific projects; and taking responsibility for tasks that could not easily be dealt with by volunteers. In 1987 the office moved to Seattle, and three consultants shared the various responsibilities. In 1991 with a staff change, NWTRCC returned to the East Coast with an office and consultant based in Maine.

Each year a National Action Conference is held to discuss the needs of the movement, set program goals, and determine priorities. The Alternative Revenue Service Campaign, described in Chapter 14, was an outgrowth of these gatherings. NWTRCC meetings are held once or twice a year to implement the decisions made at the conferences. The meetings are rotated to different parts of the country, thus making it possible for more local groups and individuals to be involved in NWTRCC. NWTRCC has grown into a national effort that is supported by more than eighty national and local affiliate organizations.

The War Tax Resistance Network

With the help of member groups, NWTRCC has developed a network of "area contacts" around the country. These area contacts are responsible for referring people to war tax resources in their areas. This may include referrals to war tax counselors, lawyers, support groups, alternative funds, or other organizations involved in war tax issues. As a result of the work area contacts are doing, more people are looking for help locally, and local groups have become stronger and have taken increased responsibility to assist war tax resisters and reach out to potential resisters. National organizations, which formerly provided much of the counseling and legal assistance, have been able to refer people to local groups. Perhaps most important, people who are looking for assistance are more often able to get the personal and timely help that local groups can provide. Since war tax resistance is a personal act, people often feel isolated in their resistance. Being able to be in touch with local people alleviates these feelings of isolation and can provide immediate assistance when unexpected situations arise.

Telephone Tax Resistance Campaign

Because telephone tax resistance is a relatively low-risk, easy form of war tax resistance (see Chapter 4), NWTRCC members decided to initiate a telephone tax resistance campaign to reach out to the thousands of people who are working for peace but still paying taxes for war. Organizing is done on the community level by local war tax resistance groups in order to encourage a more personal, decentralized effort. NWTRCC is responsible for providing educational and organizing materials, as well as support and publicity. In 1990 when Congress attached the tax to a child care bill, NWTRCC offered a forum for discussing how this affected the campaign (since the money was still deposited in federal general funds, resistance continued) and whether to make

---

NWTRCC was founded in 1982 during the rapid expansion of the war tax resistance movement.

Area contacts are responsible for referring people to war tax resources in their area.

NWTRCC has helped to minimize the feeling of isolation felt among war tax resisters.

a special effort to encourage redirection of resisted phone tax to child care programs.

Publicizing War Tax Resistance

Traditionally, war tax resisters make their resistance public at demonstrations, rallies, and other events held around the April 15 tax filing deadline. In the past few years the number of local tax time actions has grown significantly, involving perhaps 150 communities of which we are aware. In 1983 NWTRCC began offering organizing assistance to groups publicizing the actions of war tax resisters. In addition, NWTRCC undertook to publicize war tax resistance on the national media level (with press conferences, press releases, interviews) emphasizing the number of tax time activities, putting reporters in touch with war tax resisters for interviews, and providing information on the movement. The combined efforts of NWTRCC and the many local and national groups around the country have resulted in an increase in favorable reporting about war tax resistance and individual resisters, characterized by one longtime activist and resister as "the best publicity war tax resistance has ever received."

Producing Resources

The amount of support NWTRCC has received from groups and individuals around the country has made it possible to develop a number of resources on organizing, outreach, support, and counseling. Local groups are often small and thus have limited financial resources. However, many such groups contributing money to NWTRCC have made it possible to develop resources that would not otherwise have been possible.

A series of attractive brochures have been produced, relating tax resistance to many current issues. These brochures were all written and designed by NWTRCC volunteers and produced by the NWTRCC office. A series of flyers titled "Practical War Tax Resistance" includes pieces such as "Controlling Federal Tax Withholding" and "Resisting Collection." A slide show on war tax resistance was made and donated to NWTRCC. The show has proved to be an excellent organizing tool, appealing both to those new to war tax resistance and those with extensive experience. And in 1985 NWTRCC published the *War Tax Manual for Counselors and Lawyers*. The majority of this manual is original material that was written by people with many years of experience as war tax resisters and counselors. It is the first book of its kind to address the issues and problems that confront those who act as counselors and lawyers to war tax resisters. "Network News" is the newsletter of NWTRCC and is published six to ten times a year. The newsletter keeps groups and individuals in touch with the network between meetings, contains legal updates or news on critical cases, and provides organizing tips.

The work NWTRCC members have undertaken has not been easy, but it has resulted in an important success. War tax resisters with different goals, philosophies, and ideologies have successfully come together to find strength in diversity. With respect for the views of all members, NWTRCC has been able to progress toward its goal of building a movement based on personal responsibility and positive alternatives.

National War Tax Resistance Coordinating Committee (NWTRCC)
PO Box 774
Monroe, ME 04951

Kathy Levine was the first NWTRCC staff member, from 1983 to 1987.

Tax day actions occurred in 150 communities.

Network News keeps groups and individuals in touch and informed between meetings.

War Tax Resistance Resources

Some of the resources listed here provide additional information beyond what is covered in this book. Others are useful tools for organizing, leafletting, and tabling. The group that produced each resource is noted in parenthesis at the end of each item; addresses appear at the end of the listings. Contact each group for prices.

Brochures/Flyers

Our Tax Money, Our Choice: A Call to War Tax Resistance offers a basic introduction to the why's and how's of war tax resistance. (WRL)

Where Your Income Tax Money Really Goes is produced annually; a tax "pie" chart that breaks down military and other spending in the federal budget. (WRL)

EZ Peace form is a parody of the IRS 1040 to encourage some level of war tax resistance. (WRL)

Current Issues Series:
Your Taxes Pay for the War in Central America
Our Taxes Pay for the Nuclear Arms Race
Are Your Praying for Peace But Still Paying for War? A Christian Perspective
Women Say No to War Taxes
Creating a Nonviolent World Through War Tax Resistance
(NWTRCC)

Practical War Tax Resistance Series:
Controlling Federal Tax Withholding
To File or Not To File
Resisting and Surviving Collection
(NWTRCC)

For the Sake of Conscience is a series of six brochures on conscience, the law, and lobbying. (PTF)

Do Your Taxes Have to Pay for War? a flyer about conscientious objection to war taxes. (PTF)

Packets and Booklets

Some Writings on War Tax Resistance, a pamphlet which includes short essays, poems, and stories. Part of the A.J. Muste Memorial Institute Series. (WRL)

On the Duty of Civil Disobedience by Henry David Thoreau. Classic essay. Part of the A.J. Muste Memorial Institute Series. (WRL)

Peace, Taxes, God and Country by Chel Avery offers guidelines for Quakers and others concerning military taxation. (PYM)

Christian Perspectives on War Tax Opposition is a general information packet. (MCC)

Tax Packet includes various brochures and basic information. (CMTC)

Newsletters

Network News includes updates on war tax resistance news and resources. Published six to ten times a year. (NWTRCC)

The Peacemaker, a monthly newsletter including letters and stories from war tax resisters. (Peacemaker)

Conscience is a quarterly magazine of stories, news, analysis, and resources for war tax resisters. (CMTC)

Peace Tax Fund Newsletter gives special focus to news about the campaign and related Congressional activities. (PTF)

In addition to the above newsletters, other publications will sometimes carry articles on war tax resistance: *The Nonviolent Activist* (WRL), *The Catholic Worker*, *Fellowship* (FOR), *Friends Journal*, *Progressive*, *National Catholic Reporter*, and *Sojourners*.

Books and Handbooks

War Tax Manual for Counselors and Lawyers is the most detailed guidebook of war tax resistance counseling skills and legal information. (NWTRCC)

Handbook on Military Taxes and Conscience edited by Linda B. Coffin discusses war tax issues and choosing resistance from a Quaker perspective. (FWCC)

Fear God and Honor the Emperor is a manual on military tax withholding for religious employers. (FWCC)

Speaking for Conscience: A Manual for Peace Tax Fund Activists. (PTF)

Audio/Visuals

More Than a Paycheck, a 20-minute slide show produced for NWTRCC in 1984. Still an excellent introduction to war tax resistance although the political context is less timely. There's talk of an update. Check with NWTRCC.

Paying for Peace: War Tax Resistance in the United States. 30-minute video includes interviews with war tax resisters and an overview of the why's and how's of war tax resistance. Produced in 1990. (NWTRCC)

Addresses

CMTC. Conscience and Military Tax Campaign, 4534½ University Way NE, Seattle, WA 98105 (206) 547-0952

FWCC. Friends World Committee for Consultation, 1506 Race St., Philadelphia, PA 19102 (215) 241-7250

MCC. Mennonite Central Committee, 21 S. 12th St., Akron, PA 17501 (717) 859-1151

NWTRCC. National War Tax Resistance Coordinating Committee, PO Box 774, Monroe, ME 04951 (207) 525-7774

PM. Peacemakers, Box 627, Garberville, CA 95440

PTF. National Campaign for a Peace Tax Fund, 2121 Decatur Pl., NW, Washington, DC 20008 (202) 483-3751

PYM. Philadelphia Yearly Meeting Publications, 1515 Cherry St., Philadelphia, PA 19102.

WRL. War Resisters League, 339 Lafayette St., New York, NY 10012 (212) 228-0450

Many of these groups also sell posters, buttons, and other materials.

The War Tax Resistance Network
Groups, Alternative Funds, and Contacts

Alabama
Vine & Figtree Community
11076 County Rd. 267
Lanett, AL 36863

Arizona
Nuclear Resister
PO Box 43383
Tucson, AZ 85733

California
War Tax Alternative Fund
PO Box 741537
Los Angeles, CA 90004

Southern California War Tax Resistance
11622 Missouri Ave.
Los Angeles, CA 90025

Civilian Congress
2361 Mission St., #238
San Francisco, CA 94110

San Francisco Bay Area WRL
2205 34th Ave.
San Francisco, CA 94116

Committee on War Tax Alternatives
841 Esplanada Way
Stanford, CA 94305

People's Life Fund
PO Box 2422
Berkeley, CA 94702

Northern California War Tax Resistance
PO Box 2422
Berkeley, CA 94702

**Resource Center for Nonviolence/
Santa Cruz Alternative Fund**
515 Broadway
Santa Cruz, CA 95060

Sonoma County Taxes for Peace
540 Pacific Ave.
Santa Rosa, CA 95404

People for a Nuclear-Free Future
366 N. Main Street
Ft. Bragg, CA 95437

Peacemakers
PO Box 627
Garberville, CA 95440

Ukiah Valley War Tax Resistance
1 Lorraine St.
Ukiah, CA 95482

WRL/Redwoods
215A South Main Street
Ukiah, CA 95482

Northcoast War Resisters League
PO Box 875
Arcata, CA 95521

Sacramento Peace Center
1917A 16th St.
Sacramento, CA 95814

Chico Peace Center
930 Walnut
Chico, CA 95962

Colorado
Boulder War Tax Information Project
Rocky Mountain Peace Center
1520 Euclid Ave.
Boulder, CO 80302

Foothills Peace Center
805 S. Shields St.
Ft. Collins, CO 80521

Connecticut
New England Yearly Meeting Peace Tax Fund
16 Westwood Rd.
Storrs, CT 06268

New England War Resisters League
PO Box 1093
Norwich, CT 06360

New Haven War Tax Resistance Support Group
64 Edgewood Ave.
New Haven, CT 06511

Friends Peace Tax Fund
129 Long Hill Dr.
Stamford, CT 06902

District of Columbia
National Campaign for a Peace Tax Fund
2121 Decatur Place, NW
Washington, DC 20016

Nonviolence International
PO Box 39127, Friendship Stn.
Washington, DC 20008

Washington Area Alternative Fund
2111 Florida Ave.
Washington, DC 20008

National Interreligious Service Board for Conscientious Objectors (NISBCO)
Suite 750
1601 Connecticut Ave., NW
Washington, DC 20009

Sojourners
PO Box 29272
Washington, DC 20017

Washington Area War Tax Resistance
6310 Owen Place
Bethesda, MD 20817-5462

Florida

Tampa Bay Peace Education Program
130 19th Ave., SE
St. Petersburg, FL 33705

Tampa Bay War Tax Resistance Support
2701 Burlington Ave., North
St. Petersburg, FL 33713

Georgia

Tax Conversion Fund for Peace & Human Needs
1425 Miller Ave., NE
Atlanta, GA 30307

Metanoia Community
1702 Highway 40 East
St. Marys, GA 31558

Illinois

Lombard Mennonite Peace Center
528 E. Madison
Lombard, IL 60148

Covenant Community Peace Tax Group
7729 N. Hermitage Ave.
Chicago, IL 60626

Chicago Area War Tax Refusers Support Group
PO Box 408845
Chicago, IL 60640

Indiana

Church of the Brethren Fund for Life
606 N. Mill St.
N. Manchester, IN 46962

War Tax Resisters Penalty Fund/Fellowship of Reconciliation
PO Box 25
N. Manchester, IN 46962

Friends United Meeting Peace Tax Fund
101 Quaker Hill Dr.
Richmond, IN 47374

Iowa

Iowa Peace Network
4211 Grand Ave.
Des Moines, IA 50312

Kansas

Central Kansas Peace Tax Fund
409 E. Minneapolis
Salina, KS 67401

Salina Peace Coalition
c/o Center for Peace Concerns
1497 E. Iron St.
Salina, KS 67402

Kentucky

Louisville Fellowship of Reconciliation
c/o Jean Edwards
2317 Strathmoor Blvd.
Louisville, KY 40205

Peace Taxpayers
PO Box 383
Lexington, KY 40585

Maine

Maine War Tax Resistance Resource Center (So. Maine)
295 Forest Ave., #314
Portland, ME 04101

Maine War Tax Funds For Life
98 Winthrop St.
Augusta, ME 04330

Maine War Tax Resistance Resource Center (No. Maine)
2 Robinson St.
Fairfield, ME 04937

National War Tax Resistance Coordinating Committee
PO Box 774
Monroe, ME 04951

INVERT
PO Box 776
Monroe, ME 04951

Massachusetts

Pioneer Valley War Tax Resistance
PO Box 66
Wendell, MA 01379-0066

New England Yearly Meeting of Friends
901 Pleasant St.
Worcester, MA 01602

Cambridge Friends Peace Tax Fund
5 Longfellow Park
Cambridge, MA 02138

New England War Tax Resistance
Box 174, MIT Branch
Cambridge, MA 02139

A Peace of Love
PO Box 43
Fairhaven, MA 02719

Michigan

Detroit WRL
26318 Dundee
Huntington Woods, MI 48070

Ann Arbor War Tax Dissidents/Peace Tax Fund
1027 Miller Ave.
Ann Arbor, MI 48103

Conscientious Objectors to Military Taxes of Mid-Michigan
414 N. Jenison
Lansing, MI 48915

Minnesota

Minnesota War Tax Resistance
122 W. Franklin, Room 302
Minneapolis, MN 55404

Duluth War Tax Resistance
530 E. Skyline Parkway
Duluth, MN 55805

Missouri

Covenant Community of War Tax Resisters
c/o Karen Catholic Worker House
1840 Hogan
St. Louis, MO 63106

Nebraska

New Covenant Justice & Peace Center
3503 State St.
Omaha, NE 68112

New Hampshire

Nashua Peace Center
22 Meade Street
Nashua, NH 03060

New Hampshire War Tax Alternative Fund
PO Box 1072
Salem, NH 03079

Upper Valley War Tax Alternative Fund
35 School St.
Hanover, NH 03755

Dover Friends Peace Tax Fund
PO Box 98
Dover, NH 03820

New Jersey

Princeton Fund for Life
c/o Coalition for Nuclear Disarmament
40 Witherspoon St.
Princeton, NJ 08542

New Mexico

Albuquerque War Tax Alternative Fund
144 Harvard, SE
Albuquerque, NM 87106

War Tax Resisters de Santa Fe
2 Frasco Rd.
Santa Fe, NM 87505

New York

War Resisters League
339 Lafayette Street
New York, NY 10012

New York City War Tax Resistance/People's Life Fund
339 Lafayette Street
New York, NY 10012

Lawyers' Committee on Nuclear Policy
666 Broadway, 6th Floor
New York, NY 10012

Mobilization for Survival
45 John St., Suite 811
New York, NY 10038

Pax Christi Metro—N.Y.
475 Riverside Dr., Room 1371
New York, NY 10115

Westchester Alternative Tax Fund
c/o WESPAC
PO Box 488
White Plains, NY 10602

Fellowship of Reconciliation
PO Box 271
Nyack, NY 10960

Long Island WRL
PO Box 621
Rocky Point, NY 11778

Long Island Alternative Fund
2837 Pine Ave.
Lake Ronkonkoma, NY 11779

Quaker Peace Tax Fund
Albany Friends Meeting
727 Madison Ave.
Albany, NY 12208

Syracuse Peace Council
924 Burnet Ave.
Syracuse, NY 13203

Chenango Friends Peace Tax Fund
PO Box 162
Treadwell, NY 13846

Western New York Peace Center
472 Emslie St.
Buffalo, NY 14212

Rochester Military Tax Resistance
713 Monroe Ave.
Rochester, NY 14607

Ithaca War Tax Resistance
PO Box 6809
Ithaca, NY 14851

North Carolina

WRL Piedmont
604 W. Chapel Hill St.
Durham, NC 27701

Rural Southern Voice for Peace
1898 Hannah Branch Rd.
Burnsville, NC 28714

Ohio

Students for Peace and Justice/WRL
Box 22 Ohio Union
1739 N. High Street
Columbus, Ohio 43210

Yellow Springs Friends Meeting
PO Box 45
Yellow Springs, OH 45387

Oregon

Center for Peace Learning
George Fox College
Newberg, OR 97132

Oregon Community for War Tax Resisters
2305 NW Kearney, #246
Portland, OR 97210

Eugene Peaceworks/WRL
454 Wilamette St.
Eugene, OR 97401

Peace House
PO Box 524
Ashland, OR 97520

Blue Mountain Fellowship of Reconciliation
713 NW Johns Rd.
Pendleton, OR 97801

Pennsylvania

Pax Christi USA
348 E.10th St.
Erie, PA 16503

Mennonite Central Committee
21 S. 12th St.
Akron, PA 17501

Lehigh Valley War Tax Resistance Life Fund
PO Box 344
Riegelsville, PA 18077

War Tax Concerns Support Committee/ Philadelphia Yearly Meeting
1515 Cherry Street
Philadelphia, PA 19102

Philadelphia War Tax Resistance/ War Resisters League
2208 South St.
Philadelphia, PA 19146

Central Committee for Conscientious Objectors
2208 South St.
Philadelphia, PA 19146

Rhode Island

Rhode Island Alternative Fund
PO Box 2873
Providence, RI 02907

Tennessee

Swords into Plowshares
War Tax Conversion Fund
Rt. 3, Box 449
Waynesboro, TN 38485

Texas

Dallas WRL
2710 Woodmere
Dallas TX 75233

Houston Nonviolent Action/ War Resisters League
850 Jaquet
Bellaire, TX 77401

Austin War Tax Resistance
3014 Washington Square
Austin, TX 78705

Red River Peace Network (FOR/WRL)
c/o Peace Farm
HCR 2, Box 25
Panhandle, TX 79063

Vermont

Central Vermont War Tax Conversion Fund
PO Box 87
N. Montpelier, VT 05666

Tax Resisters of Conscience
RD 2, Box 442
W. Brattleboro, VT 06301

Virginia

Christians for Peace
PO Box 541
Harrisonburg, VA 22801

Richmond War Tax Alternative Group
2063 Jackson Shop Rd.
Goochland, VA 23063

Louisa Alternative Fund
Rt. 4, Box 169
Louisa, VA 23093

Washington

Western Washington Fellowship of Reconciliation
225 N. 70th St.
Seattle, WA 98103

Ministry for Music & Healing
c/o Church Council of Greater Seattle
4759 15th Ave., NE
Seattle, WA 98105

Conscience and Military Tax Campaign
4534 ½ University Way, NE
Seattle, WA 98105

Northwest Peace Tax Fund
7043 22nd Ave., NW
Seattle, WA 98117

Ground Zero Center
16159 Clear Creek Rd., NW
Poulsbo, WA 98370

Tacoma WRL/FOR
Reverend Milt Andrews
Hillside Community Church
2508 S. 38th St.
Tacoma, WA 98409

Peace & Justice Action League of Spokane
W. 320 5th Ave.
Spokane, WA 99204

West Virginia

Alderson Hospitality
PO Box 579
Alderson, WV 24910

Wisconsin

Milwaukee War Tax Resistance & Alternative Life Fund
PO Box 05206
Milwaukee, WI 53205

Southern Wisconsin Alternative Tax Fund
PO Box 3090
Madison, WI 53704

Lutheran Peace Fellowship & Fund
4329 Tokay Blvd.
Madison, WI 53711

War Resisters League and New Society Publishers

The War Resisters League (WRL) was formed in 1923 to create a mass movement against war based on the principle that wars will end when individuals refuse to participate in them. WRL advocates Gandhian nonviolence to create a democratic society free of war, racism, sexism, and human exploitation.

The radical pacifism of the League uses education and nonviolent action to contend with the complex political, social, economic, and psychological causes of war. Even where there seems to be peace, quiet deaths from starvation, poverty, and disease are as real and deadly as battlefield deaths from bullets and bombs.

Feminist thinking has brought a better understanding of the connections between militarism and sexism. It is not surprising that in a society which equates masculinity with domination, wars should develop. The spirit and style of feminism offers a striking alternative to the military psychology of America which stresses competition and aggressive (even violent) behavior.

Current programmatic activities of the League focus primarily on counter-recruitment, disarmament, shifting federal budget priorities, Stop War Toys Campaign, local organizer training and support, feminism, war tax resistance, anti-intervention, and other international and domestic issues. The national office works in conjunction with the regional office in Norwich, Connecticut, a network of more than twenty local groups, and organizers across the country to implement these programs.

Though opposed to the payment of taxes for war since its founding, the League did not begin to promote war tax resistance until the late 1940s when it issued a memo on token tax refusal. Then in the mid-1950s the WRL Executive Committee adopted a policy to refuse to withhold from staff members who were resisters. And in 1966, WRL began a nationwide campaign of telephone tax resistance in opposition to the Vietnam War. Income tax resistance also began to be promoted by the League. WRL has helped to create organizations to coordinate national war tax resistance organizing efforts.

As a result of League policy not to withhold from resisting staff and the League's refusal to cooperate with any IRS collection procedures, WRL has suffered seizures of its checking accounts and has been taken to court. Despite this harassment, the War Resisters League continues to publish literature, encourage resistance, and support the growth of the movement against paying for war.

War Resisters League
339 Lafayette St.
New York, NY 10012

Regional Office
WRL/New England
PO Box 1093
Norwich, CT 06360

New Society Publishers is a not-for-profit, worker controlled publishing house. We are proud to be the only publishing house in the United States committed to fundamental social change through nonviolent actions.

New Society Publishers is connected to a growing worldwide network of peace, feminist, religious, environmental, and human rights activists and strives to meet their needs. In ten years of publishing we have been able to offer resources which represent nonviolent alternatives in an increasingly violent world.

New Society Publishers is a project of the New Society Educational Foundation and a founding member of Coop America, a nationwide network of socially conscious businesses and consumers. We are not a subsidiary of any multinational corporation or beholden to any other organization. We hold the publishing house in trust for you, our readers and supporters, and we appreciate your contributions and feedback.

New Society Publishers
4527 Springfield Ave.
Philadelphia, PA 19143

Index

abortions, 11, 111
accelerated billings, 45
ACT-UP, 100
actions, 100-105
   counseling sessions, 114-115
Adamson, Edith, 71
"Adjustments to Income" section of form 1040, 29
advance payments from employers, 54
airport trust fund, 17
air travel excise tax, 36
alcohol excise taxes, 15, 17-18, 36
Alexander I (czar), 75
Alexander, Donald, 102
Algonquin Indians, 62
allowances, on W-4 form, 30-33
alternative funds, 10, 25, 54, 68, 57-61
   Conscience & Military Tax Campaign Escrow Fund, 60
   list of, 120-124
Alternative Revenue Service (ARS), 25, 68, 100, 109-110, 116
American Friends Service Committee (AFSC), 36, 64, 65
American Revolution, 15, 62
anarchist tax resistance, 106
Anglo-Dutch War (1672), 62
Angola, 69
appeals
   of audits, 38
   complicity argument in, 43-44
   Constitutional arguments in, 41-43
   Nuremberg Principles in, 44
   procedures for, 38-41
   to Tax Court, 39-41
appellate courts, 39-41
appointments, in audits, 38
arrests
   for actions at IRS offices, 102-103
   see also indictments; jailings of tax resisters
assessments, 38, 45
   statutes of limitations on, 55
   see also levies
Atlanta Tax Conversion Fund for Peace and Human Needs, 60
auctions of property, 48-49, 56
   actions around, 101-103
audio/visual resources, 118
audits (examinations), 38-39
   appeals from, 39-41
   of forms 1040X, 53
Australia, 69
Automated Collection System, 68
automobiles
   actions around auctions of, 101
   resisting seizures of, 56
   seizures of, 48-49, 53
   World War II tax stamps for, 64, 78

Bady, Bob, 67, 103
Baez, Joan, 64, 65, 67
Baltimore Four, 43
bank accounts
   alternative funds in, 57, 60
   levies on, 45-46, 47, 54
   service charges for levies on, 54
Bassett, Larry, 42, 67
beer, excise taxes on, 36
Belgium, 69-70
BettyJohanna, 108
blank return method, 29
blue-collar tax revolt, 108
Boardman, Elizabeth, 9
bonds
   savings, 17-18
   war, 15-17
   during World War I, 63
Bourne, Randolph, 106
Brandywine Peace Community, 103-104
Braun, Henry, 66
Brethren, Church of the, 9, 49, 62-63, 66
Britain, 70-71
brochures, 118
Bromley, Ernest, 5, 64, 78-79
   seizure of Peacemaker house and, 102
Bromley, Marion Coddington, 50, 64, 79
   seizure of Peacemaker house and, 102
   on socialist-anarchist tax resistance, 106
Broward Citizens for Peace and Justice, 101
Brown, Moses, 62
Buckley, Sally, 66
budget, federal
   feminist analysis of, 106
   military spending in, 10, 15-24
   Peace Tax Fund and, 110-112
budget authority, in federal budget, 21
Bush, George, 17, 67

Cain, Martha, 104
Cakars, Maris, 26
Callahan, Donald, 66
calls by IRS, 45, 50
Calvert, Angie O'Gorman, 65
Calvert, Robert, 9, 65, 66
Campaign for Tax Refusal (Spain), 75
Canada, 71
   bank accounts in, 53
Carter, Jimmy, 17
Catholic Worker, 65
Catlett, Richard, 29, 67, 68, 92-93
Center for Defense Information, 20
Center on Law and Pacifism, 42, 43, 50, 65, 68, 111
Central Committee for Conscientious Objectors (CCCO), 36
Chomsky, Noam, 64, 65
Chrisman, Bruce, 50, 29, 67, 90-91
cigarettes, excise taxes on, 36
Circular E (Employer's Tax Guide), 31
civil disobedience, 11, 12, 27, 103-104

   Thoreau on, 63
civil procedures
   penalties in, 47
   statutes of limitations in, 55
   see also collections; seizures
civil rights movement, 13
Civil War, 8, 15, 63
Clergy and Laity Concerned, 36
Coalition for the Homeless, 100
Cold War, 17, 64
collections (of tax funds), 12, 45-52
   alternative funds and, 57
   Fifth Amendment rights and, 42
   not filing method and, 28-29
   resisting, 53-56
   statute of limitations on, 28-29, 55
   steps leading to, 38
   of telephone taxes, 27
collective bank accounts, 54
Collective Impressions Printshop, 36
Committee for Nonviolent Action (CNVA), 26, 65
Community Church of Cincinnati, 81
Community for Creative Nonviolence, 36
complicity argument, 43-44
Conference on More Disciplined and Revolutionary Pacifist Activity (1948), 64
confrontation, 5, 10
conscience, rights of, 42-43
Conscience Canada Inc., 71
Conscience & Military Tax Campaign (CMTC), 60, 65, 109
conscientious objection, 110
Conscientious Objection to Military Tax (COMIT; Japan), 74
conscientious objection to war taxes
   Fourteen Amendment position, 43
   international campaigns for, 69-71, 74
   Peace Tax Fund Bill for, 65, 110-112
   during World War II, 64
conscription, 8
Constitution, U.S.
   Article I, Section 10 of, 107
   Article VI of, 43
   First Amendment to, 42, 107
   Fifth Amendment to, 29, 42, 49, 52, 56, 67, 107
   Ninth Amendment to, 42-43
   Fourteenth Amendment to, 43
   Sixteenth Amendment to, 15, 62, 63, 107
   Thirteenth Amendment to, 107
contempt of court, 42, 50, 64
   R. Kehler cited for, 96
   J. Nelson cited for, 83
   Robinson cited for, 83
   L. and S. Snider cited for, 66
Corner, Betsy, 5, 67, 68, 94-96, 103
corporate income taxes, 17-18, 36
corporations, family, 30
Council for a Livable World, 20
counseling sessions, 114-115

Index

Court of Appeals, U.S., 38
courts
  actions organized in and around, 104
  Constitutional arguments in, 41-44
  criminal, 49-50
  Tax Court, 39-41
  see also jailings of tax resisters
Crane, Susan, 113
credit ratings, 48
credits
  on W-4 (withholding) form, 30
  war tax, 29
crimes
  of complicity, 43-44
  war, 43
criminal courts, 49-50
criminal violations
  in collection process, 49-50
  extra dependents method and, 29
  indictments for, 56
  for not filing, 29, 47
  penalties for, 47
  statutes of limitations on, 55
  for W-4 resistance, 34
Croft, John-Ed, 53
Cuba, Arnold, 56
currency, 53, 107
customs duties, 17-18

Day, Dorothy, 65
debts from past wars, 15-17, 19-21
  resisting, 25
decision making, in alternative funds, 60-61
deductions
  FICA, 17
  military, 89
  on W-4 (withholding) form, 31
  war tax, 29, 38, 47-48
Defense, Department of, 19
Dellinger, David, 64, 65
Dellums, Ronald, 66
demonstrations at IRS offices, 100-104
dependents
  in calculating levies on wages and salaries, 46
  extra, on form 1040, 29
  on W-4 (withholding) forms, 31,34
DiGia, Ralph, 35
Doyle, Gene, 43
Doyle, Mary, 43
Draft, 8
Dunkards (Brethren), 63
Durland, William, 42, 67
Dworkin, Andrea, 106

Egnal, John, 84
Egypt, 69
employers
  First Amendment issues and, 41
  IRS definitions of, 34-35
  levies on wages or salaries of employees of, 46-47, 54-55
  negotiations with, 54, 99
  refusal to withhold taxes by, 35-36
  W-4 forms and resistance and, 34
employment agencies, 35, 55
Energy, Department of, 19
escrow accounts, 60, 65
estate taxes, 17-18
Evans, Arthur, 64
examinations **see** audits
excise taxes
  alcohol and tobacco, 36
  history of, 15
  resistance to, 18-19, 36
  telephone tax, 25-27
  for trust funds, 17
  see also telephone tax
exemptions to income taxes, 107
exempt status (on W-4 form), 34
extra dependents method, 29
  see also dependents; W-4 forms and resistance
EZ Peace form, 25, 68, 100, 109-110

failure to file, 28-29
  Catlett convicted of, 92
  Fifth Amendment method and, 29
  penalties for, 45
Falk, Richard A., 44
family corporations, 30
family trusts, 107
Farmer, Fyke, 44
federal budget, **see** budget, federal
Federal Communications Commission (FCC), on telephone tax, 26-27, 88
Federal funds, 20, 21
federal tax liens, 48
feminist tax resistance, 106
Ferlinghetti, Lawrence, 64, 65
fiat currency, 107
FICA (Federal Insurance Contributions Act), 17
Fifth Amendment method, 29
  collections and, 49
  used by right-wing tax resisters, 107
filing frequently method, 87
Final Assessment of Tax Due (form 4188), 38, 55
Final Notice Before Seizure, 45
First Amendment, 41-42
forms
  668 (Notice of Federal Tax Lien), 48
  668A, 668C, 668P, 668W (levy forms), 46-47
  1040, 27-28
  1040X (amended), 53
  2222 (bids at auctions), 48, 56
  4188 (final assessment of tax due), 38, 55
  refusal to file, 28-29
  Schedule A (itemization), 29
  using as leaflets, 100
  W-2 (report of income), 28
  W-4 (withholding), 30-36
Forsberg, Randall, 90
Fourteenth Amendment, 43
Fowler, Mike, 66, 86
France, 71-72
Franz, Marion, 113
fraud
  Monsky charged with, 89-90
  penalties for, 45
  L. Snider cleared of, 66
  statute of limitations on, 38
  W-4 resistance and, 34
Freeman, Harrop, 64
French and Indian War (1755), 62
Friends Committee on National Legislation, 20
Friends Committee on War Tax Concerns, 37
"frivolous or groundless" suits, 38, 53
"frivolous" penalty, 28, 29, 38, 45, 67, 68
  for Fifth Amendment and blank return methods, 29

Gandhi, Mohandas, 99
Gano Peacemakers, 102
Garrison, William Lloyd, 62
gasoline excise tax, 36
Germany, 72-73
gift taxes, 17-18
Ginsberg, Allen, 65
Gormly, Walter, 64, 79
grants, by alternative funds, 61
Great Britain, 70-71
Green Card applications, 51
Grenada, 5
guerrilla theater, 100
Gulf War, **see** Persian Gulf War
Gulick, Steve, 61

Handbook on Nonpayment of War Taxes (Peacemakers), 11, 63, 64
handbooks on war tax resistance, 118
Hanrahan, Clare, 98-99
harassment by IRS, 50-51
Harper, Lisa, 113
Harper, Robin, 29, 42, 84-86
Hatfield, Sen. Mark O., 66, 111
Haworth, Margaret, 42
Hedemann, Ed, 4, 5-6
Hennacy, Ammon, 79, 86
highway trust fund, 17
Himmelbauer, Bill, 66, 86
history of war tax resistance, 62-68
Houser, George, 64
houses
  auctions of, 94-95, 101-103
  resisting seizures of, 56, 93, 102-103
Hugh of Lincoln (saint), 70
Hungary, 73
Hunthausen, Raymond, 65, 67
Hutchinson, Barbara, 89
Hutterian Brethren, 63

income taxes
  Federal funds derived from, 17-18

Index

history of, 15
history of resistance to, 62-68
methods of resistance to, 27-31
resisting paying any of, 25
right-wing analyses of, 107-108
Sixteenth Amendment and, 15
withholding of, 31-37
during World War II, 64
independent contractors, 34-35
India, 13, 73
indictments, 56
during Indochina War, 65
for not filing, 92
post-Indochina War, 11, 66
for W-4 resistance, 66
see also courts; criminal violations; jailings of tax resisters
individual responsibility, 42
Indochina War, 9, 15, 19, 45
alternative funds organized during, 57
debt from, 19
Harper's war tax resistance during, 84-85
Johnson's war tax resistance during, 93
Monsky's war tax resistance during, 89-90
tax resistance to, 65-66
telephone tax during, 25-26
interest
in assessments, 45
on IRS collections, 12
on national debt, 17, 20-21
not paid by alternative funds to depositors, 57
interfund transactions (federal), 21
Internal Revenue Service (IRS), 8, 11, 14
actions organized at, 100-105
alternative funds and, 57
audits and appeals process of, 38-44
on blank returns and Fifth Amendment method, 29
collection process of, 12, 45-52
"employer" defined by, 34-35
resisting collections by, 53-56
right-wing tax resisters and, 107-108
telephone tax and, 226-27
W-4 forms and resistance and, 34, 108
see also collections; forms
international law, 43
international treaties, 43
international war tax resistance, 69-77
conferences, 69
intifada, 13, 76
Iraq, 5
Ireland, 73
Italy, 73-74
itemization, war tax deduction as, 29

Jacobs, Rep. Andy, 66
jailings of tax resisters, 49-50
of E. Bromley, 65, 78
of Catlett, 92
for contempt, 56
history of, 62-66
during Indochina War, 65-66
between Korean and Indochina Wars, 64-65
of Kehler, 96
of Leininger, 66
of McCrackin, 80-81
of Meyer, 86-87
of Mosley, 41
of Otsuka, 79-80
post-Indochina War, 68-69
of Rice, 41
of Robinson, 83-84
of Shea, 66
of L. and S. Snider, 66
of Thoreau, 63
of Tranquilli, 88-89
of W-4 resisters, 66
of N. Wild (Britain), 70
Japan, 74
jeopardy collections, 45
Jesus Christ, 12-13
Jobs with Peace, 100
Johnson, Donna, 93-94
Johnson, Lyndon B., 17
joint bank accounts, 46
"just war" theory, 41

Kehler, Randy, 5, 50, 67, 68, 94-96, 103
Kenney, Jo, 113
Kieninger, Carol, 92, 93
King William's War (1689), 62
Klaasz, Jacob, 74
Knudson, Ken, 34, 63, 65
Korean War, 15, 17, 19, 64-65
telephone tax during, 25

laws
disobedience of, 11
see also civil procedures; criminal violations
lawyers, 39, 55-56
Lawyers for Nuclear Disarmament (Britain), 71
Larzac (France), 71-72
leafletting, 100
inside IRS offices, 103-104
Leininger, John, 66
letters from IRS, 45
levies
against employers, 35-36
alternative funds and, 57
on bank accounts, 45-46, 53-54
on property, 48-49, 55
on wages or salaries, 46-47, 54-55
Levine, Kathy, 116-117
libertarian tax resistance, 106
Liberty Amendment (to repeal Sixteenth Amendment), 107
liens, 45, 48
literature
feminist analysis in, 106
leaflets, 100
resources, 118-119
living below taxable level, 29-30
loans, by alternative funds, 60
local taxes, 17, 106
Lottinville, Wayne, 27
Love, Kennett, 65
Lull and Herby v. **C.I.R.** (U.S., 1979), 42-43
Lutheran Peace Fellowship and Fund, 60
Luxembourg, 74
Lynd, Staughton, 64, 65
Lyttle, Bradford, 65

McCrackin, Maurice, 51, 53, 64, 80-81
Macdonald, Dwight, 64
Madison, James, 42
Malinowski, Jack, 66
Mangel, James, 43
marches, 100
Mason, Mary Bacon, 79
media
at court actions, 105
National War Tax Resistance Coordinating Committee contacts with, 117
on tax day, 100
Melman, Seymour, 11
Mennonite Church, 9, 50, 62, 63, 66
Mexican War (1846-1848), 15, 63
Meyer, Karl, 86-87
Himmelbauer and Fowler indicted with, 66, 86
jailing of, 50
sanctuary addresses suggested by, 55
on telephone tax resistance, 26, 65
W-4 resistance by, 34
Meyerding, Jane, 108
military deduction, 89
military spending, 8, 10, 17-24
current, 25
history of, 15-17
military trust fund, 17-18
Mills, Wilbur, 25
minimalization of income, 29-30
ministerial exemption, 107
Mitchell, Ron, 66
Mitterand, Francois, 72
Mogensen, Marti, 104
Monsky, Paul, 34, 50, 66, 67, 89-90
Montgomery Bus Boycott, 13
Moore, Nancy, 53
Morse, Pat, 67, 103
Mosley, Don, 41, 42, 68
Moss, Allen, 42
Muste, A.J., 8, 64, 65
First Amendment method used by, 41
on living below taxable level, 30

National Campaign for a Peace Tax Fund, 110-112

Index

National Campaign for War Tax Resistance (Italy), 73-74
National Council for a World Peace Tax Fund, 66
national debt, 15, 17, 19-21
National Priorities Project, 20
National War Tax Resistance, 64, 65, 66
National War Tax Resistance Coordinating Committee (NWTRCC), 56, 61, 67, 109, 115, 116-117
   on alternative funds, 61
   resources available from, 118-119
natural rights, 42
negligence penalty, 45
Nelson, Juanita, 50, 63, 64, 81-83
Nelson, Wally, 8, 54, 81-83
Netherlands, 74-75
"New Call to Peacemaking," 67
New England Non-Resistance Society, 62
New England War Tax Resistance, 57, 60-61, 64, 68, 89
newsletters on war tax resistance, 118
New Society Publishers, 125
New York City People's Life Fund, 60-61, 65, 68
New Zealand, 75
Nickerson, Wes, 102-103
noncooperation, 28, 29 97, 99
non-withheld labor, 35
Northern California People's Life Fund, 57, 60-61, 65, 68, 100
Northern California War Tax Resistance, 104
Norway, 75-76
No Tax for War in Vietnam Committee (1965), 65
not filing method, 29-30
   penalties for, 45
   used by Catlett, 92
Notice of Deficiency, 38
Notice of Federal Tax Lien (form 668), 48
Notice of Levy on Wages, Salary, and Other Income (form 668W), 46-47
nuclear power, 11, 25, 74
nuclear weapons, 8, 17, 25
   in Department of Energy budget, 19
Nuremberg Principles, 43

Ohno, Michio, 74
organizations
   alternative funds, 57-61
   Conscientious & Military Tax Campaign, 60, 65, 109
   list of, 120-124
   National War Tax Resistance Coordinating Committee, 116-117
   for peace tax fund, 110-112
   tax resistance by, 36-37
   see also religious groups

organizing
   of alternative funds, 57-61
   around IRS collections, 54-56
   of tax resistance counseling sessions, 114-115
   of war tax resistance actions, 100-105
   tax day actions, 100
Otsuka, James, 64, 79-80
outlays, in federal budget, 24

Palestine, 76
Panama, U.S. war in, 5, 19
Parks, Rosa, 13
Pascale, David, 49
passport applications, 51
past wars, debts from, 15-17, 19-21
   resisting, 25
payments, 53
   paying under protest, 112-113
Peacemakers, 26, 64, 65
   founding conference of, 63, 64, 79
   Handbook on Nonpayment of War Taxes published by, 64
   seizure of house of, 102
Peace Pledge Union (Britain), 70
Peace Tax Campaign (Australia), 69
Peace Tax Campaign (Britain), 70, 71
Peace Tax Campaign (New Zealand), 75
Peace Tax Fund, 110-112
Peace Tax Fund Committee (Canada), 71
penalties, 12, 47
   against employers, 35-36, 47
   in assessments, 45
   for employers ignoring levies, 47
   "frivolous," 28, 29, 38, 45, 67, 68
   for "frivolous or groundless" cases in Tax Court, 38, 53
   for not filing, 31, 45
   for tax resistance by organizations, 36-37
Pennsylvania Colony, 62
pensions, 46
perjury
   for claiming W-4 exempt status, 34
   W-4 resistance and, 30
Persian Gulf War, 17, 19, 67, 68, 73, 104, 106, 113
Peter (saint), 12
Petitions, to Tax Court, 39-40
Philadelphia Alternative Fund, 57-61, 68
Philadelphia War Tax Resistance, 58-59, 65, 101
Philadelphia Yearly Meeting, 41
picketing, 100
Pioneer Valley (Massachusetts) alternative fund, 58
Pioneer Valley War Tax Resistance, 97
Portugal, 69
Posse Comitatus, 107-108
post office, action at, 102-103
Presbyterian Church, United, 81

Prior, Dr. Jerilynn, 71
professional licensing, 51
property
   auctions of, actions around, 101-103
   seizures of, 48-49, 55-56
prosecutions, 49-50
   statute of limitations on, 55
   see also criminal violations; indictments; jailings of tax resisters

Quaker Peace Committee (Britain), 70
Quakers (Society of Friends), 63-64, 68
   in Britain, 70
   in Ireland, 73
   in Russia, 76

rallies, 100
Reagan, Ronald, 17, 18, 66-67, 116
real estate, auctions of, 48-49
Rece, Ellis, 66
refunds, 47-48
Regional Director of Appeals, Office of, 38
religious groups
   historic war tax resistance among, 9, 62-63
   Indochina War tax resistance by members of, 66
   international war tax resistance by, 69, 70, 71, 73, 76
   ministerial exemption and, 107
   post-Indochina War war tax resistance by, 67
   on war tax resistance, 9
religious questions, 12-13
   in First Amendment position, 41-42
   in right-wing tax resistance, 107
"Report of Individual Income Tax Examination Changes," 38
resources, 118-119
Revolutionary War, 15, 62
Rice, Max, 41, 42, 68
Richter, Dennis, 66
Riggs, Francis, 79
Riggs, Valerie, 79
rights of conscience, 42
right-wing tax resisters, 107-108
   Fifth Amendment method used by, 29
   Hutchinson, 89
Riley, Mark, 66
Robinson, Eroseanna, 64, 83-84, 86
Rome, ancient, 13
Russia, 76
Russo-Japanese War (1903), 74

safety deposit boxes, 48
salaries
   levies on, 46-47, 54-55
   see also withholding taxes
Sale, Kirkpatrick, 65
sales taxes, 17, 18

Index

SANE/Freeze, 100
sanctuary addresses, 55
Sandin, Max, 46, 79
Sargent, Doris, 26
savings bonds, 18
Schell, Jonathan, 89
Schenk, Roy, 66
Seeger, Pete, 65
seizures
   actions around auctions following, 101-103
   against War Resisters League, 35
   alternative funds to shield money from, 57
   of bank accounts, 45-46, 47, 54
   post-Indochina War, 68
   of property, 48-49, 55-56, 93, 94-96
   because of telephone tax, 53, 93
   of wages or salaries, 46-47, 54-55
self-employment, 34
service charges, by banks on levies, 54
Shakers, 62
Sharpe, Cynthia, 113
Shays, Rep. Christopher, 45
Shea, Jim, 50, 66
Sixteenth Amendment, 15
slavery, 63
small tax cases (in Tax Court), 39
Smith v. Oregon State Employment Division, 41
Smith, James, 66
Snider, Lyle, 34, 66, 90
Snider, Sue, 66
socialist-anarchist tax resistance, 106
Social Security checks, 46
Social Security numbers, 57
Social Security taxes, 29, 36
Social Security trust fund, 17
Society of Friends, **see** Quakers
Sojourners, 36
Spain, 76-77
Spanish-American War (1898), 15, 25, 63
Special Services Staff (IRS), 51, 102
state
   collection for federal taxes, 53, 97
   taxes, 17, 106
statutes of limitations
   on audits (examinations), 38
   for civil and criminal cases, 55
   on collections, 38
   on non-filing, 29
Steinem, Gloria, 65
Stuart, Lyle, 65
Supreme Court, U.S., 41
   on admission of illegally obtained information, 50-51
   on First Amendment argument, 41-42
   on international treaties and IRS code, 42-43
   on seizures of joint bank accounts, 46
Sweden, 77

Switzerland, 77
symbolic resistance, 25
Szent-Gyorgyi, Albert, 65

Taunton, Joel, 109
taxable level, 29
Tax Court, 39-41
   actions around, 104
   "frivolous or groundless" suits in, 41
tax credits
   on W-4 (withholding) form, 30
   war, 29
taxes
   history of, 15-17
   methods of resistance to, 25-37
   and military spending, history of, 15-17
   refusing all forms of, 12
   for war, 17-19
tax liens, 45, 48
Tax Refusal Committee (Peacemakers, 1948), 64-65
Tax Refusal Movement (France), 71-72
tax resistance
   by anarchists, 106
   by feminists, 106
   by right-wing, 107-108
   see also war tax resistance
tax stamps, 5, 78
Taxpayers Bill of Rights, 45
Taylor, Telford, 44
telephone tax, 17-18
   AT&T break-up and, 27
   Act for Better Child Care and, 26
   automobiles seized because of, 53
   Indochina War resistance to, 66-68
   National War Tax Resistance Coordinating Committee campaign on, 116-117
   numbers of resisters of, 66
   resistance by organizations to, 35, 36
   resisting, 25-27
   Tranquilli's resistance of, 26-27, 87-89
Templin, Ralph, 79
Thoreau, Henry David, 7, 62, 63
tobacco excise taxes, 17-18, 36
token (symbolic) resistance, 25
Tolstoy, Leo, 99
training sessions, 114-115
Tranquilli, Martha, 26-27, 50, 87-89
treaties, 42-43
Truman, Harry S, 17
trust accounts, 46
trust funds (federal), 17, 20, 21, 36

Unified Budget (federal), 20-21
United Nations
   Charter, 43
   Human Rights Commission, 71
United States Tax Court, 39-41
   actions around, 105
   "frivolous or groundless" suits in, 38, 41

United States v. **Harper** (1975), 42, 85
United States v. **Snider** (1974), 66
United States v. **Sullivan** (1927), 42
Universal Life Church, 93, 107
Universal Peace Union, 63
Urie, Caroline, 79

Van Valkenberg, Edward, 113
veterans' benefits, 19, 21, 25
Vietnam War, **see** Indochina War
violence, feminist analysis of, 106
visits by IRS, 45, 50-51

W-2 forms, 29
W-4 exempt status, 34
W-4 forms and resistance
   during Indochina War, 68
   methods of, 30-34
   not filing method and, 28-29
   prosecutions for, 50, 66
   used by right-wing tax resisters, 107-108
wages
   levies on, 46, 54-55
   see also withholding taxes
Walker, Gerald, 64, 65
War of 1812, 15, 62-63
war adjustment method, 29
war bonds, 15-17, 63
war crimes, 43, 44
war crimes deduction, 89
War Resisters League, 20, 109, 125
   IRS levies on employees not honored by, 35
   leafletting inside IRS offices by, 103
   National Action Conference (1982) of, 67
   telephone tax resistance promoted by, 26, 65
war tax credit, 29, 68
war tax deductions, 29, 38, 47-48, 68
war taxes, 17-18
   legal objections to, 110-113
War Tax Refusers Support Committee, 95-96, 103
war tax resistance
   actions organized around, 100-105
   counseling sessions on, 114-115
   history of, 62-68
   international, 69-77
   legal forms of, 110-113
   list of organizations for, 120-124
   methods of, 25-37
   motivations for, 8-9
   National War Tax Resistance Coordinating Committee for, 116-117
   philosophical and political aspects of, 11-14
   resources for, 118-119
   Thoreau on, 7
War Tax Resistance (WTR), 65
War Tax Resisters' Penalty Fund (WTRPF), 112
War Tax Revenue Act (1914), 25

Index

We the People—American Citizens Tribunal (ACT), 107
Wild, Nigel, 70
Wilson, D.D.S., Thomas A., 96-98
   professional licensing and, 51
wine, excise taxes on, 36
Wisconsin Alternative Fund, 61
withholding taxes
   in Britain, 70
   history of, 17, 63
   methods of resistance to, 27-30
   right-wing tax resisters on, 107
   during World War II, 65
women, feminist tax resistance by, 106
Women's International League for Peace and Freedom (WILPF), 64, 100
Woolman, John, 62, 102
World Peace Tax Fund Bill, 65, 66, 111
World War I, 15, 25, 63, 111
World War II, 9, 13, 15-17, 63-64
   E. Bromley's tax resistance during, 64, 78
   debt from, 19
   telephone tax during, 25
   withholding taxes during, 30
Writ of Entry, 45
Writers and Editors War Tax Protest, 64, 65

Zinn, Howard, 89